Approaches to Teaching
Wiesel's *Night*

Approaches to Teaching World Literature

Joseph Gibaldi, series editor

For a complete listing of titles,
see the last pages of this book.

Approaches to Teaching Wiesel's *Night*

Edited by

Alan Rosen

The Modern Language Association of America
New York   2007

For information about obtaining permission to reprint material from
MLA book publications, send your request by mail (see address below),
e-mail (permissions@mla.org), or fax (646 458-0030).

Library of Congress Cataloging-in-Publication Data
Approaches to teaching Wiesel's Night / edited by Alan Rosen.
p. cm. — (Approaches to teaching world literature)
Includes bibliographical references and index.
ISBN-13: 978-0-87352-589-3 (hardcover : alk. paper)
ISBN-10: 0-87352-589-2 (alk. paper)
ISBN-13: 978-0-87352-590-9 (pbk. : alk. paper)
ISBN-10: 0-87352-590-6 (alk. paper)
1. Holocaust, Jewish (1939–1945)—Study and teaching.   2. Holocaust, Jewish
(1939–1945)—Personal narratives—Study and teaching.   3. Wiesel, Elie, 1928–
Un di velt hot geshvign.   I. Rosen, Alan.
D804.33.A65 2007
940.53'18071—dc22   2007006398
ISSN 1059-1133

Cover illustration of the paperback edition: *Distribution of Soup*, by Walter Spitzer. Buchenwald,
1945. Courtesy of the Ghetto Fighters' Museum Art Archive.

Published by The Modern Language Association of America
26 Broadway, New York, New York 10004-1789
www.mla.org

CONTENTS

PREFACE TO THE SERIES

In *The Art of Teaching* Gilbert Highet wrote, "Bad teaching wastes a great deal of effort, and spoils many lives which might have been full of energy and happiness." All too many teachers have failed in their work, Highet argued, simply "because they have not thought about it." We hope that the Approaches to Teaching World Literature series, sponsored by the Modern Language Association's Publications Committee, will not only improve the craft—as well as the art—of teaching but also encourage serious and continuing discussion of the aims and methods of teaching literature.

The principal objective of the series is to collect within each volume different points of view on teaching a specific literary work, a literary tradition, or a writer widely taught at the undergraduate level. The preparation of each volume begins with a wide-ranging survey of instructors, thus enabling us to include in the volume the philosophies and approaches, thoughts and methods of scores of experienced teachers. The result is a sourcebook of material, information, and ideas on teaching the subject of the volume to undergraduates.

The series is intended to serve nonspecialists as well as specialists, inexperienced as well as experienced teachers, graduate students who wish to learn effective ways of teaching as well as senior professors who wish to compare their own approaches with the approaches of colleagues in other schools. Of course, no volume in the series can ever substitute for erudition, intelligence, creativity, and sensitivity in teaching. We hope merely that each book will point readers in useful directions; at most each will offer only a first step in the long journey to successful teaching.

Joseph Gibaldi
Series Editor

PREFACE TO THE VOLUME

In dealing with the Holocaust—the destruction of European Jewry, 1939–45—one turns first to primary sources. The sources from within the events, of which there were many, try to give a sense of what was happening at the time. Ghetto logs, reportage, journals, diaries, poems, and stories all convey the incremental constriction that the victims faced.

The victim's memoir, written in the wake of the events, has both the advantage and disadvantage of hindsight, of knowing the full extent of the catastrophe suffered by European Jewry. Elie Wiesel's *Night*, a memoir by a Hungarian Jewish survivor, has become a classic for many reasons, one of which may be the art of combining these two vantage points. Written in the aftermath of the war, *Night* nevertheless presents its story as if it is unfolding before the reader. It renders the step-by-step destruction of a teenager's routine, home, and family almost without the intrusion of the larger picture. The reader, like the victims themselves, is trapped within the events. In *Night*, then, the hindsight of the memoir is melded with the lack of knowledge characteristic of writings penned during the lived experience. Doing justice to this complex narrative strategy is thus one of the challenges facing teachers of Wiesel's memoir.

Teachers must also become familiar with Wiesel's native culture. As with the works featured in a number of volumes in the MLA series Approaches to Teaching World Literature (I think, for instance, of those dedicated to Frederick Douglass and Chinua Achebe), Wiesel's chronicle of a typical if precocious religious Jewish boy takes place in a cultural context foreign to many readers. Hence *Night*'s allusions to Jewish custom and practice deserve careful attention.

Night was the first book Wiesel wrote; he has gone on to publish fifty or so more volumes of fiction, essays, dramas, librettos, and journalism as well as commentary on Jewish religious texts and personages. He has served as a human rights advocate (for which work he was awarded the Nobel Peace Prize in 1986), as a spokesman on behalf of Holocaust victims and a chairman of the United States Holocaust Memorial Council, and as an international lecturer. His writings and lectures in French, Hebrew, and Yiddish and his lectures in English have brought his concerns to a diverse world audience. *Night* is often read through the prism of who Wiesel has become; the essays in this Approaches volume allow the memoir to be read through this lens as well as through a more historically situated one.

As the contributors attest, *Night* is taught in many different forums for many different kinds of readers. The range of commentary included here both reflects what generally is and explores what may be. Following the general format of the Approaches series, the volume's first section, "Materials," details editions, commentary, and contextual works relevant to teaching Wiesel's *Night*. The second section, "Approaches," contains the editor's introduction and seventeen essays arranged under three headings: "Historical and Cultural Contexts," "Literary Contexts," and "Courses and Classroom Strategies." Notes on contributors, a list of survey participants, a list of works cited, and an index close out the volume.

Approaches to Teaching Wiesel's Night appears fifty years after *Night* was first published, in Yiddish, under the title *Un di velt hot geshvign* ("And the World Remained Silent"). It also appears in the wake of a new translation of *Night* into English. These two events mark an auspicious occasion for bringing out this collection of teaching materials on *Night*.

NOTE

Unless otherwise stated, the edition of *Night* to which all essays refer is the translation by Marion Wiesel. Ellipses in quotations from *Night* appear in the memoir; bracketed ellipses indicate omitted text.

ACKNOWLEDGMENTS

Important conversations with Susan Suleiman over several years confirmed that a volume of this kind and in this series was worth pursuing. Several discussions with Nehemia Polen helped explore the best way to carry it out. Riki Bodenheimer, Rob Rozett, David Silverklang, and Anne Simonin shared useful contextual information. Martha Hauptman was typically generous in suggesting resources. Stacy Mayhew Clements gave me a sense of an audience beyond the academic classroom for which this book might be meaningful.

The enthusiasm and guidance of the series editor, Joseph Gibaldi, were essential to the project's realization. Anonymous readers' detailed comments at two stages of the editorial process helped shape the final product. Sara Pastel's careful copyediting refined the text throughout. I am grateful to those who filled out questionnaires on teaching *Night* and to those whose sensitive essays appear in this volume. I have learned from them all.

Students at Boston University, Bar Ilan University, and the International School for Holocaust Education at Yad Vashem have deepened my appreciation for the many approaches to *Night*. From the other end, as a student I learned how to approach *Night* from two masters, Maurice Natanson and Elie Wiesel. They and a few other masters—Phil Wall, Jim Siemon, Marx Wartofsky, Harrell Beck, and Alasdair MacIntyre—have helped me see the classroom as one of the great arenas of life and learning. My debt to them is ongoing.

As with anything I write or edit, my wife, Ruth Clements, sets an extraordinary model of excellence; she again has helped in ways too many to count. My children inspire constantly; they should be blessed to know and make a world where the scenes *Night* renders are confined solely to the past.

Part One

MATERIALS

Editions and Texts

Elie Wiesel (b. 1928) originally published his memoir in 1956 in Yiddish in Buenos Aires, where it appeared in a series commemorating Eastern European Jewish culture. Excerpts from the Yiddish have since been published in English translation. Chapter 7 serves as the first reading in the well-regarded *Anthology of Holocaust Literature*, a compilation of primary sources translated mainly from Yiddish. Edited by Jacob Glatstein, Israel Knox, and Samuel Margoshes, the collection gives a victim's perspective on the Holocaust; that the excerpt from Wiesel comes first in the collection demonstrates the respect accorded it. Other excerpts translated from the Yiddish version appear in Irving Abrahamson's *Against Silence*, a collection of Wiesel's shorter writings, as "The Deportation" and "The Beginning and the End," in Wiesel's *All Rivers Run to the Sea*, and in Wiesel's preface to the new English edition of *Night*. The full Yiddish text can be purchased at the National Yiddish Book Center or can be found in libraries (WorldCat lists twenty-four United States and Canadian university, college, and public libraries that have the text).

Wiesel's French adaptation of the memoir appeared two years later, published by Editions de Minuit, a press that had its origins in resistance to Nazi censorship during World War II. Yet Wiesel's *La nuit* was only the second concentration camp memoir published by them (Simonin, *Editions*; Simonin, personal communcation). The French version is similar to the Yiddish in almost every respect, except that Wiesel and then the publisher cut out what was considered superfluous, including the Yiddish memoir's prologue and epilogue. It can be purchased online and is available in many university libraries. Hill and Wang published the first English edition of *Night* in 1960, a translation of the French *La nuit*. Most teachers have used the Bantam edition. Bantam first published it in 1982, but Wiesel introduced some minor emendations after the initial printing; these may come to light if students end up with older Bantam editions (see Suleiman, "Do Facts Matter"). This translation has also been included in a trilogy of Wiesel's first full-length writings: in addition to *Night*, the volume includes Wiesel's first and second French novels, *Dawn* and *The Accident* (also titled *Day*). In 2006 Hill and Wang published a new English edition of *La nuit*. Translated by Marion Wiesel, the author's wife and, since the 1970s, translator of many of his publications, it features a new preface by the author. Available in a reasonably priced paperback, this edition promises to become the standard one.

Instructor's Library

Historical Context

A small book, *Night* nevertheless affords entry to the tragic intersection of modern European and Jewish history. General histories of the Holocaust (Reitlinger; Hilberg, *Destruction*; Dawidowicz; Bauer; Gilbert; Yahil) place Wiesel's chronicle of the destruction of Hungary in chilling perspective—some five million Jews had already been murdered by the time Hungary's Jews were deported to Auschwitz in 1944. These histories also address key elements of the Holocaust that one finds in *Night*: ghettos, deportations, camps, and death marches.

Essential information regarding the city and area of Wiesel's birth and boyhood—Sighet in Transylvania—can be found in the relevant entries of the *Encyclopedia Judaica* ("Sighet," "Transylvania," "Hungary," and "Rumania"). Though Transylvania was alternately under Hungarian and Romanian rule, its Jewish population was tied essentially to Hungary. The volumes on Hungarian Jewry edited or authored by Randolph Braham address the special nature of Transylvanian Jewry's tragedy. Several books on Wiesel misleadingly cast Transylvanian Jewry under the rubric of the Balkans; the *Encyclopedia Judaica* entries are more reliable. *The Heart Remembers Jewish Sziget* (Alfassi, Netzer, and Szalai), a *yizkor* book produced by former residents, was recently issued and includes an English translation of much of the material.

Ghettos and Concentration Camps

The first major wartime ghetto was established in Lodz, Poland, in spring 1940; other Polish and Lithuanian ghettos were set up over the next several years. Jews were forced to evacuate their homes and relocate to a small, densely packed area of a city. Some ghettos were enclosed by a fence or a wall, imprisoning the Jews within; other ghettos were kept open. Ghettos were generally not instituted in western, central, and southern European countries.

Hungary did not establish ghettos until Germany forced its hand. In structure, the ghettos were similar to those set up earlier in Eastern Europe. Yet the Hungarian ghettos were short-term in comparison with those in Poland and Lithuania. In Sighet the ghetto was in existence for about a month in 1944, from its establishment on 20 April to the final deportation of Sighet's Jews on 22 May. Braham sets forth the special situation of Hungary's ghettos of shorter duration and chronicles the fate of Sighet—which he lists under its Hungarian name, Máramarossziget (see the chapters "Ghettoization" and "Hungary during the War" in *Politics*).

The ghettos of Eastern Europe lingered on sometimes for years and brought into being many social, cultural, and literary phenomena that, although not directly pertinent to most of the short-lived ghettos of Hungary, help convey the Holocaust's broader dimensions. Here, too, the resources are substantial. The major histories of the Holocaust provide cursory overviews of the ghettos. In addition, Philip Friedman's short comparative survey of World War II ghettos provides a basic yet sophisticated overview. Isaiah Trunk reviews many aspects while focusing on the Jewish Councils that attempted to administer ghetto life. Christopher Browning updates the discussion on the perpetrators' reasons for establishing ghettos ("Before the 'Final Solution' "). Michael Marrus's collection of articles covers a full range of topics from the victims' perspective. Writing, literature, and dramatic performance were cultivated activities in the more long-lived ghettos (see Roskies, "Scribes" and *Literature*; Horowitz, "Voices"; on children, Zapruder; on theater, Rozit and Goldfarb).

The major histories of the Holocaust also provide overviews of the concentration camp system, including Auschwitz-Birkenau, Buna, Gleiwitz, and Buchenwald—the camps in which the Wiesels were incarcerated. Konnilyn Feig details specific camps; Yisrael Gutman and Michael Berenbaum's compilation examines Auschwitz from multiple perspectives, and many of its essays keep the victims' experience in the foreground. Debórah Dwork and Robert Jan van Pelt chronicle the prehistory of the town and the emergence of the camp. For a thoughtful view of Buchenwald from a non-Jewish inmate's perspective, see the two memoirs by Jorge Semprun. Eugen Kogon and David Hackett document Buchenwald's history, organization, and specific forms of brutality.

Issues of faith, religious practice, and theodicy are frequently seen to be at the core of *Night*. Wiesel's response to the challenge the Holocaust presented to traditional observance can be compared with the responses of other Jews, both from Hasidic points of view (Schindler; Eliach; Polen) and general ones (Berkovits; Greenberg).

Christians have also felt called to respond to the scandal of the Holocaust and, more particularly, to Wiesel's deposition. For Christians, issues of theodicy are interwoven with those of Christian responsibility (and the responsibility of Christianity) for the Holocaust. The earliest Christian response to *Night* was likely articulated in the foreword by François Mauriac, a French man of letters and an ardent Catholic. Wiesel has both described the meeting that led to Mauriac's response ("Interview") and reflected critically on it (*All Rivers*). Another Catholic writer, Eva Fleischner, has taken issue with Mauriac. Books by John K. Roth, Harry Cargas, and Carol Rittner elaborate the issues of Christian faith in the light of the Holocaust.

Holocaust Memoirs

Night is one particularly well known example of Holocaust memoirs—retrospective accounts by victims often detailing life before the war, the upheaval during the war, and some reckoning of life after the liberation of the camps in 1944 or 1945. David Patterson examines the reiterated themes of these memoirs, particularly the writing of the memoir as an act of life renewal. In "Voices from the Killing Ground" Sara Horowitz contrasts the fragmented perspective of Holocaust diaries with the retrospective view of the memoir. (Wiesel himself speaks of modeling the style of *Night* on the terse prose of the diarists.) Although Wiesel composed his memoir in his mid-twenties, he rendered it through a child's perspective. One might thus compare *Night* with diaries written during the Holocaust by children, excerpts from which have been recently translated and collected by Alexandra Zapruder. Memoirs by other survivors of Sighet, one written before Wiesel's and the others decades afterward, offer a more focused comparison (see Perl; Fried; Isacovici and Rodríguez; Halivni; Sorell). The differences in the authors' milieus and narrative approaches complement those of *Night*. Yet their repetition of the circumstances of destruction that Wiesel evokes is similarly haunting. Salomon Isacovici, whose memoir was penned in Spanish and translated into English, also gave an earlier oral memoir, an interview with the psychologist David Boder almost forty-five years before he composed his written one; it can be read online in an English transcription (Isakovitch).

Biography

There is no full-length biography of Wiesel geared for college readers. Ellen Stern's is for younger readers and, while heightening the drama, is not always responsible to facts. Books and essays on Wiesel (see Estes; Fine; Rosen) draw mainly on Wiesel's interviews, essays, and later memoirs (*All Rivers* and *And the Sea*) to narrate his life.

Books of interviews provide another point of entry to Wiesel's life and thought. Therein he often comments on *Night* and related topics (indeed, most everything he has written and undertaken is related). Of the nine books currently featuring interviews with Wiesel, the most helpful for teaching is *Elie Wiesel: Conversations*, edited by Robert Franciosi. It contains complete or excerpted interviews dating from 1961 to 2000; five are French-language interviews translated especially for the volume. In contrast with the other volumes, Franciosi's provides an excellent index that allows the teacher and reader to follow the course of a topic over the range of interviews—and thus over the course of Wiesel's career.

Critical Commentary

Two collections reprint essays on *Night*. *Modern Critical Interpretations: Elie Wiesel's* Night, edited by Harold Bloom, consists of eight essays first published between 1975 and 1995. Readers of the earlier versions of the essays have paid tribute to those of Lawrence Langer, Ellen Fine, and Ora Avni. The second volume, *Readings on* Night, edited by Wendy Mass, is designed for young adult readers, middle and high school students. Although it includes a greater number and diversity of essays than Bloom's collection, it deals with *Night* under a rigid literary framework (plot, characters, etc.) that patronizes rather than inspires its readers. The appended chronology mistakes both the day of Buchenwald's liberation and the nationality of the liberating army.

In contrast, each of the three volumes in English of collected essays on Wiesel (edited by Rosenfeld and Greenberg; Cargas; Rittner) includes sophisticated commentary on *Night*. Essays by Robert Alter ("Elie Wiesel") and Irving Halperin ("From *Night*") particularly complement those in *Modern Critical Interpretations* by considering *Night* as a basis for Wiesel's early novels. Virtually all of the full-length studies of Wiesel (Roth; Berenbaum; Fine; Estes; Brown; Davis; Sibelman; Kolbert) devote a chapter to *Night* (many of these chapters are included in Bloom's collection). Several major studies of Holocaust literature similarly discuss *Night* at length (Halperin, *Messengers*; Langer). These studies fall roughly into two approaches: narrative and religious or moral; *Night* is often discussed under both rubrics. Most major studies of Holocaust writing make at least passing reference to *Night* (see, for example Irving Howe's influential essay "Writing and the Holocaust").

The importance of Wiesel's languages (French, Yiddish, Hebrew) in relation to *Night* and to his work generally has mostly received tangential comment. Naomi Seidman, using source criticism and reception history, has argued that Wiesel's French adaptation modifies the original Yiddish significantly. Those who read *Night* in English can see for themselves by comparing the translation from the Yiddish that serves as the opening selection in Glatstein's anthology. Wiesel has commented on the primary value of Yiddish for dealing with the Holocaust in his "Marginal Thoughts on Yiddish." Yet he has chosen to write predominantly in French, in his view a rational language, in order to deal through paradox with the mystical nature of the Holocaust (see Franciosi).

Wiesel's Other Writings

Since the publication of *Night*, Wiesel has produced a steady flow of writings: novels, stories, essays, reportage, plays, librettos, as well as various shorter writings, like book reviews. Instructors mention teaching *Night* with *Dawn* and *The Accident*, two early novels; *The Forgotten*, a later novel; the essays "A Plea for the Dead" and "The Holocaust as Literary Inspiration"; and Wiesel's introduction to *The* Night *Trilogy*. Some teach courses that focus exclusively on a selection of Wiesel's writing, choosing different genres written over the course of his career.

Bibliographies

The only full-length bibliography of Wiesel's work was compiled in the mid-1970s by Molly Abramowitz. It only lists works until 1974 but nevertheless gives readers a good idea of Wiesel's enormous output in Yiddish, French, and Hebrew. Published in the United States for mainly English-language readers, Abramowitz's volume cites translations into English as well as other languages. The bibliography thus helps convey a general notion of the reception of *Night* through the early 1970s. For those interested in the contemporary response to *Night's* publication, Abramowitz lists and briefly annotates fifty-three newspaper reviews of the English edition of *Night*, most of which appeared in 1960 or 1961 (64–72). The section "Works about Elie Wiesel," which includes reference to several important early periodical essays on *Night* by Alter ("Apocalyptic Temper") and A. Alvarez, complements the reviews. Though indispensable, the annotations are not always careful with facts (Abramowitz refers to Sidra Ezrahi as "he") and can at times be misleading (the indication that Alter views Saul Bellow in contrast to Wiesel is not on target).

Wiesel's shorter writings are collected in Abrahamson's three-volume set *Against Silence*. The material varies extraordinarily, ranging from brief quotations to lengthier works such as Wiesel's first play, "Black Canopy Black Sky," and short stories. These volumes reveal easily overlooked aspects of Wiesel: his many book reviews convey a sense of him as a reader as well as writer of books; excerpts from lectures indicate the diverse forums he has addressed. Reviews, lectures, and shorter comments also show the evolution of Wiesel's work on human rights such that a reader can see its outgrowth from Wiesel's own wartime ordeal and losses. The third volume contains an index to all three volumes. *Against Silence* appends bibliographies listing the sources of the material included; materials are, however, listed not by date of publication but by title. *Against Silence's* bibliographies document exclusively primary sources; Alan Rosen's text contains a list of full-length primary work in all genres through 2002 and a selection of book-length secondary work.

In addition to the MLA Bibliography, the most recent articles on *Night* and Wiesel's other writings can be located on RAMBI, the Web site that indexes scholarly articles on Jewish topics (http://jnul.huji.ac.il/rambi/).

Specialized resources on Wiesel and *Night* can be complemented by general bibliographies on the Holocaust: Martin Sable, *Holocaust Studies: A Directory and Bibliography of Bibliographies*; Jacob Robinson and Friedman, *Guide to Jewish History under Nazi Impact*; Robinson, *The Holocaust and After: Sources and Literature in English*. Henry Friedlander, David Szonyi, and, most recently, Donald Niewyk and Francis Nicosia have compiled annotated bibliographies for the general reader; Abraham Edelheit and Hershel Edelheit's *Bibliography on Holocaust Literature* lists many sources but is cumbersome to use, bearing an index only listing authors. The supplementary second volume has a better index but is less helpful for *Night*. Braham's *The Hungarian Jewish Cat-astrophe: A Selected and Annotated Bibliography* offers a regional focus rele-vant to Wiesel's memoir, particularly the section "Personal Narratives" (192–96).

Audiovisual Materials

Night can be obtained in audio recordings: Audio Bookshelf has produced an unabridged cassette or CD edition narrated by Jeffrey Rosenblatt; Recorded Books offers a CD of Marion Wiesel's new translation read by George Guidall. In 1967, Wiesel narrated *Sighet, Sighet,* a short film documentary evoking the town of his birth, available through Alden Films. The 1994 film *Elie Wiesel Goes Home* is a valuable companion to *Sighet, Sighet*. Other useful videos con-cerning Wiesel's life and work include *Facing Hate*, featuring an interview with Bill Moyers, and *First Person Singluar*, narrated by William Hurt.

Part Two

APPROACHES

Introduction

A small book about a devastating subject, *Night* has an artistry that encompasses many strategies. One of these strategies is the parenthetical statement. Virtually no student will in a first reading notice these parentheses, which contain anything from a few words to an entire paragraph, but I have found that it pays to draw attention to them. *Night*'s parentheses reveal many different voices (caustic, informative, uneasy, discerning) and range from deft asides to shocked recognition. All share, however, the character of commentary; set off from the main text, they help convey the proper tone and emphasis.

The first instance is both stunning and exemplary. Having just received word that the wearing of the yellow star has been decreed upon Sighet's Jews, Wiesel's father, a community leader, tries to make the best of the situation: "The yellow star? So what? It's not lethal . . . " (11). In the wake of his father's consolation, however, Wiesel declares otherwise, enclosing his stinging response in parentheses: "(Poor Father! Of what then did you die?)." This caustic aside questions his father's sense of proportion. It dramatizes another instance of the clash between the wisdom of age and the audacity of youth found throughout the memoir. Yet the parentheses attempt to keep such audacity in check even as they create the rhetorical space for its impertinent voice.

Drawing attention to these mostly overlooked (or unexamined) parenthetical insertions can inspire students to reread, to attend to features of this small text that they may have taken for granted. It fosters close reading of a harrowing text in which the details could easily be lost. But the parenthetical also urges attention to the multiple voices Wiesel draws on to create his memoir, voices often of counterpoint, sometimes of conflict.

The seventeen essays collected in the "Approaches" section of this volume help us listen better to Wiesel's multiple voices. The essays approach *Night* from familiar as well as unfamiliar terrain. Most familiar perhaps will be those essays that consider the book as a Holocaust memoir, indeed, as a classic work of the genre, comparing *Night* with memoirs written by other authors and with other memoirs written by Wiesel. Less familiar will be two essays that situate *Night* in a Jewish-Yiddish context, an approach that may appear more standard than it actually is. Most readers are aware that Wiesel is Jewish and that his chronicle refers to Jewish aspects of life and death. But the teacher of *Night* is not usually versed in the manifold dimensions of tradition that shape Wiesel's memoir. Moreover, regaining the Yiddish context of *Night*'s initial publication helps readers see *Night* as one important step in the Jewish response to the Holocaust. At the other end of the spectrum are approaches that defamiliarize *Night* by including it in courses not focused on the Holocaust. *Night* takes on a different cast here, as do the readings that dwell alongside it. Other essays adapt the memoir to its diverse audiences by highlighting innovative ways of presenting *Night*. Literary to the core, *Night* nonetheless speaks to a gamut of disciplines. Thus the essayists contributing to the volume are historians, psychologists, and theologians, as well as literary critics.

The essays placed under the heading "Historical and Cultural Context" both broaden and narrow the focus to guide a reader to crucial contexts. Wiesel's memoir is not simply an account of any victim but that of a religious Jewish boy who views his experience through the media of Jewish life. References to prayer, blessings, holidays, learning, and religious books abound in the family setting and in the succeeding period bereft of it. Nehemia Polen provides a primer in the history, rituals, and texts of the Jewish experience, with a particular accent on the Hasidic contribution, yet the premise of his review is that neither Hasidism nor Wiesel's account and experience can be understood without the background of classical Jewish life. Only with a proper understanding of this context can Wiesel's narrative be fully appreciated as a counternarrative.

The counternarrative set in motion by the Holocaust per se begins with the ghetto, the forced removal from home bringing about a disruption of life's normal routines. At this point, however, families were still for the most part intact. This disruption was taken another step by the forced deportations of Hungary's Jews to Auschwitz. Simone Gigliotti, a cultural historian based in New Zealand, analyzes what it means to focus on the underexamined dimension of the deportations through *Night*. The emotional violations recorded in *Night* compel historians (and classrooms dealing with Holocaust history), in Gigliotti's terms, to destabilize cognitive analysis. Although pitched to historians, this essay also sets chapter 2 of *Night* in a rich context that returns the reader to the chapter's detail.

Often invoked as the symbol of the Holocaust's devastating evil, the Auschwitz concentration camp was a locale with a history, organization, and geography. Michael Berenbaum introduces those aspects of the camp while weaving in Wiesel's personal response to the camp's "madness and confusion." Berenbaum's reference to terms, population, and punishments places Auschwitz on a map and suggests how Wiesel's experience may or may not be viewed as typical. While Polen and Berenbaum begin to tease out *Night*'s response to theodicy, Alan L. Berger elaborates what he terms Wiesel's "protest from within faith." He details how Wiesel's later memoirs, taking stock of his life after the war and reviewing again his life before and during it, stay with questions first raised in *Night* while giving a fuller picture of the life of faith out of which they arise.

The Holocaust surely deserves to be seen in the context of history. But *Night*, for all its historical detail, is not a historical treatise or essay. The second section of essays, "Literary Contexts," shifts from a focus on history and culture to an appreciation of *Night* as a work of literature. As a richly crafted memoir drafted in Hebrew, written in Yiddish, adapted into French, and translated into English and dozens of other languages, *Night* intersects with a variety of literary traditions. Foremost among these is Yiddish, the language of its initial publication. Jan Schwarz's essay on the memoir's Yiddish context parallels Polen's chapter on *Night*'s Jewish background. Schwarz also fills in a Jewish context. He traces the memoir's publication as part of a series of Yiddish volumes largely devoted to writing about the Holocaust, recalls the audience of the Yiddish *Night* (an audience already familiar with the Holocaust memoir's conventions), and surveys the basic writings on the Holocaust in Yiddish in the mid-1950s. He rightly concludes that *Night*'s appearance was not by any means unique; this rich context gives us different eyes with which to read. The adaptation into French directed *Night* to a different audience. But here, too, as Judith Clark Schaneman shows us, it is useful to compare *La nuit* with other French Holocaust survivor literature, particularly the novels and memoirs written by Anna Langfus and Charlotte Delbo. This comparison allows the special features of *Night* to come into view while introducing students to less-well-known but still formidable chroniclers.

There is yet a third context: Hungary. Hungary resolutely held onto its Jews until late in the war; indeed, most of Europe's Jews had been annihilated by then. Rita Horváth suggests that this late date shapes Hungarian Holocaust writing generally, above all by intensifying the self-conscious act of witnessing. By locating *Night* among these memoirs and by comparing it with Imre Kertész's *Fateless*, Horváth offers us another frame—one that is often lost sight of or never fully acknowledged.

These various cultural frames allow different aspects of *Night* to emerge. By narrowing the focus, Susanne Klingenstein's step-by-step reading of chapter 1 reveals the artistry that underlies *Night*'s simple prose. Finely attentive to the narrative roles of the Jewish calendar and intertextual allusion, Klingenstein examines the chapter's carefully paced account of Jewish Sighet's decimation, thereby offering a judicious entry point to Wiesel's memoir. In contrast and complement, David Patterson looks at *Night* against the broad backdrop of Holocaust memoirs. He argues that the act of writing a Holocaust memoir is wedded to the hope of recovery. *Night* can then be measured (appreciated, read) in relation to general patterns, with other texts providing contrasting examples. In this vein, Jonathan Druker speaks of teaching *Night* with Primo Levi's memoir, *Survival in Auschwitz*. The two memoirists are bound by their time spent in Auschwitz and by a career of writing that constantly weighed the implications of that period. Pairing them is thus natural. Yet the two hailed from different Jewish worlds and chronicled their experience in different idioms. Druker shows how, without claiming these two memoirs as definitive, the pairing can extend greatly a classroom appreciation for the range of response.

The concept of witness underlies approaches to the Holocaust generally and to *Night* in particular. For that reason, Michael Bernard-Donals's approach to the role of witness in *Night* is decidedly provocative: the memoir teaches us, to his mind, not so much about witness as about the "limits of witnessing." Such recognition comes by way of "three principal pedagogical issues"—issues that also have been crucial to critical theory's confrontation with the Holocaust: the problem of witness and memory, the problem of the sublime and trauma, and the problem of history.

The final section of essays, "Courses and Classroom Strategies," makes explicit the diverse forums in which *Night* today finds an audience—whether in university, college, or high school, in classes devoted to the Holocaust or in those in which the Holocaust only enters through *Night*. Some essays stress the conceptual approach to *Night* as enabled by a certain course syllabus (Eisenstein, Lewis); others highlight innovative teaching methods (Lassner, Frost, Darsa, Roth).

Courses in critical thinking, a staple of university education, argue for the values of analysis and demonstrate the weakness of casual thought and belief. Paul Eisenstein shows how well such a course can benefit by the enigmatic questions that *Night* raises and how, in turn, *Night's* challenge to conventional notions often goes beyond the critique presented by Sophocles, Dante, and Shakespeare. Eisenstein's essay (and the course that it chronicles) highlights Wiesel's special contribution among the literary monuments of European culture. Teaching *Night* in courses dedicated specifically to the Holocaust brings another set of demands and opportunities. Reflecting on her course called The Representation of the Holocaust in Literature and Film, Phyllis Lassner argues that collaborative learning, either in pairs or small groups, can help make the most of the emotional intensity generated by reading *Night* and the search for an adequate language of response. Further, Lassner uses Wiesel's essay "A Plea for the Dead" to model for students the "midrashic discourse of questions and commentary" with which they can engage *Night*. By doing so, she enables multiple Wiesel voices to play a role in eliciting the students' own voices.

For the psychologist Christopher J. Frost, *Night's* insistent questions on identity shape the approach to this theme in an interdisciplinary course entitled Science, Religion, and the Quest for Meaning. Students' group projects integrate the issue of identity into the broader investigation of the Holocaust. Poignantly, Frost's story of his journey to present-day Romania models how the quest for meaning and identity in *Night* can find expression in day-to-day ethics. In Kevin Lewis's course Spiritual Autobiography, *Night* is again in the company of great books, this time more contemporary ones, which enables the unconventional nature of Wiesel's autobiography to come through. Lewis, too, draws on Wiesel's later life and writing to illuminate *Night's* strategies, but his interest is more existential than narrative. Wiesel's description of a post-Holocaust journey to India leads to an interrogation of Western civilization in the light of the Holocaust while suggesting the terms required to embrace again the West's tainted culture.

Testimony has various modes, each of which, when used judiciously, can enhance the others. Jan Darsa, an educator working largely with a high school audience, tells how video testimony complements *Night's* literary witness and suggests a classroom sequence that alternates readings from *Night* with video segments, weaving a testimonial fabric of voice and text. For John K. Roth, *Night* provokes questions that in turn serve as a guide for his general course on the Holocaust. These questions—historical, interpretive, and reactive—emerge from a reading of the memoir and are then channeled into the remainder of the syllabus. Given Roth's position as an eminent Christian thinker on the Holocaust's implications, the questions also revolve around Christian response to the Holocaust, including the contribution of Christian antisemitism to the Holocaust—issues that Roth traces to his ongoing dialogue with *Night* and subsequent Wiesel writings.

These essays on teaching *Night* set out an array of pedagogical issues and problems. What is perhaps less clearly stressed is the pain, for teacher and student alike, that comes with reading such grim scenes. Nothing can blunt the pain of the story *Night* tells. Nor perhaps should anything. Indeed, Wiesel has told the story of a parent who, learning that on reading *Night* her child had nightmares, asked the author what could be done. He responded that, to his mind, one should be worried if after reading *Night* one did not have nightmares. If nightmares begin the process, a critical language can give it shape. Teachers can help give language to this dark emotion. Hence the teacher must be ready to listen to students who grope for what to say and to aid them in becoming articulate. Reading *Night* can bring about a crisis; the essays in this volume set forth strategies whereby, at the very least, such a crisis can be addressed.

Night as Counternarrative: The Jewish Background

Nehemia Polen

Elie Wiesel's *Night* records the events that crushed the faith of a young boy growing up in a world of faith. It is a counternarrative to the narrative he was told as a child, to the stories, traditions, and values with which he grew up. Only the merest glimpses of that world appear in *Night*, which focuses relentlessly on collapse and destruction. Yet to understand the scope of the tragedy, to comprehend its full weight and existential burden, one must hold in mind a vision of the orderly world that preceded the collapse, in particular the religion into which Wiesel was born and the faith that nurtured him.

The religion is Judaism, a multitiered system of belief and practice based on the Hebrew Bible (*The Holy Scriptures*). The core of the Bible is the Pentateuch—the five books of Moses, whose core in turn can be seen as the assertion that humans are made in the image of God (Gen. 1.26; cf. Gen. 5.1) and the commandment to love our neighbor as ourselves (Lev. 19.18). These two great principles illumine the Ten Commandments, especially the prohibition against murder on the one hand and the call to honor our parents—God's life-bestowing agents—on the other. The events in *Night* are a direct challenge to the values embedded in these commandments. The will of the perpetrators can be seen as triumphing over the will of the author of the commandments, the God of Israel. The narrator of *Night*, young Eliezer, observes that the only one who kept his promises to the Jews was Hitler. What about the identity of the ones who did not keep their promises? The reader no doubt thinks of the Allies, the politicians, the Jewish communal leaders. But it should not be forgotten that the first one to make promises to the Jews was the Jewish God: promises of peace and blessing, of honor and achievement, of dignity and wisdom to inspire others. To appreciate the intensity of *Night*, one must hear it as a cry of betrayal.

The Bible points to the two great triads that would govern Jewish thought in all periods: God, Torah, and Israel; Creation, revelation, and redemption.

> *God* in the Bible is a passionate personality: concerned about his creation, yearning for relationship with his creatures, capable of anger but also of compassion, mercy, and forgiveness.
>
> *Torah*, the record of the divine-human encounter, includes a broad variety of genres and works: story and law, prose and poetry, ethics and worship. In the fullness of the biblical canon, the word *Torah* came to comprise the great prophetic visions of Isaiah, the joyous faith of the Psalms, the gnomic wisdom of Proverbs, the incisive questioning of Job, the knotty skepticism of Ecclesiasties, the fragrant eros of Song of Songs, the love and devotion of Ruth. The Torah is thus a sacred scripture that eludes monochromatic definition, that always and at all points breathes expansively with many voices and radiates multiple perspectives.
>
> *Israel* is the people entrusted with the covenant, God's message of Torah, and charged with the responsibility to create a culture of blessing—of bounteous growth, generosity, and mutual respect—throughout the world, beginning in the land promised to their forefather Abraham. If Israel remains faithful to the covenant, it is promised peace, material prosperity, and spiritual distinction: "a kingdom of priests and a holy nation" (Exod. 19.6).

> *Creation* means that the world is not an accidental emergence but the volitional product of a good Creator who surveyed his work and "saw that it was very good" (Gen. 1.31).
>
> *Revelation* refers to God's gift of the Torah and more broadly to the wisdom immanent in the world and the human capacity to discover it and live in harmony with it. "The Torah of the Lord is perfect, restoring the soul" (Ps. 19.8).
>
> *Redemption* points to a subtle telos woven into the fabric of creation, a bias for growth and repair, and the hope for a return of all things to their place and their dignity in God's good time. It underlies the fundamental optimism that pervades the Hebrew Bible despite repeated tragedy and trauma. This disposition to optimism is found at the end of the Pentateuch, with Moses's abundant blessing to all Israel; at the close of the Prophets, with the promise of Elijah's return and the restoration of "the heart of the fathers to the children, and the heart of the children to the fathers" (Mal. 3.24); and at the conclusion of the

Writings—and thus the Hebrew Bible as a whole—with the proclama-
tion to the Jewish exiles by the Persian king Cyrus encouraging those
who wished to return to Jerusalem and rebuild their Temple: "the Lord
his God is with him—let him go up" (2 Chron. 36.23).

From the Hebrew Bible Judaism received its basic ideas of sacred time (Sabbath and festivals); sacred place (Jerusalem, the Land of Israel, and the Temple), holiness and ethics; visions of an ideal future age (the messianic idea), and
the quest for a direct experience of the divine (Jewish mysticism, known in
some periods as kabbalah). While the biblical prophets could be overwhelmed
at times by the power and immediacy of the divine presence, by the later books
of the Bible, and certainly throughout the Second Temple period (fifth century
BCE to first century CE), a tendency arose for God to recede from direct view.
The main body of Jews came to believe that prophecy had ceased, that miracles
were largely a thing of the past, and that although God could still be approached in prayer, his presence was to be perceived in the "still small voice" (1
Kings 19.12), in echoes and hints of the sacred rather than in the overtly miraculous events of the fast-receding foundational period. Especially after the Romans destroyed the Second Temple (70 CE) many Jews searched for God in
their sacred texts and traditions, through study and sober deliberation. These
tendencies eventually culminated in Rabbinic Judaism and its classic works: the
Mishnah, the Midrash, and the Talmud.

The legacy of the early rabbis (first through sixth centuries CE) is a Judaism
of modesty and balance, a low-profile religion that adapts to the loss of political
power and prepares to survive and even flourish under conditions of exile and
adversity. Rabbinic Judaism is a robust, fault-tolerant system that governs by
mutual consent rooted in ideals of literacy and a shared culture of learning. In
this society the voice of God is to be heard not in thunder but in the give-and-
take of Talmudic debate. The divine light no longer shines visibly from the
Temple but can be seen emerging from the interstitial spaces of master-disciple
transmission and collegial discussion. In the rabbinic religion of intertextual
play, God is the connecting link between generations, sustaining the dialogue
between distant texts that are endlessly juxtaposed and related in new ways,
jostling one another in provocative camaraderie. Rabbinic Jews believe in God
with as much passion as their biblical forebears, but for them God hovers in the
background, offstage, holding the script in his hands with love and care, observing the unfolding action with great interest and hope.

A central characteristic of God in the Bible is power—power to intervene in
history, to deliver from danger, and to free from bondage. In rabbinic literature,
by contrast, God is often portrayed as vulnerable and (at least overtly) disem-
powered, cultivating the virtues of patience and receptivity—just like his people. This theology receives its most striking expression in those rabbinic passages that portray God in prayer or weeping and mourning, actually shedding
tears over the destruction of his house in Jerusalem and the exile of his people.

Closely associated with this image of God is the theme of the Shechinah, God's manifest presence, which feels the pain of suffering humanity and accompanies the Jews in their wanderings, providing comfort and hope of redemption.

The Talmudic corpus exceeds the expansive diversity of the Hebrew Bible by many orders of magnitude. It is an encyclopedic body of literature, whose wisdom has captivated and challenged generation upon generation of scholars and lay readers. It would be futile to attempt a summary here, other than to suggest that the resistance to encapsulation is itself part of the message: human nature is difficult, religion is complex, but there is hope in both, and the wise course is to remember that there are no easy answers and that every small opportunity to do good and to grow in learning and spirit must be seized enthusiastically.

Finally, there is one rabbinic aphorism that, in the light of our focus here, has an eerie and ominous ring: From the day the Temple was destroyed, prophecy was taken away from the prophets, but at times it emerges from the voices of little children—and madmen.

The Middle Ages saw the flowering of philosophical approaches to Jewish theology, as exemplified by the writings of Moses Maimonides (1135–1204). Maimonides struggled to remove all anthropomorphic conceptions of the deity; but while his austere theology was enormously influential, a counterapproach arose that delighted in imagining God in vivid language and poetic figures. This approach, known as kabbalah, reached its classical expression in the thirteenth century with the appearance of the Zohar, a work of astonishing literary, religious, and imaginative creativity.

The basic ideas and concerns of Jewish mysticism come from a close reading of Genesis, chapter 1. The first idea is the creative power of language. In Genesis, God creates the world by speaking; thus every utterance, every particle of language—especially the Hebrew language—has infinite power and significance. Jewish mysticism displays an endless fascination with all aspects of Hebrew, not just the semantic surface of utterances but also the details of letters—their shapes, sounds, numerical values, permutations, and combinations. The second main idea comes toward the end of the first chapter of Genesis, when God creates human beings—male and female—in his image. For the kabbalists, this act is more than a metaphor or a noble sentiment expressive of human dignity. The divine image is a true correspondence inscribed in the human body as well as in human emotion, intellect, and spirit; every aspect of human morphology corresponds to some aspect of divine being and life.

The ten modes of divine manifestation, or stages in God's self-disclosure, are the sefirot, the basic structures of kabbalistic theory. This theory is complex and ramified, but for our purposes it is helpful to note just a few basic patterns. On the kabbalistic tree of life (the map of emanation from the unknowable absolute to our created world) there are three vertical columns. The right column represents energy of infinite love and expansiveness. The left column embodies judgmental rigor and the setting of limits. The central column resolves these two polar forces in a beautiful, harmonious balance. There is a vertical polarity as well. The highest position represents pure bestowal, and the lowest represents pure receptivity. The emphasis of the system as a whole is on reaching balance and equipoise and on the realization that each sefirah includes all the others in a supple and endless dance of energies. The kabbalistic practitioner strives for harmony in all aspects of life and especially for ethical commitment to giving to others, which prepares the kabbalist to be a receptive vessel for the divine flow of bounty and light. For the traditional kabbalist the best way to ensure that one's life is in balanced correspondence to the divine realm is by adherence to the Torah's system of moral and ritual practices.

While some scholars were fascinated with kabbalah for its intellectual sophistication and challenge, most devotees were on a personal religious quest to experience the infinite. For the kabbalist the entire universe is alive with the presence of God. Kabbalistic texts frequently quote Isaiah 6.3, "the whole earth is full of His glory." There are sparks of the divine everywhere, waiting to be redeemed—that is, transformed and raised to a higher state of being, aided by the compassionate attentiveness of the kabbalistic practitioner.

One aspect of kabbalistic thinking is the nonlinearity of small actions. In this view, we cannot judge the implications of a deed by applying rational criteria alone, by looking only at surface appearances. Since the upper world and the lower, physical plane are linked at every point, a good deed, even a good word or kindly thought, may redound throughout the universe with infinite power and blessing. Of course the opposite is true as well: negative energy can multiply exponentially with demonic virulence and fury. One mode of kabbalistic practice addresses this issue, attempting to sweeten—that is, sublimate and transform—negative forces in benign and positive directions. This aspect of kabbalah results in the near apotheosis of the human being, since the cosmic system as a whole is exquisitely sensitive and responsive to human initiative. As the kabbalists put it, "arousal above [on the heavenly plane] follows arousal below [on the terrestrial, human plane]" (Zohar 1.235a, 3.105a).

We now come to the Hasidic movement, which first flourished in the Jewish communities of eighteenth-century Russia and Poland. Hasidism embraces all aspects of the tradition it inherited: the creator deity of the Bible who in his love chooses Israel and who can be entreated in prayer; the tender compassionate father and divine teacher of Rabbinic Midrash; the abstract God of the Jewish philosophers; the unknown and unnameable absolute of kabbalah who self-discloses in the sefirot; the all-pervasive immanent presence verging at the edge of pantheism; and the popular deity of the common folk—a familiar member of the family, just as in the days of Abraham, Isaac, and Jacob in Genesis—enigmatic, elusive, sometimes obstinate, as all family members can be at times, but by no means a stranger. This last description might be considered a cornerstone of Hasidic theology: God should not be a stranger.

Hasidism's founding figure is Rabbi Israel ben Eliezer (d. 1760), known as the Baal Shem Tov ("Master of the Good Name"). He endeared himself to the common folk as a wonder-working kabbalist, healer, and shamanistic intercessor for the beleaguered Jewish people, but he also attracted a small inner circle of rabbinic scholars, opening their eyes and hearts with his profound panentheism—the experiential awareness of God's presence everywhere.

The Baal Shem Tov's major contributions are attitudinal and experiential rather than theoretical. They include:

> Fearlessness: since God is everywhere, evil is ultimately an illusion, and there is nothing to fear but God.
>
> A joyful, robust embrace of this world as God's arena.
>
> Emphasis on religious pleasure: every religious act should strive for ecstasy, a rush of intense communion at the moment of joining with the divine. In particular, intense, ecstatic prayer is the very core of religious life.
>
> The uniqueness of the individual, the centrality and sacredness of each personality, along with the appreciation of diversity in a changing religious universe.

The innovation in Hasidic social structure is the zaddik, the saint who is the center of the community and its link to heaven. The zaddik is responsible for his entire community, and the efficacy of his prayer channels blessing to the people. In return, the followers, or Hasidim, venerate their master and give him their fervent devotion. But the real grace is not in the zaddik or in the Hasidic community but in the bond between them that nurtures and enriches them all.

Hasidism conveys its teachings by direct contact between master and disciple, as well as in books that record the master's discourses, usually expositions of biblical passages. But perhaps Hasidic wisdom is best embodied in its tales and stories. Hasidic tales from the classic period represent such values as faith in God and in the zaddik; the power of prayer, inwardness, devotion, and simplicity; and the importance of seeing things from another perspective. Embracing these values almost invariably means seeing things from the side of the powerless, the disenfranchised, those who otherwise would not have a voice. The tales emphasize the importance of small changes that are immediate and accessible, in contrast to larger, systemic changes whose effects will be felt much later.

The Hasidic tale carried in one's heart functions by itself as a kind of teacher or mentor. To possess a fund of tales is to cultivate an inner voice providing perspective, poise, and grounding, a reservoir that can point to a new purchase on circumstances and assist in proceeding with wisdom and integrity.

While Hasidism was a central component of the culture of Sighet Jewry before the destruction, much of the spirit a religiously sensitive young man would have absorbed was simply the common legacy of the traditional Eastern European Jewish community. A core value of the common legacy was respect. Even inanimate objects were treated with respect: food was never thrown about or handled in an indifferent manner. Books, especially sacred books, were treated with reverence; when stacked, care was taken to place the Bible on top, with other books arranged in a sequence reflecting their place in the canonical hierarchy. Worn, aged books were not discarded but were laid to rest. Of course parents were treated with reverence: a child would not interrupt a parent, sit in the parent's seat at table, or call him or her by name. In some communities children only addressed parents and teachers in the third person.

This was the common ground of Jewish life. But those who embodied the ideal of *mentshlichkeit* (humanity, heightened ethical sensibility) went much further, dignifying every encounter with young and old, friend and stranger, rich and poor and holding in mind the constant awareness that all human beings embody the image of God and that all creatures bear a divine spark. Householders knew and followed the Talmudic dictum that pets and farm animals must be fed before the family sat down to table.

Finally, despite the focus on parents and the elderly, traditional Jewish society was very child centered. Children were prized not just as God's blessing for the future but also as inheritors of the Torah. Parents would go without food in order to pay for a child's education.

One of the holiest and most poignant moments of the week was at the onset of the Sabbath, on Friday evening, when parents would bless their children. With the gentle glow of the Sabbath candles as a backdrop, all children—from infants to adults with families of their own—would hear the ancient biblical words ("May the Lord bless you and keep you. . . ."; Num. 6.24–26) uttered with deep love, parental hands resting on their heads. The blessing would conclude with the parents' deepest personal wishes for their children, perhaps articulated only in the silence of a caressing gaze.

Here we return to the biblical ideal of blessing, which implies bestowal of bounty and success as well as acknowledgment—the recognition of the preciousness and significance of the other and the awareness that we only come into ourselves by recognizing and acknowledging the being of the other. To bless is to rejoice in the connectedness of similarity and in the integrity of difference—even in one's own children.

With this brief picture of Judaism and Jewish values in mind, we can see clearly how *Night* functions as a counternarrative, almost a counter-Torah. While the pages of *Night* contain no direct quotation of a classical Jewish text, the texts and traditions are always there, offstage, moaning and mourning quietly. Judaism hovers as a disembodied ghost, a broken faith, a dark nimbus casting shadow and no light. Both the Jews and the Judaism of Eliezer's childhood have been murdered.

In the beginning of *Night*, God is strong, and Eliezer's faith is strong. By the end of the memoir, the God of Eliezer's childhood stands defeated, crushed. To be sure, there are biblical precedents that one can point to: the book of Lamentations, passages in Job, Jeremiah, and the Psalms. Yet these books contain at least a glimmer of hope; alongside the passages of despair, one can point to verses of consolation and hope and even joy. There is nothing like this relief in the unrelenting horror of *Night*.

To find appropriate resources for grappling with the world of *Night*, one might turn to classic Rabbinic literature. For it is in the Talmud and Midrash where, as noted above, a theology of divine vulnerability and disempowerment comes to be articulated, where the Shechinah suffers with humanity and wanders in exile with the Jewish people.

Deuteronomy presents a seemingly uncomplicated religious calculus: the good are rewarded, the wicked punished. While Job probes and challenges this approach, the rabbis begin to problematize the whole calculus. The fact is we don't always know why the good suffer and the wicked prosper. And just as the righteous are not always blameless, the wicked may have redeeming features, may deserve our sympathy. The Mishnah teaches that when a criminal is put to death for his crime, the divine presence, the Shechinah, suffers with him (Sanhedrin 46a). Rabbi Meir (second century CE) taught that a hanged criminal must be let down immediately and respectfully buried. To allow the body to linger in its mortification and disgrace is an offense against human dignity and against God, in whose image all humans are made, the just and the wicked alike (Sanhedrin 46b).

It is only by embracing a God of vulnerability, of self-restraint and apparent powerlessness that Judaism was able to survive the loss of the Temple in Jerusalem and of national independence. These trends are intensified in the world of kabbalah, whose texts are filled with images of the Shechinah's fall, of her suffering and shame. The complexity and suppleness of kabbalistic theology, however, leave room for a domain of divine transcendence, assuring the eventual triumph of goodness and blessing, of God's original plan for creation, so that the Shechinah will be raised from the dust and the world and God will achieve fullness and completeness.

These theories put into relief one of the most vivid images of *Night*: that of the little angel, the child dying in slow agony on the gallows. In this context, the famous words, "Where He is? This is where—hanging here from this gallows . . ." (65) take on a new aspect. It is indeed God who is on the gallows, suffering—not for humanity but with humanity, indeed as humanity. And children embody the sacred in a particularly vibrant form. As the Zohar puts it, the face of a schoolchild is the face of the Shechinah, the growing edge of the divine, oriented to the world, beaming hope.

If *Night* chronicles the defeat of God the divine father, it is also the story of the ruin of Eliezer's human father. When we first encounter the father, he appears strong and wise, compassionate but somewhat distant. Notably, he dismissed the reports of grave danger; it was he who made the decision not to attempt escape.

Gradually, as the horrors unfold, the relationship between father and son changes. Eliezer sees his father weep for the first time (19). The son has discovered his father's vulnerability and realizes that his father is dependent on him for survival. His father is beaten, but Eliezer does not respond, does nothing to intervene, and is filled with remorse and shame (39). Later his father is beaten again, with even more savagery. Eliezer is angry—not at the perpetrator but at his father, for not knowing how to avoid the wrath of his tormentor. Eliezer thinks of how to move away from his father, to avoid being beaten himself (54). On another occasion, because his father cannot march in step and is repeatedly punished on account of it, Eliezer becomes his teacher, giving him lessons in marching in rhythm (55).

Eliezer's struggle against the temptation to treat his father as a burden emerges as a central theme of the memoir. After discovering that a certain son had abandoned his father, he prays, "Oh God, Master of the Universe, give me the strength never to do what Rabbi Eliahu's son has done" (91). Eliezer comes to realize that his own task of survival is made more difficult by his commitment to his father. Nevertheless he does not abandon him but remains faithful to the end.

It is hard not to see Eliezer's struggle to remain faithful to his father under impossible conditions as reflecting his fight to retain some relationship with the God of his childhood. The world of *Night* had no sacred time, no sacred place, no sacred ritual, no sacred text, no comfort of family or of tradition. But the great challenge was, How could Eliezer abandon his divine father just when Eliezer needed him the most? No, the real question was even more painful: How could he abandon his divine father just when God needed Eliezer the most?

Night provides no answer to this question. Indeed, as the memoir comes to an end, the loss and collapse seem to be total. "Since my father's death, nothing mattered to me anymore. . . . I no longer thought of my father, or my mother" (113). There is no coda, no note of hope, no glimmer of light. The narrator supplies no biblical verse, no rabbinic aphorism, no Hasidic tale to alleviate the gloom. (These would come later, in subsequent works, to be written at a later stage in the author's life.)

And yet. In the very last scene, Eliezer has survived, has been liberated from Buchenwald, and finds himself in a hospital hovering for two weeks between life and death. Summoning all his strength, he gets up, wanting to see himself in the mirror hanging on the wall, for the first time since the ghetto.

> From the depths of the mirror, a corpse was contemplating me.
> The look in his eyes as he gazed at me has never left me.   (115)

What the narrator sees is shocking, a shattered self. Yet the last word, "me," makes it clear that that shattered self is not to be identified with the narrator. The corpse's eyes that looked back from the mirror, "his eyes," were not those of the chronicler; the narrator has recovered self-awareness, has found a voice, has a face beyond the image in the mirror. The mirror did more than reflect the present in inexorable fixity; by its very starkness, it broke open a window on the future.

Here we are reminded of a Talmudic story, which—consistent with the rest of *Night*—the author does not cite but which may nevertheless illumine this final, arresting image of the memoir. The Talmud records that Simeon the Just—considered the last truly saintly high priest of the Jerusalem Temple (second century BCE), whose countenance shone with a godly light—was reluctant to partake of the sacrifice of the Nazirite, the man or woman who had sought holiness by forswearing wine, growing long hair and then shearing it, and avoiding impurity. Simeon was afraid that the Nazirite's ascetic vow was taken in haste, for mixed motives, perhaps for reasons of religious exhibitionism. On one occasion, however, Simeon fully approved of a Nazirite's vow. There was a handsome young man who had beautiful eyes and long locks of hair perfectly framing his striking features. He was unaware of his comeliness, having never seen his image in a mirror. Once he went to draw water from a well and saw his own face gazing back at him. Becoming aware of his physical charms for the first time, he felt the strange stirrings of temptation and sin, so he immediately decided to devote his lustrous hair, indeed his life, to God by taking the vow of the Nazirite (Nedarim 9b).

Perhaps the narrator of *Night*, seeing the ghost in the mirror for the first time, is moved to follow the path of the post-Holocaust Nazirite. He knew that the eyes in the mirror would never leave him. They called to temptation—not that of lust but of collapse and despair. But he would choose to direct his own gaze to the future, to tell the tale, to introduce a new generation to the world that was destroyed, to participate in the sacred task of rebuilding. Can one think of a more sacred response to the face in the mirror?

Night and the Teaching of History: The Trauma of Transit

Simone Gigliotti

I am a historian who teaches in the field of modern Europe, particularly its histories and representation of racism, state violence, forced migration, and colonial expansion. My most well developed specialization is the Holocaust and World War II, and I have taught courses on these topics to undergraduate students in Australia, New Zealand, and the Caribbean, using historical sources, film, witness testimony, and literature. My research concerns one of the most traumatic moments of entrapment and forced displacement in World War II, arguably in the modern period, the Nazi-organized mass deportations of Jews all over Europe to the main extermination camps in occupied Poland. It is in the effort to understand how deportees experienced this mass transit and forced migration as both event and representation that Elie Wiesel's *Night* proves pivotal and instructive.

From October 1941 until the end of 1944, an estimated three million Jews were transported from major ghettos to their deaths by trains under the orders of Hitler and the Nazi regime. The inhumane, claustrophobic, and debilitating conditions deportees experienced in the train journeys are some of the last and most illuminating untold episodes of captivity and displacement in the Holocaust.

Instructors focusing on deportation journeys face multiple options. First, they can examine the historical and political background, considering deportations as a major territorial displacement and forced relocation of the Jews, an intensification of Nazi anti-Jewish policy that began in 1933 with the introduction of antisemitic legislation and racial persecution. Second, instructors can nationalize this approach by focusing on country-specific histories of invasion, occupation, collaboration, and the impact on Jewish communities in Poland, Hungary, and France, where the euphemism for the mass murder for the Jews, the "Final Solution of the Jewish Question" (hereafter the final solution) was implemented by the Nazi regime during World War II. After the Nazi invasion of Poland, in September 1939, the country was occupied and divided into several administrative areas. One was the *Generalgouvernement*, and it included the cities of Warsaw, Krakow, Radom, and Lublin. This area contained the majority of Poland's Jewish population in ghettos, and thus the number of deportations from it were high.

A third option is to integrate victim and survivor testimony into either approach, to illuminate how Nazi deportation policy was received and represented by its victims. This essay considers the third approach. It enters the space of traumatic transit, largely detoured by historians, by examining Wiesel's Holocaust memoir *Night*. What does *Night* reveal about the deportation experience that historians writing about the Holocaust cannot? In what ways does the journey represent a microcosm of social collapse? How does Wiesel's representation of transit add to the teaching of the history of deportations?

Historians have, overwhelmingly, represented Nazi deportation policy in ways that confirm a stereotype of an efficient bureaucracy employed in the business of mass murder. Using mainly perpetrator documents, historians have reconstructed a procedure for deportations that identified the logistical determinants and financing of transports across Europe; the contribution of national railways from Germany and occupied Greece, Poland, and France; and the administrative and legal complexities that classified a person as "deportable." Despite their important contribution, these approaches echo the perpetrators' view of their victims as objects of a process. They leave the reader at the station platform as the trains depart, outside the deportees' traumatic confinement. The narrative journey of deportation resumes on the platforms of arrival at the concentration camps.

Before investigating *Night* and its themes, it is necessary to provide a context for the function of deportations in the development of the final solution. The decision-making process and the emergence of Hitler's order for the final solution are topics of ongoing debate among historians (see Browning; Cesarani; Gerlach; Jäckel; Longerich; and Roseman, *Wannsee Conference*). By adopting this contextual approach, instructors can introduce a larger historical narrative in which to place *Night*.

How can historians' narratives of deportation as a process and victims interpretation of it intersect? Raul Hilberg and Alfred C. Mierzejewski emphasize the logistical features of deportation, such as scheduling Jews on *Sonderzüge* ("special trains") to fit within existing timetables, the application of concession fares to transports of four hundred or more Jews, free travel for children under four, Jewish self-financing of the one-way journeys with expropriated property, and the coordination of the SS and the *Deutsche Reichsbahn* (German Railways) to implement it. Their analyses provide a critical foundation for interpreting Nazi approaches and contradictions: the use of boxcars and cattle cars for most deportations was evidence of the perpetrators' view of their victims as subhuman and continued the dehumanization that was a central theme of Nazi antisemitic ideology. Transportation to "the East" was presented to victims as relocation (there were provisions of food and clothing and luggage requirements) and as a means of survival, so as to encourage deportees' compliance and agreement in boarding the train. If this was a faithful representation, then why inflict such intolerable conditions as spatial compression, climactic assault, and humiliation of the victims? These conditions conspired to overwhelm them physically and psychologically and made their preparedness for alleged labor in "the East" all the more unlikely.

The deportees' anticipation of work, however, depended on the believability of rumours and the knowledge of what was happening to those Jews who were forcibly resettled, and this information varied greatly in select occupied areas and ghettos. At the time of Wiesel's deportation with his family, in the spring of 1944, news of gassings of Jews at Treblinka, which had been occurring since the summer of 1942, and the connotation of a trip to "the East" as a journey of no return were still largely unknown among Sighet's prospective deportees. Instructors thus need to situate Wiesel's narrative of life in Sighet, in northern Transylvania, Romania: the region's annexation by Hungary in 1940, the Nazi occupation of Hungary in late March 1944, and finally the ghettoization of Sighet's Jews. This coverage of the historical background can condition students, in the very least, to the context of the uncertainty, isolation, and incarceration faced by Jewish communities in many small towns like Wiesel's and to the departure scene in *Night*: "The synagogue resembled a large railroad station: baggage and tears" (22).

Wiesel's testimony of deportation transports the reader into a physical and historically distinct space of trauma that resists easy interpretation. His account of the conditions of transit—the compression of bodies, the separation of families, the lack of material provisions, the terror of temporal uncertainty, and the profound abandonment represented by the isolation of human beings in a cattle car en route to death—has been corroborated in countless other testimonies. Of course, there was no typical deportation experience, as individual narrative, context, time of deportation, duration of journey, number of people in each car, and other factors determined each victim's response.

And yet despite the journey's narrative and historical function—providing a passage from one form of incarceration to something altogether unimaginable—these transit experiences have been largely seen in abstraction, too traumatic, emotional, and subjective to be of important historical use. On entering the space of the cattle car, readers become suspended travelers and invasive witnesses to unspeakable trauma and the degradation of human beings. What can testimonies of this experience—so singular, extreme, and disturbing—do for historical approaches to the Holocaust? I argue that testimonies of deportation destabilize cognitive control of historical representation as a factually legitimated, ordered, and chronologically constructed event. Instructors might use these testimonies to investigate this destabilization of factual control, in addition to the erasure of trauma in historical representation; the role of emotion in narrative history; and the adoption of a sensory paradigm, as offered by the physiological response to the train journey, in interpretations of witnessing.

Mobility and immobility were constant companions of Wiesel's even before his involuntary departure from Sighet. In the synagogue, where Wiesel and others were awaiting deportation, the scene was desperate and chaotic. The next day, when they were marched to the station, the Hungarian police forced them into the cattle car. Wiesel described the experience thus:

> [E]ighty persons in each one. They handed us some bread, a few pails of water. They checked the bars on the windows to make sure they would not

come loose. The cars were sealed. One person was placed in charge of every
car: if someone managed to escape, that person would be shot.   (22)

Wiesel paints an image of imprisonment—bars, limited vision, and surveillance. Historians might contest his count of eighty people in the cattle car on
the grounds that numbers vary substantially among survivors' accounts. His es-
timate would require some documentation from SS records about the number
of people in that transport. Whether or not the exact number of people can be
verified, as Wiesel does not say how that number was arrived at, does not
negate the impression of suffocation, the feeling of intense overcrowding, and
the destruction of intimacy and personal boundaries, conditions common in
many deportees' accounts.

Wiesel's account of the deportation offers a rare type of witnessing. Owing to
the hermetic architecture and overwhelming darkness of the cattle car, the narrator's memory of what happened during the journey seemed less influenced by
what he saw than by what his other senses told him, and his witnessing became
an embodied act that displaced the reliance on vision. In embodied witnessing,
what one feels, smells, hears, and cannot see constantly threaten one's sanity,
faith, and any hope for normality, however defiantly construed. (This effect is
especially evident in Wiesel's representation of Mrs. Schächter.) The heat from
bodily compression and the thirst from lack of water produced desperation and
tension, as well as a loosening of the bondage to accepted convention.

Spatial compression in deportation journeys was prefaced with overcrowding
in ghettos, although the threat to practicing civility and the performance of private acts in public was not as common. Whatever remained in the ghetto of an
individual's or family's physical belongings and identity was further expropriated for the deportation journey, since deportees were only permitted to take a
specified weight of luggage and clothes. These material expropriations were in-
comparable, however, to the subversion of conventional behavior, practice, and
response and the effect of this subversion on individual and communal adjust-
ment to the journey, including the victims' management of some irritating deportees. Wiesel's journey became a time of release of inhibitions and erotic
feeling, the darkness of night acting as an anonymous stimulant:

> Freed of normal constraints, some of the young let go of their inhibitions
> and, under cover of darkness, caressed one another, without any thought
> of others, alone in the world. The others pretended not to notice.   (23)

The uncertainty of the train's destination produced a need for the preservation of food and water, and the labor of surveillance and preventing escape was
transferred from the German guards to the deportees themselves. This mode of
management and control aimed to instill intense fear and terror in the deportees during the journey. Attempts at escape were punished through violence
against the majority.

Although Wiesel's representation of the cattle car journey is not unlike many others at this point, the historian might be nervous about the lack of reference to time and chronology in *Night*. When was Wiesel moved into the ghetto? When was he deported and with whom? How many days did the journey take? But arguably such questions, evidence of a need to ground these events in wartime reality, do not bring us much closer to interpreting the historical utility of Wiesel's journey. While such questions should be answered, they are not the only pertinent questions. What questions, then, can be asked of the relation between chronology and intensifying trauma, between time and testimony? How does the train journey escape historical time and destabilize cognitive control?

It is in the journey where time and chronology are no longer defined by quantifiable units but, in Wiesel's memory, by traumatic events that punctuate time's passage from day to night. One of the more unsettling episodes occurs in the uncontrolled and periodically terrifying screams of Mrs. Schächter, a woman who was traveling with her ten-year-old son and whose husband and two elder sons were inadvertently deported previously without her. She yelled, "Fire! I see a fire! I see a fire!" as she looked out through the barred windows of the cattle car (24). Her screams are shocking, not only because of what fire has come to symbolize from a postwar perspective but also because the deportees could see "[o]nly the darkness of night" (25). Wiesel reports her continuing visions, as though her descent into delusion was marked by increasingly vivid and animated scenes of fire. Her screams created a collective trauma in the wagon:

> Our terror could no longer be contained. Our nerves had reached a breaking point. Our very skin was aching. It was as though madness had infected all of us. We gave up. A few young men forced her to sit down, then bound and gagged her.   (25–26)

Here Wiesel narrates how, during the temporary muting of Mrs. Schächter's screams, the train's rhythmic movement added an air of welcome routine to the journey. Yet her insistent cries soon intensified, finally culminating in "Look at the fire! Look at the flames! Flames everywhere . . ." (26; ellipses in orig.). The physical violence that silenced her screaming, as Wiesel tells it, became accepted in the carriage, not because violence was an acceptable practice but because, in the space of the cattle car, a degree of toleration and management had to be imposed for the mental preservation of the majority. The ferocity of the men's blows was a reflection of deportees' repression of their possible fate, for she was a reminder of what they feared—surrender to delirium and incomprehension.

Mrs. Schächter finally paused in her outbursts, but again her muteness was only temporary. The darkness of night, as I interpret from Wiesel's figurative and literal use of it, was the catalyst for an uninhibited truth too painful to comprehend and the canvas on which the flames yet again saturated her vision:

> Toward evening she began to shout again:
> "The fire, over there!"
> She was pointing somewhere in the distance, always the same place. No one felt like beating her anymore. The heat, the thirst, the stench, the lack of air, were suffocating us. Yet all that was nothing compared to her screams, which tore us apart. A few more days and all of us would have started to scream. (26)

As the train arrived at Auschwitz, Mrs. Schächter's vision was confirmed:

> And as the train stopped, this time we saw flames rising from a tall chimney into a black sky.
> Mrs. Schächter had fallen silent on her own. Mute again, indifferent, absent, she had returned to her corner. (28)

Wiesel's narration of Mrs. Schächter's public outbursts of her private torment—predictions, when read retrospectively—carries the reader into a space not accessible from reading historians' accounts of deportation. The illumination of the journey's assault on the senses, such as the piercing volume of Mrs. Schächter's screams, renders this experience as one of continuous reliving, a psychologically relentless transit moment of no escape. The moment occurred in historical time, as a part of Wiesel's narrative, but also outside it, in "traumatic time"; the journey experience is disjointed and highlights the psychological descent and terror of the victims, as well as their complete abandonment.

The themes in Wiesel's narrative common to other victims' accounts—the eradication of privacy, the erosion of intimacy, the relaxation of social convention regulating erotic and violent behavior, the humiliation of using the pail to defecate or urinate, and the communal spatial exchange for sleeping and standing that developed among deportees—explode the bureaucratic presentation of deportation as relocation, a journey to a work camp. It is the deportation journey that functions as the stripping or shedding stage of the self from the past, from social convention and expectations of improvement and promise. The physical and psychological endurance of the days of travel undo, essentially, one's ability to retain resolve, moral strength, and purpose. If the deportees were under the impression that they were meant to survive the trip, instructors may also use the deportations as evidence of a major corrective to the controversial perception of deportees as ostensibly voluntary, willing, and docile victims. Instructors can reflect on the deception of the Nazi image of relocation that characterized deportation journeys and the undoing of that image: the deplorable conditions of transit, the number of deportees crammed into each car, and the almost immediate killing of women and children, the sick and the elderly who arrived at the camps. The differences in the types of carriages used—passenger cars for Jews from Western Europe and cattle cars for Jews in the *Generalgouvernement* and more distant regions such as Greece—reinforced the Nazi perception of civilized, assimilated Jewry in the West and so-called primitive Jewry in the East. While the method of transport was not always consistent, these distinctions reflected the pretense of travel in those areas where resistance may have been encountered.

When used with other testimonies of deportation (e.g., Bretholz and Olesker; Heilman; Hillesum; Klüger; Kuperhand and Kuperhand; Levi; Greene and Kumar), survivor narratives can further corroborate and legitimate what historians have represented as a well-rehearsed process of identification, extraction from the community, and transportation. Deportation was an administrative and detached process that involved the Jewish councils, acting on Nazi instruction to compile deportation lists; the Jewish police, assisting in roundups; and, finally, the use of railways, which required the aid of auxiliary officers who guarded deportation trains and railway workers who patrolled the stations. In addition to causing us to rethink the realm of ordinary workers and antisemitic perpetrators involved in this task, the testimonies give a voice and identity not only to those victims who survived but also to those who, in Primo Levi's words, "drowned" and are obscured in the anonymity of the magnitude of six million deaths.

The moments of trauma in *Night*'s deportation narrative complicate the teaching of deportation history, but this complication seems essential when integrating testimony. While I have suggested ways of situating *Night* in a historical context of the final solution and the Nazi occupation of Hungary, I have not yet considered key issues that arise when intersecting traumatic testimony with historical narratives. The interpretive distinctions between truth and fiction, between historical evidence and fabrication, have proved crucial in the reading of testimonies and memoirs of Holocaust survivors. It is no surprise that historians need more to convince them to incorporate testimonies and memoirs into undergraduate courses on the Holocaust. How can testimonies be validated in the absence of independent corroborating material? What happens to the claims in memoirs if one or more detail of the recollection is proved to be false or historically inaccurate? How can historians use, as an exercise in pedagogy and ethical rewitnessing, the traumatic and emotional testimonies of persecution and atrocity that threaten to defy rational comprehension? Indeed, the dissonance between the ostensible rationality and order of perpetrator documents and the irrationality of survivor texts arguably remains a major point of interpretive dispute among historians and other scholars. Perpetrator documents, from Hitler decrees to orders for evacuation or deportation, present events in a regimented fashion, in euphemistic language that disguises the actual persecution and murder of Jews, thus rendering in documentation, language, and practice an erasure and, ultimately, a convenient denial of the commission of genocide. Survivor testimonies, written or recorded at the time of persecution (such as ghetto chronicles) or after liberation from a position of refuge, are attempts at rewriting the persecuted self in narrative form, exercises in self-censorship that render individual versions of persecution, but not the traumatic depth of it. A consistent dialectic in survivor representations of the Holocaust is thus the need to rewitness the event through temporal displacement and journeying; the literary journey, however, not unlike oral recordings or video testimonies, exposes the inability of language to achieve this sense of actuality and experience and falls inevitably short of satisfying the positivist criterion of writing history as it really was.

Testimonies of deportation should not be construed so rigidly. Occurring in historical time, this aspect of the Holocaust experience presents the instructors with a coalition of interdisciplinary approaches:

> Historical: the mapping of a general historical context, the location of Jewish communities across Europe, the assault to dispersion and relative safety occasioned by the Wannsee Conference, and the results of this conference in European-wide mass deportations of Jews
>
> Aesthetic and linguistic: the Nazi presentation of deportation in language, documentation, and practice as a travel experience to induce the compliance of deportees
>
> Corporeal, spatial, geographic: the assault to the physical body and psychological self during the journey, the spatial dimensions of compression and its impact on the interpretation of trauma, the journey as a study of embodiment and abjection
>
> Literary or interpretive: the journey's escape from bounded time in testimony
>
> Narrative or (auto)biographical: the utility of writing and speaking to impose logic and order over chaotic and emotional memories

In sum, my purpose is to outline how historians can address perceived limitations of emotional, traumatic testimony and see it as integral to the history of the Holocaust. Though I have concentrated exclusively on *Night*, instructors can use other critical literature on interpretations of testimony (Agamben; Bernard-Donals and Glejzer; Felman and Laub; Hartman; LaCapra; Lang; Liebsch; Roseman, "Surviving"; Rothberg; Stone). Crucial to this mediation of traumatic testimony are Wiesel's own recollections, one of which has been published in English as *All Rivers Run to the Sea*. In this book, Wiesel includes reflections on the writing of his deportation narrative. His intention, he makes clear, is not to repeat his account of *Night* but to "review that testimony as I see

it now. Was I explicit enough? Did I miss what was essential? Did I serve memory well? In fact, if I had to do it over again, I would change nothing in my deposition" (79). Wiesel collapses past and present, and his writing functions as a
ticket without expiry to his deportation memories, as if he is a permanent trav-
eler on that train:

> We arrived at the station, where the cattle cars were waiting. Ever since
> my book *Night* I have pursued those nocturnal trains that crossed the
> devastated continent. Their shadow haunts my writing. They symbolize
> solitude, distress, and the relentless march of Jewish multitudes toward
> agony and death. I freeze every time I hear a train whistle.   (74)

Night and the Encounter with Auschwitz

Michael Berenbaum

When Elie Wiesel, his family, and his community arrived at Auschwitz, they were not familiar with the name of the camp. Yet before their tragic arrival, more than 600,000 Jews had been killed there. Once on the scene, Wiesel quickly learns the rules. The desire for resistance, for instance, is quelled by "sage" advice: "We mustn't give up hope, even now as the sword hangs over our heads" (31). Wiesel soon faces *selektion*, parting from his mother and sister forever—the first indication of the new reality he faced. Arrival at Auschwitz marked the transition from a world of sanity and clarity to a world of madness and confusion—the beginning of a journey into night.

Auschwitz was actually three camps in one: a prison camp, Auschwitz I; a death camp, Auschwitz II, also known as Birkenau ("Birch Tree"); and a slave labor camp, Auschwitz III, or Buna-Monowitz, which was many camps stretching over miles.

The prison camp was established first, in 1940, and housed Polish prisoners. Birkenau, the death camp, was established in 1942, when it became clear to the Germans that the existing facility could not handle the burdens of the "Final Solution of the Jewish Question" that was being implemented throughout Europe. Killing at Birkenau was conducted in four crematoriums. To accommodate the arrival of 437,402 Hungarian Jews on 147 trains, a railroad spur was built directly into the camp's selection ramp. In total, there were 44 parallel railroad tracks at Auschwitz. For a basis of comparison, New York's Pennsylvania Station uses 21 parallel tracks to accommodate hundreds of thousands of people a week. Auschwitz II was thus chosen as a death camp because the infrastructure was in place to facilitate the transport of Jews to their death. The slave labor camp system surrounding Auschwitz proper increased dramatically in size and scope as German corporations augmented their investment in the area and their commitment to a seemingly unending supply of cheap labor.

A mosaic of victims inhabited Auschwitz. Polish prisoners were in Auschwitz I. Gypsies were gassed with the Jews in Birkenau. Soviet prisoners of war, mostly young and able-bodied men, were in Auschwitz I and in Auschwitz III, the industrial complex of Buna-Monowitz, where they were joined by foreign forced laborers—men and women. Germans ran the camp, but some Germans and people of German nationality—referred to as *Volksdeutsch*—were prisoners or camp functionaries. Of all the camp inmates, the Jews lived the most with the shadow of death. They could be killed at any moment for any or no reason. Closest to the Jewish situation was that of the Gypsies. Virtually the camp's entire Gypsy population—almost 20,000 people—was killed in the summer of 1944 in the gas chambers. Between 1.1 and 1.3 million people were killed at Auschwitz (9 in 10 were Jews). To arrive at this figure, the chief historian of

Auschwitz, Franticek Piper, took the total number of people deported to Auschwitz and then subtracted the number of people who survived, the number who were transferred from Auschwitz to other camps, and the few who escaped. The remainder was the number of people murdered in the camp.

Religious Struggle

Wiesel's description of life in Auschwitz is personal. As a religious Jew, he laces his depiction with religious themes. Because he experienced Auschwitz with his father, the father-son motif is evident as well. The story has meaning because of his relationship with God and his relationship with his father. Both change. Wiesel experiences his first alienation from God as everyone recites Kaddish, the traditional Jewish prayer for the dead: "For the first time, I felt anger rising within me. Why should I sanctify His name?" (33). This rebellious religious attitude intensifies in the next months. An attitude of remembrance as a response to atrocity also persists throughout Wiesel's work:

> Never shall I forget that night, the first night in camp. [. . .]
> Never shall I forget those things, even were I condemned to live as long as God Himself.
> Never.   (34)

He cannot escape speaking of God in dealing with the ultimate manifestation of the anti-God at Auschwitz.

For Wiesel, Auschwitz poses theology questions that culminate in the High Holidays and themes of sin and forgiveness, atonement, and mercy and justice—themes that are incompatible with what he is experiencing in the camp. Thus each word uttered by the prayer leader drives Wiesel further away from God, causing him to reverse the traditional hierarchy: "I was the accuser, God the accused" (68). Wiesel adopts the stance of "an observer, a stranger," in his rebellion. The SS show their scorn for the Jewish God with the *selektion* on (or soon after) Yom Kippur. The traditional prayer U'Netaneh Tokef proclaims:

> On Rosh Hashanah it is written and on Yom Kippur it is sealed . . . Who shall live and who shall die . . . who by fire and who by water . . . Yet repentance, prayer, and charity shall avert the harsh decree.

The SS mock the prayer, not in words but in deed. They decide who shall live and who shall die. Wiesel accedes to his father's request and does not fast on Yom Kippur. As he nibbles his crust of bread, he encounters a void—the absence where presence had been.

Several times, Wiesel depicts his father receiving punishment in Auschwitz. The first time, Wiesel does not respond and feels guilty. The second time he is angry, not at Idek, the *Kapo* inflicting punishment, but at his father for not knowing how to avoid Idek's outbursts. He comments, "That was what life in a concentration camp had made of me . . ." (54; ellipses in orig.). The Germans used incarcerated inmates to help run the concentration and death camps; a *Kapo* acted as a prisoner foreman.

Sonderkommando

Sonderkommando were the special units that worked in the vicinity of the crematoriums and saw the Jews in the dressing room before they perished in the gas chamber. Afterward, the *Sonderkommando* removed the bodies from the crematoriums. The Germans reserved for themselves the crucial tasks; they alone decided who would live and who would die. They alone put the gas in the gas chambers, and they alone declared the dead, dead—using Red Cross vehicles since the final pronouncement of death was regarded as a medical function.

The Walking Dead

Wiesel uses another concentration camp term, *Muselman*, the walking dead. The term refers to those prisoners who had lost all will to live and whose almost lifeless presence could rob those on the brink of despair of the strength and tenacity needed for survival. The *Muselmänner* were often shunned because virtually every prisoner could see himself or herself slipping into a similar state and giving up. Because he was young and the factories at Buna-Monowitz needed workers, Wiesel was selected to live on arrival at the camp. The old, the very young, women with children (such as his mother and his sister Tzipora but not his two older sisters, then young adult women), and the infirm were sent immediately to die.

Wiesel describes how the Allied bombing of Buna-Monowitz was a hopeful event for the inmates: "Every bomb that hit filled us with joy, gave us renewed confidence" (60). Why the labor camp of Buna was bombed but the killing center of Birkenau was not remains controversial. Bombing Birkenau was considered briefly in the summer of 1944 (during the period Wiesel was at Auschwitz) but was rejected. On 4 July 1944, John J. McCloy, assistant secretary of war, wrote to the director of the War Refugee Board to explain that bombing the camps would have required "the diversion of considerable air support essential to the success of our forces" and would have been of "very doubtful efficacy." As such, the bombing operation "does not appear justified" (qtd. in Neufeld and Berenbaum 260). In contrast, the bombing of Buna-Monowitz was a high priority because of its synthetic oil factory. Even so, some historians debate whether bombing the death camps was militarily feasible. But bombing the death camps was never actually considered. The project was never tasked, which would have required the gathering of all information regarding Auschwitz at one desk (connecting the dots, to use post-9/11 language). A low priority for bombing Auschwitz fit in with Allied policy in general. No serious effort was made to rescue the victims; winning the war was the sole consideration.

Wiesel also describes the hanging of three prisoners for acts of resistance, among them a young boy too light to die, too brave to tell what he knows. (Interestingly, Wiesel does not repeat the description of the child in his later memoir, written more than four decades after *Night*.) As he passes the three hanging prisoners, someone asks, "where is God?" He hears an inner voice answering, "hanging here from this gallows" (65). The scene deliberately resembles the crucifixion. What is Wiesel saying about God at Auschwitz? This image has endured, and many Jews interpret death at Auschwitz as a crucifixion without resurrection and without redemptive value.

Death Marches

Toward the end of *Night*, Wiesel depicts the death march: the forced evacuation from Auschwitz in January 1945. It is in this context that he narrates his fateful decision to leave the infirmary and the ultimate struggle of each of the prisoners between the will to live and the desire to die and be at peace. He speaks of betrayal and abandonment as each person battles for himself; few have the inner resources to help others. Wiesel prays to the God he no longer believes in for the strength not to abandon his father.

The historian Daniel Jonah Goldhagen has described the death marches as the "ambulatory analogue to the cattle car" (328). They were the antithesis of the deportations, which for two and a half years brought the Jews to centralized killing centers. The death marches were a process of dispersal, sending the prisoners off on various paths toward Germany, which on the brink of defeat was receiving the Jews it had once expelled. The Germans wanted to prevent these prisoners from being captured and perhaps also wanted to hold on to them as cannon fodder before the advancing Allied armies. Sixty thousand prisoners began a long westward march from Auschwitz without much—and some without any—food, without a place to sleep or rest, and without a place to perform even the most basic biological functions. The walking skeletons soon became corpses. For many, these marches were the most difficult part of their experience, for the prisoners were now engaged not in a battle against an external enemy but in an inner struggle between the need for rest, the yearning for quiescence, and the ever-diminishing will to live. To pause, to rest, or even to fall behind was to die in the snow.

They walked from Auschwitz in the dead of winter, walked until all strength waned, and after an open train ride in January, they arrived in Buchenwald, a concentration camp near Weimar, Germany. At this point, Wiesel's father is a broken man, a *Muselman*, one of the walking dead who have given up on life and can no longer go on. Wiesel argues with his father, argues with the death that he has chosen. When sirens force Wiesel to seek shelter, he leaves his father behind.

At his father's death Wiesel comments: "And deep inside me, if I could have searched the recesses of my feeble conscience, I might have found something like: Free at last!" (112). The months thereafter, from January to liberation on 11 April, are henceforth without meaning: "nothing mattered to me anymore" (113). Ill after liberation, Wiesel eventually is able to look in a mirror, only to be faced with a corpse: "The look in his eyes as he gazed at me has never left me" (115). The transformation is complete. Auschwitz has taken Wiesel, a boy who did not even question why he prayed, and shown him the utter absence of God. Yet the guilt he feels for his behavior shows that he has maintained a sense of normal morality in the world of Auschwitz's immorality.

Further Reading

I recommend Primo Levi's *Survival in Auschwitz* and Gisella Perl's *I Was a Doctor at Auschwitz*, an excerpt of which is available with other women's narratives in a book edited by Carol Rittner and John K. Roth, *Different Voices: Women and the Holocaust*. For historical perspective, I recommend Debórah Dwork and Robert Jan van Pelt's excellent *Auschwitz: 1270 to the Present* and the book that Yisrael Gutman and I edited, *Anatomy of the Auschwitz Death Camp*. Peter Hellman's *The Auschwitz Album* reproduces photographs of Hungarian Jews at Auschwitz.

A visit to a Holocaust museum is appropriate. There are many in the United States (in Washington, Los Angeles, New York, Detroit, Dallas, Houston, Saint Petersburg, and elsewhere) as well as in Israel (Yad Vashem). One may also consider a pilgrimage to the site itself. The museum at Auschwitz is powerful, vast, and important. So too is the museum at Majdanek, another Nazi death camp in occupied Poland, which, unlike Auschwitz, was captured intact by the Russians before the fleeing Germans could destroy it. The memorials at the death camps Treblinka and Belzec in Poland are exceptionally powerful; the museum at Belzec helps explain the history of the site. Bibliographies, videographies, a list of resources, and resource centers for studying the concentration camps are also available online (www.ushmm.org; www.yadvashem.org; www.mjhnyc.org; www.wiesenthal.com).

Faith and God during the Holocaust:
Teaching *Night* with the Later Memoirs

Alan L. Berger

Night begins with Wiesel as a God-intoxicated teenager in Sighet, Transylvania, and ends in Buchenwald, Germany, with the author looking in a mirror for the first time since he had been in the ghetto. Instead of his own reflection, he sees the image of a corpse staring back at him. Between these two episodes, Wiesel's life and theological innocence have been shattered. The Holocaust consumed his mother, Sarah; his youngest sister, Tzipora; his father, Shlomo; and his childhood faith in God. Surprisingly, in defiance of logic, Wiesel attests in his subsequent two-volume memoir, *All Rivers Run to the Sea: Memoirs* and *And the Sea Is Never Full: Memoirs, 1969–*, and later interviews that he did not lose faith during the Holocaust.

This essay discusses the importance of *Night*, a text I have been reading and teaching for nearly three decades, in understanding Wiesel's ongoing trial of God and his attempt to re-fuse Jewish faith after Auschwitz. The memoir, he claims, is both the end and the beginning of everything. In analyzing what ended and what began, I ask and respond to four questions. How does reading *Night* on its own differ from reading it in tandem with the memoirs and later interviews? How does teaching *Night* in dialogue with *All Rivers* and *And the Sea* shape students' reading of the earlier memoir? What is Wiesel's understanding of the purpose of literature and the role of the witness as author? How do students respond when they encounter this material? I conclude with a meditation on how *Night* has influenced my students.

Protest Theology

Night is the fundamental text for understanding Wiesel's reflections on God and faith after Auschwitz. Unlike other coming-of-age works, this memoir deals with death rather than the unfolding of life. The text, written after a ten-year period of silence following his liberation from Buchenwald, is an argument against, and with, God and is the foundation of his quest for a plausible post-Holocaust Judaism. The author seeks to fathom the secret of theodicy. He writes famously of his first night in the death camp Auschwitz-Birkenau: "Never shall I forget that night" (34). The problem for Wiesel is that the Holocaust can be explained neither with nor without God.

Wiesel's memoir is suffused with paradox. In Auschwitz his God is murdered, yet he speaks of God living for an eternity. On Rosh Hashanah, the Jewish New Year, he rebels against this deity: "I was alone, terribly alone in a world without God, without man. [. . .] I was nothing but ashes now, but I felt myself to be stronger than this Almighty to whom my life had been bound for so long"

(68). Wiesel's theological anguish reaches its apogee when he witnesses the execution of a child, "a sad-eyed angel." To a prisoner's question—"Where is God?"—the author hears a voice from within respond, "hanging here from this gallows . . ." (65). But Wiesel does not stop at this apparent point of theological no return. While he ceased to pray, he still aligns himself with the stance of biblical figures such as Habakkuk and Job, who did not deny God's existence but questioned his ways. "I was not denying His existence," Wiesel attests, "but I doubted His absolute justice" (45).

Reading **Night** *on Its Own*

Student readings of *Night* tend to focus on two relationships, Wiesel to his father and the author to God. Eliezer and Shlomo Wiesel depended on each other for survival. Students are very sensitive to the relationship issue in *Night*. One of my students reported that after reading Wiesel's memoir, in a single evening, he thought very seriously about his own relationship with his father. Despite all the time the two had spent together, he realized that he had never told his father that he loved him. Sobbing, he called his father and confided his love to him. In *All Rivers*, however, Wiesel describes a more contentious, pre-Holocaust relationship with his father, who—in the youth's eyes—was more available to Sighet's Jewish community than to his son.

Wiesel's relationship to God is more complex. Reading *Night* alone, some students conclude that God himself died in Auschwitz. Faith is also among the victims. We discuss the fact that, for the author, God hanging on the gallows refers to the death of the young Eliezer's pre-Auschwitz faith in a redeeming God. The silence of God in the death camp is theologically deafening. With the passage of time, however, Wiesel modifies his position. Students read in his cantata *Ani Maamin* ("I Believe") that the silence of God is God. The cantata's title is taken from the attestation, "I believe with perfect faith in the coming of the messiah, even though he may tarry," the twelfth of the thirteen principles of Jewish faith articulated by the philosopher Maimonides (1135–1204).

Significantly, Wiesel himself explicitly rejects the death-of-God position. He writes, "I have never renounced my faith in God. I have risen against His justice, protested His silence and sometimes His absence, but my anger rises up within the faith and not outside it" (*All Rivers* 84). Commenting further on the paradox of post-Auschwitz faith, the author writes, "Sometimes we must accept the pain of faith so as not to lose it" (84). Concerning God, Wiesel once told an interviewer that ever since *Night* he has been trying to find "an occupation for God. Just as I was always obsessed with the question of what was God doing then, I want to know what God is doing now" (Cargas, *Conversation* 81).

Wiesel views the task of the writer as correcting injustice. He attests that he wrote *Night* "to testify, to stop the dead from dying, to justify my own survival" (*All Rivers* 239). Yet language itself is problematic. He writes "not *with* words but *against* words" (Abrahamson 1: 62n12). Students learn to understand that the witness as author seeks to communicate silence. Frequently, what is not said bears equal, or greater, weight as what is directly stated. Retelling an incident in which emaciated prisoners fight over a crumb of bread, Wiesel notes that a son killed his father for the bread and was, in turn, killed by other prisoners. Of all the things that he could have said, Wiesel chose to write, "I was sixteen" (102).

Night retells events in the Holocaust and renders judgment on them. Wiesel juxtaposes normative Jewish teaching about history as the unfolding of God's plan and the murder of the chosen people by inverting biblical archetypes. Instead of the exodus to freedom, the memoir describes an anti-exodus: extinction, not deliverance, awaits the Jewish people. The symbolic abandonment of Isaac by Abraham in the biblical account of the Akedah is supplanted by sons abandoning their fathers during the Holocaust. On the one hand, *Night* raises and apparently dismisses traditional responses to catastrophe. The moral and theological chaos engendered by Auschwitz overwhelms the biblical message of hope for the Jewish people and the promise of judgment against their enemies.

In *Night*, Wiesel reports two cases of prisoners who lost the will to live because they could no longer accept traditional teachings about the existence of evil and the purpose of suffering. One of them, Akiba Drumer, who, like Wiesel, was deeply immersed in mystical Judaism, sang Hasidic melodies in Auschwitz. Akiba believed traditional assertions that God tests those he loves. Furthermore, the relentlessness of divine punishment, he attests, emphasizes God's deep concern for his people. But once Akiba "felt the first chinks in his faith, he lost all incentive to fight and opened the door to death" (77). Once he no longer believed, survival was out of the question. Another prisoner, a learned Polish rabbi, concludes that given the existence of Auschwitz, it is impossible for him, or anyone, to believe in a merciful God.

Wiesel frequently refers to himself in the third person as a teller of tales. But his passion is equally theological. Storytelling in the Jewish tradition is a significant way of engaging theological issues. Biblical thought, midrash (rabbinic commentary), and Hasidic stories all convey Jewish theology. Thus when one scholar calls Wiesel "the most important Jewish storyteller of the twentieth century" (Rubenstein 146), he means that the Nobel laureate is a formidable theologian who, as a teller of tales, can raise and reraise fundamental questions about the Holocaust, humanity, and God. Wiesel prefers questions to answers. A *question*, which contains the word *quest*, brings people together and keeps dialogue alive.

The Witness as Author

Since the publication of *Night*, Wiesel has written more than forty books dealing with the Jewish experience. Although the author maintains that he has only written directly about the Holocaust in his first memoir, the Shoah is the framing event for all his observations. His other books include novels, essays, plays, biblical and Hasidic portraits, cantatas, dialogues, and his two-volume memoir.

These two volumes—in which Wiesel bears witness to his continuing testimony and whose titles are taken from the biblical book of Ecclesiastes—cover a wide range of topics. In addition to revisiting the question of God's justice, they introduce another important aspect of Wiesel's writings, the role of witness as author. Supplementing *All Rivers* and *And the Sea*, Wiesel has given many interviews that shed light on *Night* and that my students find invaluable in helping them better understand the author's position on the role of the writer and the meaning of faith after Auschwitz.

Students are struck by the sheer size difference between *Night* and the other memoirs, which appeared nearly forty years, a biblical generation, later. They come to understand that Wiesel is now taking stock of his life. Reviewing his earlier testimony, he says that he would "change nothing in [his] deposition" (*All Rivers* 79). But he does reveal information omitted earlier. In Auschwitz Wiesel studied sacred texts with a former head of a rabbinic academy who had committed them to memory. The two studied while on their work detail. Furthermore, Wiesel continued to pray in the camps, although his faith was wounded (*And the Sea* 70). These revelations help students grapple with Wiesel's theological dilemma. On the one hand, he needed the consolation of religion and ritual, as well as his father's love, to endure the camps. On the other hand, years later he writes of being "mired in a religious crisis . . . the God of my childhood was tormenting me" (*All Rivers* 293). Ironically, he notes that it was in Jerusalem where he "first felt the need to protest against divine justice and injustice" (293). Thus the later memoirs are both a continuation of and a commentary on *Night*.

The Role of Faith

Students delve deeper into Wiesel's embrace of paradox when they read about the author's personal faith during his time at Auschwitz. Teaching Wiesel's views on faith and God in class, I assign my students specific sections of his memoirs. In the first volume Wiesel confides that in the camps he had "neither the strength nor the time for theological meditation or metaphysical speculation about the attributes of the Master of the Universe" (83). Instead, he immersed himself in Jewish ritual, putting on phylacteries on weekdays and humming "Shabbat songs" while at work on Saturday. Commenting on the meaning of his actions, Wiesel observes that in part it was to please his father, "to show him I was determined to remain a Jew even in the accursed kingdom" (82).

By presenting *Night* with the later memoirs, I provide students with the opportunity of understanding the significance of Wiesel's ten years of silence following the Holocaust. They learn that immediately after the war Wiesel was taken to a children's home in France where he elected to stay with the observant youths. While there he wrote in a diary every day. Furthermore, this decade of silence was a time of reflection and study. The young survivor, seeking to understand the meaning of his experience, read and studied secular sources that were completely new to him: philosophy, psychology, and literature. He also learned French—the language in which he writes to this day. Wiesel told an interviewer that he needed French as "one needs a new home, a new address, a new code" (Moss-Coane 171).

Students also learn about the author's travel to India during his decade of silence and his formulation of questions after Auschwitz. In India he observed firsthand, and rejected, the notion of reincarnation as a response to suffering. "I can accept and bear my own suffering," he writes, "but not that of others" (*All Rivers* 225). Wiesel confides that his protest theology only emerged when he "began studying philosophy and learned how to ask certain questions" (Moss-Coane 167). But the author's protest from within the faith is characteristic of Jewish history, from the Bible through Hasidism (an eighteenth-century Jewish mystical movement), and includes the questioning of God during and after the Holocaust.

My students find that a key to understanding Wiesel's image of God emerges from this decade of silence. This period was a process of theological growth and maturity for the author of *Night*. Although he may not have stated it in these terms, Wiesel was searching for a credible post-Auschwitz theology. His teacher during this period was the mysterious Shushani, an alias for Mordechai Rosenbaum. Described as both genius and madman, Shushani had been a child prodigy. He had an exceptional memory and was the master of many languages. Shushani taught his disciple how to deepen his understanding of theodicy and the nature of God. Specifically, Wiesel learned two important lessons that helped him formulate his theology of protest.

The first lesson for Wiesel, and my students, is that man "is defined by what troubles him, not by what reassures him." The author stresses in *All Rivers* that he "needed to be forced to start all over" (124). The God of his childhood hung on the gallows. What post-Auschwitz divine image could the young survivor accept? Wiesel reports that Shushani berates him for living and searching in error. In addition to sections of the memoirs, I have my students read Wiesel's tribute to his late mentor in *Legends of Our Time*. There the master tells his disciple that his indictment of God is based on a naive understanding of the deity. "God," Shushani proclaimed, "means movement and not explanation" (93). Yet Wiesel remains firm in his belief that, while God himself may have been suffering during the Holocaust, "He could have—should have—interrupted His own suffering by calling a halt to the martyrdom of innocents" (*All Rivers* 105).

The second lesson is contained in Wiesel's reflection on his mentor's own mission. "He upset the believer by demonstrating the fragility of his faith, he shook the heretic by making him feel the torments of the void" (*All Rivers* 129). Students recognize that Wiesel adopts the mission of his mentor as his own. He writes:

> I disturb the believer because I dare to put questions to God, the source of all faith. I disturb the miscreant because, despite my doubts and ques-

tions, I refuse to break with the religious and mystical universe that has shaped my own. Most of all, I disturb those who are comfortably settled within a system—be it political, psychological, or theological.

(*All Rivers* 336–37)

The writer's post-Holocaust role is to disturb rather than entertain his readers.

Student Response

Students respond in a variety of ways when reading *Night* in dialogue with the later memoirs. Concerning Wiesel's embrace of paradox in writing of faith and the post-Holocaust images of God, I assign the sections "Childhood," "Darkness," "God's Suffering," and "New York" from *All Rivers*. In *And the Sea* I have my students read "Scars" and "Understanding." Each of these sections provides a distinct angle of Wiesel's vision. "Childhood" describes the author's family and the way Jewish mysticism and the Bible infused his youth. The other five sections reveal the continuing dialogue between Wiesel's faith and doubt. God after Auschwitz is clearly not the deity in whom the young Wiesel believed so fervently. Today Wiesel speaks of his faith as being "wounded" (Wiesel and Heffner 54) and attests, "It is because I still believe in God that I argue with Him" (*And the Sea* 70).

Responses reflect student awareness of Wiesel's ongoing journey. The students speak of the growth and change in Wiesel's position concerning God. The wounds, many students believe, are still there, although perhaps not as raw. Furthermore, students begin to see that Wiesel employs memory as a drive to action. The author does not wallow in maudlin sentimentality. Instead, he works on behalf of humanity to seek a bettering of the human condition. In the author's words, "I do not want my past to become your future" ("Have You Learned" 6). Other students observe that reading *All Rivers* and *And the Sea* with *Night* reveals that surviving is an ongoing process. The two-volume memoir, in this reading, is a working through of the author's Holocaust trauma.

Learning that Wiesel kept his faith while in Auschwitz helps deepen student awareness of what it means to write a memoir of the Holocaust. The author's struggle with the issue of theodicy, his study of various secular disciplines, and his decade of silence enabled Wiesel to write a memoir that is both a history and an interpretation of his experience. Reading *Night* in conjunction with the later memoirs and interviews, students learn several valuable lessons. They have a greater awareness of the depravity of the death camps, and they gain a fuller and more nuanced understanding of the fundamental theological issues posed by the Holocaust. Students also begin to appreciate the limitations of language: words themselves are inadequate—yet necessary. Finally, my students are struck by the integrity of the author and his determination to seek a better future for humanity.

The Original Yiddish Text and the Context of *Night*

Jan Schwarz

Elie Wiesel published his first book in Yiddish in 1956. Titled *Un di velt hot geshvign* ("And the World Remained Silent"), it was volume 117 in the Yiddish book series Dos poylishe yidntum ("Polish Jewry"), published in Buenos Aires in the aftermath of World War II. Two years later, Wiesel rendered the Yiddish memoir into French and retitled it *La nuit*. While the English volume, *Night*, is translated from the French, seven excerpts from *Un di velt* have appeared in English translation (Glatstein, Knox, and Margoshes; Abrahamson; Wiesel, *All Rivers*; Wiesel, *Night*, Preface).

Wiesel mentions that he first wrote his "account of the concentration camp years—in Yiddish" in his cabin on the boat from Marseille to São Paulo in 1954:

> I wrote feverishly, breathlessly, without rereading. I wrote to testify, to stop the dead from dying, to justify my own survival. I wrote to speak to those who were gone. As long as I spoke to them, they would live on, at least in my memory. My vow of silence would soon be fulfilled; next year would mark the tenth anniversary of my liberation. (*All Rivers* 239–40)

In "An Interview unlike Any Other," Wiesel refers to this vow not to speak of his concentration camp experiences for at least ten years. He points out that his mistrust of words and his lack of an approach to "describe the undescribable" made him decide to wait "long enough to see clearly" (15). Wiesel mentions that he was introduced to Mark Turkov, "a Jewish book publisher" (*All Rivers*

241), on the boat's stopover in Montevideo. Turkov showed interest in Wiesel's manuscript and promised that he would publish it: "In December [1955] I received from Buenos Aires the first copy of my Yiddish testimony 'And the World Stayed Silent,' which I had finished on the boat to Brazil" (*All Rivers* 277).

According to *Leksikon fun der nayer yidisher literatur* ("Biographical Dictionary of Modern Yiddish Literature"), Wiesel's debut as writer, the novella *A bagegenish* ("An Encounter"), appeared in Paris in 1947 ("Wiesel, Eliezer"). In the following years, Wiesel contributed short stories, journalistic pieces, reviews, and reportages to Yiddish journals and newspapers in Paris and New York. His novel *Shtile heldn* ("Quiet Heroes") was serialized in the New York journal *Der amerikaner*. In addition to working as a foreign correspondent for the Israeli newspaper *Yediot akhanot*, Wiesel became a staff member at the Yiddish daily *Forverts* in 1956 and befriended Yiddish writers in New York in the 1950s and 1960s (*All Rivers* 342–44).

Wiesel's relation to Yiddish has a number of significant aspects:

> I love Yiddish because it has been with me from the cradle. It was in Yiddish that I spoke my first words and expressed my first fears. It is a bridge to my childhood years. . . . I need Yiddish to laugh and cry, to celebrate and express regret, to delve into my memories anew. Is there a better language for evoking the past, with all its horror? Without Yiddish the literature of the Holocaust would have no soul. I know that had I not written my first account in Yiddish, I would have written no others.
>
> (*All Rivers* 292)

Turkov was the editor of *Dos poylishe yidntum*, a publishing project that was begun in 1946 and that had reached the hundred-volume point when Turkov met Wiesel, in 1954. He had narrowly escaped the Nazi invasion of Poland, on 1 September 1939, and fled to Buenos Aires. Born in Warsaw in 1904, he became a journalist for the Yiddish press in interwar Poland, covering sports and political debates in the Polish Sejm (Parliament). Turkov and his three brothers, the actors Sygmunt Turkov, Yitskhok Turkov, and Jonas Turkov, were typical representatives of the secular Jewish intelligentsia in Warsaw, home to Europe's largest Jewish community. Its 300,000 Jews constituted one-third of the city's total population, and its vibrant Yiddish culture provided a model for Dos poylishe yidntum (see J. Schwarz).

The book series was published with remarkable speed. In the first years following the war, approximately two books a month were published, with an average print run of 2,500. Many books were quickly sold out, and second editions were published. Books were shipped to the major Yiddish cultural centers in Poland, the displaced persons' camps among the *sheyres ha'pleyte* ("the survivors"), North and South America, and Israel. Most of the series's first hundred volumes were memoirs, diaries, and eyewitness accounts from the ghettos and camps. Moreover, in contrast to the hundreds of *yizker bikher* ("memorial books") that focused on particular towns and cities and were often composed by amateur writers, the volumes of Dos poylishe yidntum presented broad topics related to the Holocaust and were written by professional writers. Included in the series were the memoirs and diaries of Hillel Seidman, Joseph Kermish, Jonas Turkov, and Shmerke Katcherginsky, all of whom remain important primary sources for the history of the Warsaw and Vilna ghettos. The most immediate issues facing Polish Jewry in the aftermath of the Holocaust were addressed in Yiddish writers' travelogues about their visits to Poland, such as Khayim Shoskes's *Poyln—1946* ("Poland—1946"; vol. 8). In addition to providing historical documentation, belles lettres, and memoirs, Dos poylishe yidntum served as a launching pad for young Yiddish writers such as Mordechai Strigler and Eliezer (Elie) Wiesel, who published their first Holocaust memoirs in the series. Dos poylishe yidntum re-created the idea of secular Yiddish culture after its heartland in Poland had been destroyed.

Similar to the prolific output of Yiddish writers in New York, Paris, Moscow (until Stalin purged the Soviet Yiddish cultural establishment from 1948 to 1952), and Tel Aviv, Dos poylishe yidntum emphasized cultural continuity and renewal. In assessing the impressive output of Yiddish works in the decade after the Holocaust, Shmuel Niger, the dean of Yiddish criticism, pointed out that most of these works drew their inspiration from the past:

> While Yiddish lyrical poetry expresses other tones than that of *El Male Rakhamim* [memorial prayer], Yiddish prose is still immersed in the world that is no more. It is still a literature of memoirs, chronicles, history. . . . The series of more than one hundred books that the youngest, most active and productive Yiddish publisher has published these past ten years is not coincidently called "Polish Jewry." Even *The Golden Chain* and other publications in Israel which rarely reflect the new life that is being built mostly look to the past.   (7)

A group of young Yiddish writers, most of them survivors of the ghettos and camps, breathed new life in the aging Yiddish literary world in New York, Buenos Aires, Paris, and Tel Aviv in the late 1940s and early 1950s. Among them were Chaim Grade, Avraham Sutzkever, Isaiah Spiegel, Yehuda Elberg, Rokhl Korn, Chava Rosenfarb, Strigler, and Wiesel, all born in the 1910s and 1920s. Strigler's output in Dos poylishe yidntum was breathtaking. Between 1947 and 1955, he published six memoirs about his experiences in German labor and extermination camps as well as two historical novels. Among his contributions were *Maydanek* (1947; vol. 20), *In di fabrikn fun toyt* (1948; "In the Factories of Death"; vol. 32), *Verk-tse* (vols. 64–65), *Goyroles* ("Destinies"; vols. 85–86), and *Georemt mit vint* ("Embraced by the Wind"; vols. 108–09). In an introduction to *Maydanek* dated May 1946, Strigler presented his program for a new Yiddish literature:

What has been written about our historical period has only touched the surface. The essence has not yet been disclosed. And something must be told about the internal pain, the deep psychological struggle and essential human sadness of a generation's terrifying death . . . Unlike young writers among other people who write about sun, air, light and the joy of life, this brutal destiny has made me the chronicler of my holy people's destruction. . . . **The world, even the Jewish world doesn't know what really happened! And they must know! To the last detail. . . .**

(8; boldface in orig.)

Characteristic of Strigler's work is its fusion of fiction and chronicle, psychological portraiture and testimony in delineating human degradation and resistance. Chaim Grade's 1953 novella, "My Quarrel with Hersh Rasseyner," which appeared in English translation in *Commentary Magazine*, is about the debate between two childhood friends who survived the Holocaust and then meet in Paris in 1948. The story articulated internal Jewish issues of religious faith, continuity, and relation to the gentile world. *The Seven Little Lanes*, the third part of Grade's autobiographical novel *My Mother's Sabbath Days* (1955), addressed survivor guilt and expressions of revenge among survivors in the ruins of the Vilna ghetto. Typical of the Yiddish response to the Holocaust in the first decade after the war, Grade's and Strigler's work continued a social realist style that originated with the classical Yiddish writer Mendele Moykher Sforim's neo-*maskilic* work in the late nineteenth century.

The Yiddish poet Avraham Sutzkever, a survivor of the Vilna ghetto, arrived in Palestine in 1947 and began to publish the Yiddish literary journal *Di goldene keyt* ("The Golden Chain") with financial support from the Histadrut, the central labor union. The journal was the most important vehicle for high-quality Yiddish literary and critical work in the post-Holocaust period until it ceased publication in 1995. Its name was a reference to the classical Yiddish writer I. L. Peretz's play about the decline of three generations of a Hasidic dynasty. The journal was modeled on Peretz's vision for a Yiddish culture merging Jewish content with contemporary literary trends. *Di goldene keyt* and Dos poylishe yidntum expressed an optimistic faith in the continuity of Yiddish literature in the aftermath of the Holocaust. Sutzkever's poetry written in the Vilna ghetto and his surrealist prose poem "Green Aquarium" (1953–54) about his incarceration in the Vilna ghetto presented the absurd, impenetrable inner world of the survivor in a complex modernist poetics.

Ka-Tzetnik's *Hoyz fun di lyalkes* (*House of Dolls*), published as volume 115 in Dos poylishe yidntum a few months before Wiesel's *Un di velt*, was a Yiddish translation of the author's Hebrew novel about the prostitution of Jewish women by the gestapo. The work appeared in an English translation in 1955 and was republished in Yiddish in Tel Aviv in 1958. Ka-Tzetnik, a pseudonym for Yehiel De-Nur, was a survivor of Auschwitz and one of the first Israeli authors to write about the Holocaust. A whole generation of Israelis learned about the Holocaust primarily through his Hebrew books, including *Salaman-drah* (1946; *Sunrise over Hell* [1977]), *Bet ha-bubot* (1953; *House of Dolls*), and *Ha-Sha'on asher me-'al la-rosh* (1960; "The Clock Overhead"), which detail the horrors of Auschwitz, including torture, cannibalism, and sexual abuse of children. Wiesel praised the author for his courage and artistic originality in depicting human life on the "planet" Auschwitz: "He is a witness in the highest sense of the word, a witness who took a piece of fire with him from the conflagration of the Holocaust . . ." ("Ka-Zetnik"). In short, Wiesel's Yiddish book entered a varied field of Yiddish Holocaust literature at a time when few works in non-Jewish languages dealt with these issues.

Wiesel uses a number of strategies in *Un di velt* that are special to an audience of Jewish readers and to the conventions of Yiddish literature.

> The yard—a market place: valuable things, expensive carpets, silver candelabras, chale-covers, spice boxes, holiday prayer books, everyday prayer books were scattered on the dirty earth, under the too blue heaven. Like they never had a master, like there was no master in the universe. *Without a law and without a judge*. Everything is abandoned, frighteningly abandoned. When a human ceases to be a human, the world ceases to be a world.   (30)[1]

In addition to specifying the exact kinds of ritual objects that have been "frighteningly abandoned," Wiesel's narrative includes the Hebrew expression "les din veles dayen" ("without a law and without a judge"), thereby framing the yard as a godless universe. A few pages later, Wiesel uses the same rhetorical method to describe the abandoned ghetto:

> Open rooms everywhere. Doors and windows—wide open, like after a fire, after total destruction. An abandoned world. *Let all who are hungry come and take*, all can come and take what they desire.   (34; emphasis added)

Wiesel employs the Aramaic phrase "kol dichfin yeitei veyikach" ("let all who are hungry come and take"), a phrase that in its original form ("let all who are hungry come and eat") introduces the Passover seder. He alters the traditional phrase to highlight the absurdity of Jewish religious observance in the midst of the evacuation of Jews from the Sighet ghetto during Passover in 1944. This reference situates the description in a religious framework by mocking the phrase's sacred meaning in the extreme conditions of the ghetto.

Wiesel's use of metanarrative signifiers also draws on the conventions of Yiddish literature. Although these signifiers interrupt the narrative flow and are stylistically awkward, they add a distinct moral perspective and emotional pathos to the narrator's voice. Here are two typical examples:

> And now, writing these lines, I still see him standing in the shadow of the block, leaning on a wooden pole, bent over me. I still see his eyes that

threw flames of rage on the surrounding world, flames of rage that, through me, will eternally remind all humanity that because of its silence, its criminal indifference, Germany was transformed into a sacrificial altar for the Jewish people.   (140)

Strange: writing these lines, I don't believe them. It seems as if I am writing a horror novel. A novel it is forbidden to read at night. It is impossible to believe that everything I write in fact happened to me. And—only ten years ago.   (210)

The metanarrative signifiers provide a glimpse into the mind of the narrator in the process of narration as well as situate the events in a historical context ("only ten years ago"). They bring the narrator closer to the reader. This intimacy is further emphasized by the narrator's frequent address to "the dear reader" and "dear friend." This rhetoric of intimacy between narrator and reader has been a staple of modern Yiddish literature from its inception in the late nineteenth century. The flame of rage in his father's eyes in the first quotation obligates Wiesel to remind "the world" of its "criminal passivity" during the Holocaust. The book is dedicated to Wiesel's mother, father, and sister "killed by the German murderers." This formula is typically employed in the dedication to Holocaust memoirs in Dos poylishe yidntum.

The title of the last section of *Un di velt* is appropriately "The End and the Beginning." Wiesel's rejection of "the image of myself after death" (*All Rivers* 319) brings him back to life. His shattering the mirror is followed by his first note set down for his testimony: "After I got better, I stayed in bed for several days, jotting down notes for the work that you, dear reader, now hold in your hands" (320). Although Wiesel intends his testimony to refute that the "Germans and anti-Semites tell the world that the story of six million Jewish victims is but a myth" (320), he recognizes the powerlessness of his words to make the world break its silence. By shattering the mirror Wiesel is able to resist succumbing to the image of himself as a corpse. In that sense, Wiesel's point that "had I not written my first account in Yiddish, I would have written no others" indicates that if not for his defiance of death in the act of bearing witness, he would not have survived.

The original Yiddish text and context of *Night* reveal a set of responses to the Holocaust mostly unknown outside the Yiddish cultural world. They are very different from what has become known as "Holocaust literature," which remains primarily an English-language phenomenon (including works translated into English). Original responses to the Holocaust in Yiddish and Hebrew in anthologies such as *Anthology of Holocaust Literature* (Glatstein, Knox, and Margoshes), *From a Ruined Garden: The Memorial Books of Polish Jewry* (Kugelmass and Boyarin), and *The Literature of Destruction: Jewish Responses to Catastrophe* (Roskies) can add much to our knowledge of how Jewish survivors drew on their religious, cultural, and literary traditions. This body of Jewish Holocaust memoirs and testimonies provides an invaluable source for the context and literary means of expression originating in the long history of Jewish responses to catastrophe. Moreover, these works significantly revise the enshrined notion of the survivors' silence until the Adolf Eichmann trial in Jerusalem in 1961. Instead, Yiddish testimonies such as those in Dos poylishe yidntum indicate the existence of a vibrant Jewish discourse that empowered survivors to express and share their experiences in Yiddish. The surrounding world, Jewish and non-Jewish, was almost entirely unaware of the voluminous creativity in Yiddish. The issue was not that of silence of the survivors; rather, it was the world's indifference to hearing the survivors' own voices in Yiddish.

Night remains one of the seminal texts of Holocaust literature. This great achievement, however, would not have been possible without the Yiddish literary revival in the late 1940s and 1950s, when Wiesel was starting out as a Yiddish writer. Writers mostly unknown outside the Yiddish and Hebrew literary world such as Strigler, Ka-Tzetnik, Grade, and Sutzkever provided a context for Wiesel in his quest to discover his distinct literary voice, offering a vibrant Jewish literary tradition and models for articulating his Holocaust experiences. Moreover, Turkov's interest in Wiesel in 1954 in Montevideo and subsequent publication of *Un di velt* in Dos poylishe yidntum provided the young writer with a Jewish readership. This happened at a time when Holocaust literature in non-Jewish languages was a rare exception, in stark contrast to its proliferation in our current cultural landscape.

NOTE

[1] All translations from Yiddish works are mine except for those translated in *Against Silence* and *All Rivers*.

Teaching *La nuit* in Comparative Contexts

Judith Clark Schaneman

In my personal reading history, no text has touched me more profoundly than Elie Wiesel's *La nuit*. My first encounter with it prompted the choice of a dissertation topic, introducing me not only to Wiesel but also to the body of writing by Holocaust survivors. And yet I hesitated to introduce *La nuit* to students in my undergraduate literature classes, unsure of the approach that would adequately respect the truth of this slim volume.

I first taught *La nuit* in a course on contemporary French culture, pairing it with Alain Resnais's documentary *Nuit et brouillard*. Students reacted positively—and often emotionally—to this pairing, but the presentation of *La nuit* as a historical document also allowed them to relegate the experience to a distant past, thereby acknowledging the atrocities of the camps without truly engaging them. In subsequent years, I have taught *La nuit* in several contexts that attempt to create a historical as well as a more personal connection between reader and text. One approach that has proved effective is placing *La nuit* within comparative contexts that encourage students to reflect on the text in parallel with other similar (or dissimilar) narratives.[1]

In teaching *La nuit*, I believe it is essential to return to the poignant moment when a crowded boxcar carrying Eliezer and his family arrives at Auschwitz. Those who can see out report the name of the station, but no one reacts because no one has ever heard it before. At this moment, a last brief surge of hope allows those inside to imagine that they have survived the worst (50). Already, however, we, the readers, realize the futility of that hope; what lies beyond the station remains not only unimagined but unimaginable. As Charlotte Delbo writes in *Aucun de nous ne reviendra*,

> Ils ne savent pas qu'à cette gare-là on n'arrive pas.
> Ils attendent le pire—ils n'attendent pas l'inconcevable.   (10–11)

> They do not know there is no arriving in this station.
> They expect the worst—not the unthinkable.
> > (*Auschwitz and After* 4)

For those of us who inhabit the post-Holocaust universe, the word *Auschwitz* not only conveys meaning but risks becoming an abstract symbol, "an evasion through verbal encapsulation" that enables us to contain ultimate evil as an aberration confined within a distinct historical moment (Ezrahi 2). As teachers of Holocaust literature, and specifically of *La nuit*, we must face the challenge of assisting our students in understanding, however faintly, the reality of the *univers concentrationnaire*. When even its survivors have categorized this experience as beyond the grasp of language and imagination, the task before us is indeed daunting.

By treating *La nuit* as a historical text, we run the risk of acknowledgment without comprehension. We cannot ignore the complexities inherent in engaging a generation of students who have no doubt read about the Holocaust in history textbooks, probably viewed its less than conscientious depictions in made-for-television movies, and frame their reading in this limited knowledge of distant brutality. If, on the other hand, we approach *La nuit* on the more personal level of memoir or autobiography, the experiences of one survivor may be diminished by our failure to position them clearly within the historical context of six million deaths.

In one sense, we confront the same dilemmas with which the survivor-writers struggled as they constructed their texts. For this reason, before approaching the text itself, it seems important to consider the development of Holocaust literature, its early critical reception and its impact on traditional artistic structures. Although some survivors published accounts of the camps shortly after the end of the war, others like Delbo wrote initially for themselves, making their texts public only after the texts had "stood the test of time" (*Auschwitz and After* x). Still others, like Wiesel, read voraciously about the event but refrained from writing until significantly after their liberation (Suleiman, "War Memories" 48).

To assist students in understanding the complexities surrounding the decision to memorialize the Holocaust in writing, it is important to situate these first texts within the literary context of the late 1950s and early 1960s. Therefore, before the class addresses the texts themselves, I outline for students the challenges that Holocaust texts posed to traditional concepts of art and beauty, the consequences of committing the experiences of the camps to written form, and the fear that this act might ultimately trivialize their suffering and horror.

After a brief introduction, students are able to engage in a productive discussion of topics such as Theodor Adorno's often cited "to write poetry after Auschwitz is barbaric," the relevance of literature in a post-Holocaust world, or the alternative response of silence (34). As they contemplate these questions, students become increasingly cognizant of the difficulties Holocaust writers confront in attempting to render their experiences accessible both intellectually and emotionally to those who had no firsthand knowledge of the *univers concentrationnaire*.[2] To accomplish this objective, the Holocaust writer needs to address at least three major areas of difficulty: the inadequacy of language, the encounter with a historical experience that outstripped imagination, and the inability of traditional literary structures to translate the event.

Before they begin reading *La nuit*, I ask students to consider these obstacles. To understand the inadequacy of language, we begin by discussing David Rousset's Holocaust idiom "l'univers concentrationnaire," an invention that emphatically established the camps as a world apart. Not only did this autonomous kingdom create its own vocabulary such as *Sonderkommando* and *Kapo*, words that remain untranslatable and therefore ultimately unknowable (Ezrahi 10), but, as Primo Levi insists in his memoir *Survival in Auschwitz*, even common terms like *hunger* or *fatigue* became incomprehensible outside the camps (123). As an in-class activity, I ask students to recall a moment in which they were extremely cold, tired, hungry, or thirsty and to briefly describe that experience in writing so that we can understand the intensity of the writers' feelings. Although such an approach might be criticized for diminishing the horror of the camps by equating it to the commonplace experiences of relatively privileged American undergraduates, students find it extremely difficult to communicate the intensity of even a mundane experience of deprivation and therefore seem to become more sensitive to the intensity of physical anguish in *La nuit*.

The Holocaust experience also transforms the relation between the writer and the imagination. Rather than conjure images of the absurd, the macabre, or the grotesque, as did such predecessors as Charles Baudelaire or Edgar Allan Poe, the Holocaust writer attempts to re-create a lived past so absurd and irrational that even survivors may have difficulty believing its reality. Although this is an extremely complex topic about which much has been written, building on the previous exercise, students can begin to grasp its significance by engaging in a discussion of literary devices such as metaphor and simile that have traditionally served to bridge the writer's experience and that of the reading public. When asked to identify a possible metaphor for life in the camps, students will invariably suggest "hell." In small groups, they then discuss the reasons for which this metaphor is an inadequate and inappropriate comparison. These conversations usually produce multiple perspectives ranging from the presumptive guilt of those tormented in hell to the realization that since we have no firsthand experience of hell, this metaphor fails to connect us with the events of the camps.

Finally, the entire enterprise of literature must be brought into question. If literature structures reality and reflects in that formulative process the culture that gives it birth, how can the literature of the Holocaust conform itself to the absurd chaos and perverse logic of the camps while simultaneously remaining comprehensible to the uninitiated reader? To communicate understandably with the reader, must the writer betray the capricious, irrational, and chaotic reality of the Holocaust experience?

To address this question with students, it seems helpful to present *La nuit* within a comparative framework of two contemporaneous texts, Delbo's *Aucun de nous ne reviendra* and Anna Langfus's *Le sel et le soufre*. Using recognizable but distinctive narrative strategies ranging from fiction to autobiography to poetic memoir, each author attempts to convey the essence of a wartime experience. This approach brings together three persons clearly separated by biography but ultimately united by the Holocaust.

For readers not familiar with Delbo and Langfus or their writing, a brief biography of each is perhaps instructive. Born near Paris in 1913, Delbo, the oldest of the three writers under consideration, is also the only one who is not Jewish. In 1940, she was already married and worked as an assistant to the French actor and director Louis Jouvet. When the German army occupied Paris, Delbo was touring South America with Jouvet's theatrical troop. Despite her employer's protestations, she soon decided to rejoin her husband, Georges Dudach, in France. The couple participated actively in the resistance movement until their arrest by French police in March 1942.

Two months later, after being turned over to the gestapo, Delbo's husband was executed. Delbo remained imprisoned in France until 1943, when, on 24 January, she was one of 230 women deported to Auschwitz, an event she commemorated in *Le convoi du 24 janvier*. In 1944, she was relocated to Ravensbrück before being released to the Red Cross for health reasons near the end of the war. At her liberation, Delbo returned to France where she worked for the United Nations and the Centre Nacional de la Recherche Scientifique. She began writing about her wartime experiences shortly after her repatriation but, like many survivors of the camps, published nothing until the 1960s. Her collected work, which often defies traditional categorization by genre, includes memoirs and plays that testify to her determination to bear witness to the inhumanity of the camps. Delbo died of cancer in 1985.

Seven years younger than Delbo, Langfus, the daughter of a wealthy assimilated Jewish family, was raised in Poland. She married at seventeen and with her husband was studying at a technical university in Belgium. In September 1939, the couple was spending the summer vacation with family in their native Lublin. Rather than be evacuated to the ghetto in Varsovie, they tried unsuccessfully to escape to the country. Langfus's husband was taken hostage and executed. Although Langfus herself was spared imprisonment in the concentration camps, she suffered deprivation, torture, betrayal, and confinement in a ghetto. Few details of her wartime experiences have been recorded, but it is often assumed that they are reflected in those of the protagonist of *Le sel et le soufre*, her first novel.

In 1947, Langfus entered France as a refugee. She first worked at an orphanage and later taught mathematics. She married another refugee whom she had known in Poland before the war and gave birth to a daughter. The family lived in Sarcelles, where Langfus participated actively in promoting the cultural life of the new city. Although she had barely acknowledged her Jewish origins before the Nazi invasion of Poland, she now became particularly committed to Jewish organizations and even traveled to Israel. She also resumed her prewar interest in writing and, between 1960 and 1965, published three novels centered on wartime experiences of survival and the survivors' efforts to rebuild their lives. Her second novel, *Les bagages de sable*, garnered the prestigious Prix Goncourt in 1962. Langfus died at forty-six in 1966.

Despite dissimilarities in their biographies, the narratives of Wiesel, Delbo, and Langfus resonate with one another, thereby confirming in the accounts of three distinctive individuals the commonality of horror in the *univers concentrationnaire*. Although each of their texts offers powerful insights into the Holocaust experience, together they complement and amplify one another, further enhancing the readers' understanding of the events they depict. A question is often raised about the authors' relation to French and to France, with the expectation of greater similarities between Wiesel and Langfus. In the context of the works addressed in this essay, however, parallels between Delbo's and Wiesel's texts appear more pronounced, suggesting that imprisonment in the camps was the crucial common denominator. If we consider each writer's trilogy, the commonalities between Wiesel and Langfus become much more evident as their protagonist-survivors struggle to adapt to life in a foreign country.

Comparisons of the narrative strategies employed by each author have proved an effective method for gaining access to *La nuit*. Although I initially hesitated to take such an openly literary approach fearing diminishment of the content through an emphasis on narrative techniques, it seems to facilitate discussion of the events themselves as well as of the strategies used to recount them. Focusing on the texts as literature allows students to engage in conversation about them without seeming to question the events or experiences and usually leads to a more meaningful encounter with them.

This approach can also enable the instructor to engage in a more traditional analysis of the French text. Although stylistic considerations of Wiesel as a nonnative writer of French or an assessment of the influence of the Racinian tragedies he read to master the language are probably beyond the linguistic capabilities of most undergraduate students, other questions can be effective in opening up the text. As they read, students may be asked to note the progressive losses that reduce Eliezer to a stomach (87) or a cadaver (178). Throughout the text, however, in contrast to the dehumanizing effects of the camps, moments of resistant humanity quietly suggest the possibility of survival and reconstructed post-Holocaust existence. Overwhelmed by the horrors described, students often miss the subtle moments of hope unless they are specifically encouraged to look for them.

Similarly, focusing on the vocabulary of remembrance can heighten students' appreciation of the text. By examining not only the words themselves but also their tense or form and the identity of those who use them, students can gain an awareness of the impact of the camps on survivors. The verbs *se souvenir* and *se rappeler* are repeated throughout *La nuit*, but on his first night in Auschwitz, Eliezer responds to his father's question about remembering Mrs. Schächter with a linguistic reversal that mirrors the reversals of the camps: "Jamais je n'oublierai" (60). The statement seems to enclose memory in a prison of negativity and condemns the protagonist to eternal remembrance in the future tense. A few pages later, the verb *se souvenir* reappears, this time in the affirmative command of an SS officer (66). The message to be remembered, however, is the reality of Auschwitz. Finally, a comparison of the unexpectedly lyrical passage containing Eliezer's vow of remembrance on his first night at Auschwitz with the Song of Moses in Exodus 15.1–18 can further reveal the reversals of life in the camps.

Because Delbo's memoir consists of short, often poetic fragments arranged without regard for chronology, it is relatively easy to find passages that relate to and illuminate sections of *La nuit*. The first selection in *Aucun de nous ne reviendra*, a prose poem entitled "Rue de l'arrivée, rue du départ," enhances our understanding of the fleeting hope that accompanied the arrival at Auschwitz. In the initial segment, Delbo describes a scene familiar to anyone who has been to a train station:

> Il y a les gens qui arrivent. Ils cherchent des yeux dans la foule de ceux qui attendent. Ils les embrassent et ils disent qu'ils sont fatigués du voyage.
> Il y a les gens qui partent. Ils disent au revoir à ceux qui ne partent pas et ils embrassent les enfants.   (9)

> People arrive. They look through the crowd of those who are waiting, those who await them. They kiss them and say the trip exhausted them.
> People leave. They say good-bye to those who are not leaving and hug the children.   (*Auschwitz and After* 3)

After establishing this shared human experience from everyday life, Delbo continues to evoke that station "où ceux qui arrivent ne sont jamais arrivés, où ceux qui sont partis ne sont jamais revenus" (9; "where those who arrive have never arrived, where those who have left never came back" [*Auschwitz and After* 3]). It is, Delbo concludes, "la plus grande gare du monde" (9; "the largest station in the world" [*Auschwitz and After* 3]). Although Delbo, unlike Wiesel and Langfus, does not specifically detail her pre-Holocaust life, the selection affords us a brief glimpse of this world that encourages a discussion of the arrival of Eliezer and his family at Auschwitz and the devastating loss of familiar patterns of life that preceded this moment.

An awareness of moments and seasons, not as specific events but as components of the never ending routine in the camps, suggests additional comparisons between Wiesel and Delbo. Whereas Wiesel maintains a chronological structure in *La nuit*, Delbo tends to emphasize one element of life in the camps in seemingly disconnected segments. By placing these texts next to each other, we sense not only the monotonous repetition of inhuman brutality but also the intensity of individual moments. Both writers ground their texts in the seasons, occasionally marking those moments where nature's beauty temporarily counters the agony of the camps. One such passage, a fleeting paragraph about spring, might easily be overlooked by the reader of *La nuit* (69). By pairing it with Delbo's selection entitled "La tulipe," we realize the importance of these moments lived beyond the barbed-wire boundaries of the camp as sad reminders of the world outside the *univers concentrationnaire*. Other passages from *Aucun de nous ne reviendra* involving roll calls, night, and winter also present opportunities for fruitful examination.

Both Wiesel and Delbo attempt to convey to their readers the physical deprivation suffered in the camps. Throughout *La nuit*, Eliezer's hunger constitutes a repeated motif. Deprived of all that had previously given him identity, in the camp Eliezer finds himself reduced to a stomach whose only interest is the daily ration of bread and soup. In a passage entitled "La soif" ("Thirst"), Delbo first remembers thirst in stories about desert explorers rescued on the verge of death by the serendipitous arrival of fresh provisions. From this connection, she then affirms that the thirst of which she writes is not comparable, for in the camps there will be no rescuers. After describing the torment of a thirst so severe that it impedes speech, Delbo centers on a single experience where, like Eliezer, she is fixated on only one objective: "Reste une idée fixe: boire" (116; "One obsession remains: to drink" [*Auschwitz and After* 71]). Like Wiesel's hunger, Delbo's obsession for water brings with it the recognition of her diminished humanity as she refuses the pleading look of Aurore, a fellow prisoner too weak to quench her thirst alone. The repeated expressions of hunger in *La nuit* read in parallel with the intensely felt section on thirst in *Aucun de nous ne reviendra* recall the earlier discussion of Levi's contention that *hunger, cold, fear*, or *pain* in the *univers concentrationnaire* in no way correlates to those same words "used by free men who lived in comfort and suffering in their homes" (*Survival* 123).

The sense of human diminishment to a physical shell in both Wiesel and Delbo raises the crucial question of identity. This issue has had the greatest resonance with undergraduate students, many of whom are struggling, albeit on a significantly different level, with constructing their own adult identities. By considering those elements that determine their perceptions of self as well as the identities attributed to them by others, students become more sensitive to the severity of loss that reduces Eliezer to the unrecognizable image of a cadaver reflected in the mirror of the final lines of *La nuit*.

Langfus's first novel, *Le sel et le soufre*, affords insights into questions of identity as it traces a young woman's transformation—or, perhaps more aptly, her deformation—from shocked disbelief as German bombs shatter a calm September afternoon in her Polish homeland to her cynical anguish when, after having been abandoned by her retreating Nazi captors, she returns to her home, now occupied by strangers. As in *La nuit*, *Le sel et le soufre* begins with scenes of a pre-Holocaust existence; readers armed with post-Holocaust knowledge are initially perplexed by the persistence of hope as they chart all that has been lost—from material possessions to physical security to family and relationships. These successive losses rob the protagonists of even their most basic identity; Eliezer is reduced to the numbers A-7713 tattooed on his left arm, and readers of Langfus's novel know the protagonist only as Maria, a name she has taken from false identification papers.

Although Langfus's protagonist evades imprisonment in the camps, she nevertheless experiences multiple betrayals at the hands of those whom circumstance compels her to trust. Powerless to act independently, Maria often finds herself obligated to accept promises of assistance at face value even when she has reason to doubt her benefactors' sincerity. More troubling still is the realization that she is no longer able to predict who will betray her using prewar suppositions of an orderly, rational universe. Only her Jewish ancestry, the one identity she had previously rejected, possesses an arbitrary power to determine her fate.

What separates Maria and Eliezer is the question of their religious background. Langfus's novels lack the Jewish imagery that permeates Wiesel's work. For Eliezer, the culminating loss of the Holocaust was the anguished sensation of God's absence, the apparent devastation of the meaningful core of his existence. In the novels that came after the first memoir, Wiesel's protagonists strive to reconstruct their lives in part by revitalizing that core of meaning. For Maria, the pre-Holocaust center is the self, protected and assured by family and friends. Interrogated by her German captors, Maria confesses her only crime: "Je ne pensais qu'à moi, à ma petite vie personnelle" (197; "I only thought about myself, my own personal life").[3] Grounded in herself and her personal happiness, Maria realizes that the forced recognition of her Jewish origins diminishes her in the eyes of the Nazis and in the minds of those she had once called friends and countrymen. In the novel's final pages, Maria's disillusionment as an assimilated Jew betrayed by a misplaced faith in humanity leaves her seemingly bereft of resources from which to rebuild her life. At the end of Le sel et le soufre, Maria, like Eliezer, survives isolated in a post-Holocaust world. Deprived of relationships that formerly sustained them and alienated even from themselves, Eliezer and Maria seem to echo the lament of Mado, a French deportee, whose testimony Delbo records in Mesure de nos jours: "Je ne suis pas vivante. Je suis morte à Auschwitz et personne ne le voit" (66; "I'm not alive. I died at Auschwitz but no one knows it" [Auschwitz and After 267]).

The concluding pages of these texts, culminating in Delbo's haunting declaration "Aucun de nous n'aurait dû revenir" (Aucun de nous 183; "None of us was meant to return" [Auschwitz and After 114]), signal a final problematic aspect of teaching La nuit. Unless we are teaching a specialized course on Holocaust literature, it is unlikely that we will read with our students other texts by these authors. And yet each author continued to write of the Holocaust experience and the struggle to rebuild lives in the post-Holocaust world: Delbo in Une connaissance inutile and Mesure de nos jours;[4] Langfus in Les bagages de sable and Saute, Barbara; and Wiesel in L'aube and Le jour.

These trilogies document survivors' efforts to deal with memories of the camps as they sought to rebuild their lives. Having reentered the world as empty physical shells who, in Delbo's words, must constantly train themselves to "reprendre la forme d'un vivant dans la vie" (Mesure 11; "to assume once again the shape of a living being in this life"), they soon realized that even the simplest daily task required a conscious effort:

> Marcher, parler, répondre aux questions, dire où l'on veut aller, y aller. J'avais oublié. L'avais-je jamais su? Je ne voyais ni comment m'y prendre ni par où commencer.   (Mesure 11)

> Walk, speak, answer questions, state where you want to go, go there. I had forgotten all this. Had I ever known it? I had no idea what to do and where to begin.   (*Auschwitz and After* 236)

Unless we can continue the survivors' stories in the post-Holocaust world, we risk leaving their telling incomplete. Although none of the texts mentioned above presents us with an unambiguously positive conclusion, *Le jour*; *Saute, Barbara*; and *Mesure de nos jours* do permit faint glimmers of hope for authentic lives after Auschwitz. Realizing that the pre-Holocaust past can never be restored, each writer nevertheless suggests the possibility of a rebuilt future centered on renewed relationships in the present. At the conclusion of Wiesel's *Le jour*, after surviving a life-threatening accident, the narrator leaves the hospital leaning on Kathleen for support. Although he has only resolved to be a better liar to alleviate Kathleen's concerns, he has at least determined to continue living. Similarly, at the conclusion of *Saute, Barbara*, the protagonist Michael appears to be as alone as he was at the beginning of the novel, but, for the first time, he posits a tentative affirmation for his future: "la vie . . . pourrait être possible" (206; "life might be possible"). Gradually his words become more hopeful, progressing from the conditional to present tense as he repeats, "La vie est possible" (231; "Life is possible"). Alone in a foreign land, Michael approaches a stranger to ask the time. This question, a symbol for Langfus of membership in humanity, connects Michael, however tenuously, to another. Finally, in the closing pages of *Mesure de nos jours*, Delbo also signals the importance of reestablishing connections that will enable the survivor to rejoin the human community.

> Je ne sais pas
> si vous pouvez faire encore
> quelque chose de moi
> Si vous avez le courage d'essayer. . . . (212)

> I do not know
> if you can still
> make something of me
> If you have the courage to try. . . . (*Auschwitz and After* 352)

The importance of the pronoun *vous* in this short poem emphasizes the significance of acceptance by the larger community if the survivor is to be able to resume a life. Our teaching of *La nuit* remains unfinished unless we also suggest this slender thread of humanity subtly woven in the survivors' stories.

NOTES

[1] In addition to the civilization course referenced above, I have taught *La nuit* in French to undergraduate majors and minors in upper-level twentieth-century literature

courses. Typically, a few of the students had studied for at least a semester in a French-speaking country, and most students were able to function in the language at the low to mid levels of advanced proficiency. The classes were conducted in French, and students were expected to use the language in their discussion of the text. Because of its emotional impact, however, I often allowed students the opportunity to spend one class or partial class in English.

I currently incorporate *La nuit* in a course entitled Narratives of Childhood. Cross-listed in humanities and French, the course satisfies the requirement for an interdisciplinary upper-level capstone course in the general education program at my institution. Instruction is in English, but students enrolled for French credit complete reading and writing assignments in French. Depending on the number of French students, their interest in the topic, and their level of proficiency, students may spend a supplemental hour each week discussing the texts in French. The course uses both film and print to engage historical, cultural, and psychological perspectives of childhood as we explore the question of memory in the writing of authors such as Marcel Proust, Marguerite Duras, and Patrick Chamoiseau and the films of directors like François Truffaut, Louis Malle, and Claire Denis.

[2] My remarks in class are in French, but, because the ensuing discussion involves theoretical abstractions that require superior-level language skills, allowing it to proceed in English produces a more animated, interactive conversation in which students vigorously engage various points of view.

[3] Unless otherwise referenced, all translations are my own.

[4] *Aucun de nous, Une connaissance inutile*, and *Mesure de nos jours* were published as *Auschwitz et après* in 1970.

Wiesel and Kertész: *Night* in the Context of Hungarian Holocaust Literature

Rita Horváth

Two Nobel Prizes, those of Elie Wiesel and Imre Kertész, guarantee that the story of the Jews of Hungary will be a (or perhaps even the) representative story of the Holocaust. In their major works—Wiesel in *Night*, a memoir, and Kertész in *Fatelessness*, an autobiographical novel—both writers narrate in stages what happened to them in the Holocaust: the home from which the narrator was uprooted, the discrimination under the aegis of the yellow star, the ghetto or the transit camp, deportation, arrival at Auschwitz, deterioration in the camp, terms of survival, and, finally, entry into the post-Holocaust era. These stages follow conventions of Holocaust narratives established very early. We find these conventions already in the survivors' accounts of their experiences recorded in the protocols in 1945 to 1946 by the National Relief Committee for Deportees in Hungary.[1]

Although there are various historical reasons for the prominence of narratives created by Jews who were deported from Hungary, I would like to highlight one that is related both to the special features of the Holocaust in Hungary and to the predicament of the survivors. Since the Jewry of Hungary was systematically destroyed at a very late stage of World War II—it was the last sizable Jewish community annihilated in Europe—its story is fraught with cognitive and ethical questions connected to the value and possibility of witnessing and listening to witnesses. The overwhelming majority of Hungarian survivors[2] express the feeling that had they listened better to witnesses telling unbelievable tales about the destruction of the Jews all over Europe under Nazi rule, they would have behaved differently during the destruction of their communities. The survivors are constantly tortured by this feeling in the aftermath of the Holocaust, when they are faced with the task of becoming witnesses to the events and the trauma of the Holocaust.

The first phase of the history of the Holocaust in Hungary, the phase of the Hungarian anti-Jewish policy, began in the spring of 1938, when the first anti-Jewish law was passed in the Hungarian parliament. In this period, the Hungarian regime, by employing anti-Jewish legislation, gradually and systematically eliminated the Jews from the economic and social spheres.

Even though the Hungarian regime demonstrated its murderous hatred toward the Jews—by massacres at Kamenets-Podolsk[3] and at Délvidék (Braham, *Politics* 34–37) and by the institution of forced labor in the Hungarian army—the Jews of Hungary lived in relative safety until March 1944. They experienced neither the gradual disintegration during years spent in ghettos, as did the Jews of Poland, nor the deportation of whole communities to work in inhuman conditions, as did the Jews of Romania who were deported to Transnistria.

The safety of the Jews of Hungary ended abruptly when the German army occupied Hungary on 19 March 1944 and began the second phase of the Holocaust in Hungary, the German anti-Jewish policy.[4] The destruction of most of the Jews of Hungary then happened very quickly.[5] In the short span of a few months, between April and July 1944, the Germans, with the active and efficient help of the Hungarian authorities, sent the majority of the Jewish population of Hungary to the concentration camps.

The special characteristics of the destruction of the Jewish community in Hungary—its belatedness, quickness, and well-organized efficiency—raised questions that have tortured survivors ever since: Why did not the Jews of Hungary try to flee or go into hiding? What did they actually know in the spring and summer of 1944 about the Nazi regime and the fate of the Jews in the countries occupied by the army of the Third Reich? Why did they not believe the witnesses of unbelievable atrocities? Why did they not hide at least those children and women for whom somebody offered a hiding place or false papers? All the accounts written by Jews who were living within the borders of Hungary in 1944 are full of these questions.[6] The survivors cannot decide what they had actually known at the time, and in their writings emerges a traumatic picture of self-deception, illusion, of knowing and not knowing. Because Jews in Hungary lived in relative safety until such a late stage of the war, their assessment of their situation is quite different from the terrified and vague anticipations of other European Jewish communities. Autobiographical and even scholarly writings by Hungarian survivors simultaneously claim that the Jews were completely ignorant about the meaning of ghettoization and deportation and that they had some knowledge, some sound information about the fate of the Jews in Europe.

Randolph L. Braham, the doyen of the historians scrutinizing the Holocaust of the Jews of Hungary, identifies the existence of uninformed Jewish masses as the central issue of the Hungarian Holocaust. Braham turns this problem into a sharp ethical criticism of the Jewish leadership in Hungary, the Jewish Councils, since according to Braham it would have been the duty of the well-informed leaders to warn the masses about their inevitable fate:

> In retrospect, [the Jewish Councils's] major mistake appears to have been their failure to keep the Jewish masses informed about the Nazis' drive against the Jews in German-dominated Europe. The perpetuation of this posture after the German occupation of Hungary proved fatal. This silence constitutes perhaps the most controversial chapter of the Holocaust in Hungary.   (*Politics* 87)

In the same book, however, Braham acknowledges that the Jews of Hungary did have sources of information concerning the systematic mass murder of the

Jews at the hands of the Nazis. The three most important sources that Braham enumerates were Jews fleeing from Poland and Slovakia; Hungarian forced laborers returning from the Eastern front; and the members of the various Zionist youth organizations, the *halutzim*, who had access to information known to the official Jewish leadership—they knew about the content of the so-called Auschwitz-Protocol[7]—and who traveled in the provinces to inform the Jews. Even though many Jewish refugees from Poland found their way to Sighet (Alfassi, Netzer, and Szalai, "Holocaust" 70), Wiesel's hometown, Wiesel in *Night* emphasizes a fourth source of information: his master, Moishe the Beadle, who survived the Kamenets-Podolsk massacre and returned to Sighet to warn the Jews.[8]

Thus the question of what the Jews of Hungary knew, believed, and were willing or capable of believing is complex. For the survivors deported from Hungary this question is especially torturous, because they feel that they could have done something to prevent what happened to them and to their loved ones. From a post-Holocaust perspective, it seems that more people could have survived had they chosen to cross the front lines or go into hiding. Gyuri Köves, the adolescent protagonist of *Fatelessness*, points out that the victims had choices because they had some knowledge and thus had chosen to participate in their own destruction:

> They [the neighbors of the Köves family] too had taken their own steps. They too had known, foreseen, everything beforehand, they too had said farewell to my father [when he was taken to forced labor] as if we had already buried him, and even later on all they had squabbled about was whether I should take the suburban train or the bus to Auschwitz. . . .
>
> (*Fatelessness* 260)[9]

Wiesel connects the problem of passivity to that of ignoring witnesses. He bitterly recounts every missed opportunity to escape that emerged after Moishe the Beadle's witness account: the Wiesel family did not try to obtain emigration permits to go to Palestine, and they did not take the opportunity to go into hiding in a place their old servant, Maria, offered. They refused to be separated, even though Moishe the Beadle told them the tragic story of a family that chose to remain together: "Tobie, the tailor who begged to die before his sons were killed" (7).[10] At the same time, however, Eliezer, *Night*'s protagonist, claims complete ignorance by showing how unintelligible and mad an inmate's accusations sounded to the deportees of Sighet on their arrival at Auschwitz:

> "Sons of bitches, why have you come here? Tell me, why?" [. . .] "Shut up, you moron, or I'll tear you to pieces! You should have hanged yourselves rather than come here. Didn't you know what was in store for you here in Auschwitz? You didn't know? In 1944?" True. We didn't know. Nobody had told us.   (30)

The mixture of knowing and not knowing stems from not being able to listen to witnesses and not being able to become credible witnesses.

Holocaust narratives of Jews deported from Hungary not only reveal special aspects of the problems of witnessing but also, by showing that these problems are part of the predeportation era and the aftermath of the Holocaust, connect two domains—the realms before and after the Holocaust—that are usually perceived as disconnected. They focus on the problems of witnessing as already inherent in the events of the Holocaust. Both Wiesel and Kertész establish a connection between predeportation era and the aftermath of the Holocaust through the problems of witnessing.

Wiesel links the Holocaust and its aftermath by his emphasis on two witness figures, Moishe the Beadle, who dominates the predeportation period, and Mrs. Schächter, who is the central figure during the train ride to Auschwitz. They both demonstrate aspects of the survivor-witness, aspects of what the protagonist of *Night* will become after surviving the concentration camps. Survivors share with Moishe the maddening predicament of not being understood or even listened to,[11] but they also share the belatedness and madness of Mrs. Schächter's testimony, whose frightening truth cannot save anyone anymore, since the deported people were beyond help. The survivor is a combination of these two forms of witness: he can do nothing, his world is annihilated, but by insisting on telling what has happened he still hopes to save people from a future Holocaust. Moishe the Beadle was not mad, he had a goal that he failed to achieve, to save the Jews of Sighet,[12] who thought him mad. Mrs. Schächter, on the contrary, was mad, but her truth was not any less relevant. Wiesel brings together post-Holocaust reality with the events of the Holocaust by making the protagonist experience for a moment the predicament of being a witness. Eliezer, who is one of Moishe's unresponsive audience, feels that the old man whom he had to wake up with the news of deportation thinks him mad:

> I went into the house of one of my father's friends. I woke the head of the household, a man with a gray beard and the gaze of a dreamer. [. . .] "You must ready yourself for the journey! Tomorrow you will be expelled, you and your family, you and all the other Jews." [. . .] He had no idea what I was talking about. He probably thought I had lost my mind.   (14–15)

The protagonist of *Fatelessness*, who is trying to construct himself as an authentic human being—for him synonymous with becoming a witness of the Holocaust—refuses to see the events of the Holocaust as something accidental, unconnected to the times preceding and following it, which is how his old neighbors, who lived through the worst times of the Holocaust in Budapest, prefer to view it. In *Fatelessness*, we can follow step by step how the protagonist becomes a conscious witness through a series of actual acts of witnessing. He realizes additional aspects of his fate as a witness during every meeting with people who either were not deported or want to forget everything. He meets with a series of people against whose attitudes he forms his own stance.

Gyuri travels back to Hungary with a group of young men. He still wears his striped coat,[13] and on his way home, in a town that the film script based on *Fatelessness* (also written by Kertész) identifies as Pozsony (today Bratislava, Slovakia), Jews who were not in concentration camps ask him whether he knows anything about their loved ones. Because of their questions, Gyuri realizes that even Jews, the ones who were not deported, have no idea or emotionally cannot afford to have an idea about the concentration camp reality.

> They inquired whether we had come from the concentration camps and interrogated a lot of us, me included, as to whether one had chanced to meet up with some relative, someone with such and such a name. I told them that in a concentration camp people generally did not have much use for names. Then they would endeavor to describe the external appearance, hair color, and distinctive features, so I tried to get them to see that it was pointless, since most people changed a lot in the camps.
>
> (*Fatelessness* 241)

Also in Pozsony, Gyuri is accosted by a Holocaust denier. As he realizes the person's intentions, his language loses the guide quality that it had acquired in the camps. At the beginning of the conversation he still uses it and talks about the camp universe in the present tense:

> He was curious to know—which made me smile a little—if I had seen the gas chambers. I told him that if I had, then we wouldn't be having this conversation. "Well, yes," he said, "but were there really any gas chambers?" [And I answered, "Yes, of course, among other things there are also gas chambers. It all depends," I added, "which camp followed which customs. In Auschwitz, for instance, we can expect them."]
>
> (*Fateless* 176)[14]

Because of the Holocaust denier, Gyuri has discovered the existence of a hostile group besides those who are not hostile but somehow able to hold onto their pre-Holocaust innocence and do not or cannot make an effort to understand the concentration camp universe. The existence of uncomprehending Jews was not enough to bring about the linguistic change, but the existence of Holocaust denial was, because it made Gyuri lose his unconditional goodwill toward his fellow human beings who could find themselves at any moment imprisoned in concentration camps.

Gyuri Köves has two more important meetings, one with a leftist journalist who wants to take Gyuri's testimony and one with his old neighbors, who were there to say good-bye to Gyuri's father when he was drafted for forced labor. In addition to these meetings, the protagonist observes Jews at the building of the National Relief Committee for Deportees, who returned to their normal pre-Holocaust behavior and attitudes without any reflection:

> Some wore striped coats like mine, but others were already dressed in civilian attire, with white shirts and neckties, and with their hands linked behind their backs they were once again discussing important affairs of state, just as they had done before going to Auschwitz.   (*Fateless* 177)[15]

The conversations, together with the sight of these Jews, form Gyuri Köves's stand as a witness.

The Holocaust writings of those who lived within the borders of Hungary in 1944 are thus unique in that they focus upon the urgent and traumatic issues of witnessing and being able to listen to witnesses as already inherent in the story of the Holocaust. Reading Wiesel's *Night* in the context of Hungarian Holocaust literature, and especially in the context of Kertész's *Fatelessness*, brings this issue to the fore.

NOTES

[1] In the Hungarian Jewish Archives there are 3,662 numbered and a few unnumbered protocols (see Horváth).

[2] The terms "Hungarian Jews" and "Hungarian survivors" do not necessarily coincide with the self-definition of the survivors. I use these terms only to denote Jews who were living within the borders of Hungary in 1944 and, therefore, were deported from Hungary. The peace treaty that ended World War I assigned almost two-thirds of Hungary to its neighboring states, Czechoslovakia, Romania, Yugoslavia, and Austria. In 1938, as a result of the First Vienna Award, and in the first years of World War II, Hungary regained much of its formerly lost territories. Thus many Jews living in neighboring countries came under Hungarian rule. At the end of World War II, Hungary again lost these territories.

[3] The massacre at Kamenets-Podolsk is the one that Moishe the Beadle survived. Jews whose Hungarian citizenship was found questionable by the Hungarian authorities were expelled from Hungary. "The extermination of the Jews deported from Hungary was carried out on August 27–28 [1941]. . . . Surrounded by units of the SS, their Ukranian hirelings, and reportedly a Hungarian sapper platoon composed of Swabians, they, together with the indigenous Jews of Kamenets-Podolsk, were compelled to march about ten miles to a series of craters caused by bombings. There they were ordered to undress, after that they were machine-gunned. . . . In his Operational Report USSR No. 80, dated September 11, 1941, [SS-Obergruppenführer Franz] Jäckeln put the total number of those shot at Kamenets-Podolsk at 23,600—the first five-figure massacre in the

Nazis' Final Solution Program. Of these, approximately 16,000 were Jews from Hungary" (Braham, *Politics* 34).

[4] This phase lasted a little more than a year, from the German occupation of Hungary until April 1945, when the country was liberated from German rule. Ghettoization, deportation, and massacres of Jews characterized this period.

[5] Wiesel writes, "From that moment on, everything happened very quickly. The race toward death had begun" (10).

[6] David Weiss Halivni, like Wiesel and Kertész, was an adolescent when he was deported from Hungary. Like Wiesel, he lived in Sighet. He also describes at great length the complex question of what the people in the ghetto of Sighet were prepared to know concerning their fate.

[7] The Auschwitz-Protocol was prepared by the Slovakian Jewish leadership based on the testimony of two Slovakian Jews, Rudolf Vrba and Alfred Wetzler, who escaped from Auschwitz on 7 April 1944.

[8] Sighet's yizkor book identifies Moishe the Beadle as "Mose Lieberman, the *samash* [sic] of the *Eitz Haim* synagogue," the only person who returned to Sighet after being expelled as a non-Hungarian citizen (Alfassi, Netzer, and Szalai, "Holocaust" 71–72).

[9] There are now two English translations of Kertész's novel, which render even the title of Kertész's novel differently: *Fateless*, translated by Wilson and Wilson (1996), and *Fatelessness*, translated by Wilkinson (2004). I mostly use the more recent translation since it is generally closer to the original Hungarian.

[10] In a horrible way, Eliezer and his father experience the terror stemming from the deceptive joy of not being separated immediately on the ramps of Auschwitz: "His [the father's] voice was terribly sad. I understood that he did not wish to see what they would do to me. He did not wish to see his only son go up in flames" (33). The narration almost sets this scene up as a cruel punishment for not listening to Tobie's story.

[11] Wiesel painfully describes how, after the "foreign" Jews were deported from Sighet and Moishe the Beadle came back with his terrifying testimony, life not only returned to normal but people became more and more optimistic (8).

[12] Eliezer talks about the Jews of Sighet, but he includes himself fully only after the return of Moishe the Beadle, whom he himself does not believe. At this point, Eliezer includes himself in the community destined to be destroyed: "And so we, the Jews of Sighet, waited for better days that surely were soon to come" (8).

[13] Kertész demonstrates the protagonist's as yet unconscious decision to become a witness by showing his thoughts about not parting from his inmate uniform: "I might have picked out a decent jacket from the storehouse perhaps, but in the end I made do with the trusty old striped garment, unchanged except for lacking the number and triangle, that had done me good service up till then; indeed, I specifically opted for it, one could say insisted on it, for this way at least there would be no misunderstandings, I reckoned, apart from which I found it very comfortable, practical, and cool to wear, at least right then, during the summer" (*Fatelessness* 239–40).

[14] In this particular quotation, the earlier translation, Wilson and Wilson's, is closer. The section in brackets is my translation, necessary to use in this instance because neither English translation conveys that Gyuri talks about the camp universe in the present tense.

[15] I again use here the Wilson and Wilson translation, which is closer to the meaning of the Hungarian.

Night's Literary Art:
A Close Reading of Chapter 1

Susanne Klingenstein

Wiesel's accomplishments in *Night* include the memoir's astounding brevity as well as the clear organization of the story in symmetrically arranged chapters[1] strung along a historically accurate chronological timeline. This neat arrangement coincides with a symbolically charged calendar (moving from spring to spring) and a psychological progression (moving from innocence to knowledge). In addition, there are the memoir's disciplined focus on a few themes (father and son, coming-of-age, initiation, disintegration of language, crisis of faith) and the rhythmic repetition of a few images (fire, gates, journey). The soul-shattering content of the narrative is presented with such clarity that the reader is not flooded with too much information and is thus allowed to become unsettled only by the emotional impact of the narrated events.

What needs to be made clear to students, however, is that *Night's* elegant simplicity is deceptive. Wiesel's great artistic achievement consists in the transformation of an overwhelming, inexplicable, highly irrational experience into a graspable story that proceeds smoothly and linearly from point to point. Yet Wiesel's storytelling is neither simple nor simplifying but tremendously sophisticated.

A close reading of the first chapter can illuminate Wiesel's extraordinary literary craftsmanship. The first chapter of *Night* depicts the transformation of the members of Sighet's Jewish community into German prisoners. It sets the memoir's tone and introduces many of the text's important themes.

It was a stroke of brilliance to open the French text with Moishe the Beadle. He is marginal to the events in the way prophets are marginal to the events they foretell. His description in the 1958 French text is deliberately vague and sentimental so that he comes across as a type rather than a specific individual.[2] Moishe functions as a guide to unknown territories. He initiates the narrator into the world of kabbalah, and after his return from his deportation he attempts to introduce the Jews of Sighet to the world of death. He warns them of the future he has seen. The 1956 Yiddish text calls him explicitly a *navi* ("prophet") and, more particularly, one of the *nevi'im fun khurbn* ("prophets of destruction" [*Un di velt* 12]). He lives up to his name Moishe ("Moses") by having seen the future, gotten a taste of it, but not fully entered it (the biblical Moses is allowed to see the Promised Land but, on account of an earlier act of disobedience, is not allowed to enter it). Moishe disappears from the text as soon as the realization of the future begins with the entry of the Germans into Sighet.

Like most prophets who bring bad news, Moishe is not believed in his town. The townspeople think he is crazy. Indeed, the description of Moishe by the disbelieving narrator recalls nothing so much as the literary stock figure of the wise fool, the fool with the visionary gift, whose advice runs counter to reason and convention. Most important, however, Moishe is a type of the memoir's narrator. He has survived the vision of horrors and has returned to tell the tale, and, as many survivors feared would happen to them if they told their stories, he is not believed. In the Yiddish text, Moishe derives the strength (*koyekh*) to return to Sighet from his mission to warn his fellow Jews of their impending death. When they do not believe him, he is a broken man (*Un di velt* 11–14). He sinks into silence.

As the boy Eliezer's guide through the unknown territories of Jewish mysticism and as the Jewish community's guide through the world of the camps, Moishe provides access to both worlds, as Wiesel would later do as a writer and teacher. The trope of silence that became strongly associated with survivor memoirs—on account of the authors' crisis of language when faced with narrating the unprecedented—is prefigured in Moishe, but only in a minor key. After his miraculous return from his deportation by the Germans, Moishe is confident that he can adequately report what he has seen and lived through in the territory of evil. Yet he has lost his ability to function as a teacher of Jewish mysticism. Before his deportation, his teaching included telling a version of the parable that had become famous by the mid-1950s as the *Türhüter Parabel* ("parable of the gatekeeper") in chapter 10 of Franz Kafka's novel *The Trial*. In Moishe's teaching, as in the priest's telling of the parable in Kafka's text, the message to the seeker is that the answer to profound spiritual questions does not come from the outside but is found within each seeker. The parable is paradoxical because in it the speaker, teaching the neophyte, abdicates his role as teacher, arguing implicitly that his proper role is to be silent (or laconic), as the gatekeeper in Kafka's parable is silent throughout the time of the seeker's presence outside the gate.

It is only after Moishe has been established as a presence in *Night* that the narrator introduces his father. Immediately one feels a tension. The father is described as a stern, unsentimental, highly respected figure who puts the public good above his own family. Moishe, however, an alternative father figure, is sensitive to the narrator's spiritual needs. The bond between Eliezer and Moishe is strengthened in the course of their mystic studies, which they undertake against the father's wishes. Eliezer ends up throwing his spiritual lot in with Moishe: "I became convinced that Moishe the Beadle would help me enter eternity, into that time when question and answer would become ONE" (5). The allusion here is to the *coincidentia oppositorum* ("coinciding of opposites"), a key concept in Jewish but especially in Christian mysticism that describes the resolution of all contradictions in God.[3]

When Moishe returned from his deportation and failed execution to tell his story, he found precise words to convey the facts. But he could no longer speak to his student Eliezer about God or kabbalah. The events of history have replaced the contemplation of God. As Moishe, the mystic, sees reality clearly, the townsfolk continue to cultivate "dangerous illusion."[4] Although the narrator had been among those who questioned Moishe's testimony, he emerges as crazy

Moishe's faithful disciple and thus, paradoxically, as the only clearly thinking Jew in Sighet when he asks his father to purchase emigration papers to Palestine. But the father refuses to listen to his son.

After Moishe has sunk into silence, the narrator's focus shifts to the unfolding of the historic events and their effect on the Jews of Sighet, which is nil as "life seemed normal once again" (7). Subtly, the narrator introduces a new theme, that of the simultaneity of religious and historic time. The reaction of the Jews to the news of Stalingrad, the bombardment of Germany, and the opening of a second front was to wait "for better days that surely were soon to come" (8). One can read this sentence straight, but one can also hear in it inflections of the millennial expectation expressed throughout the daily prayers. The duality of the time zones in which the Jews of Sighet live—on the one hand, the historic time of Hungary's turn toward fascism and occupation by the Germans, and on the other hand, the rhythm of the daily prayers and the succession of holidays with their eschatological concept of history and attendant expectation of redemption—dominates the rest of the chapter. This duality of factual history and eschatology functions implicitly as a central device to explain the indifference or apathy of the Jews to the historic events in the larger world around them. When the narrator remarks on the occasion of the ascent of the fascists to power in Budapest that "it was all in the abstract" (9), he points to a consequence of the intense daily immersion in the world of Jewish faith: the patriarchs and Moses become a presence of greater immediacy and significance than the leaders of the Nyilas party in Hungary's capital. When the narrator in the first sentence of the Yiddish text points to foolish faith (*narishe emune*) and trust (*betokhn*) as the source (*kval*) of the Jews' misfortunes (*umglikn*), he means precisely their exclusive immersion into a frame of reference that is disconnected from the reality of the environment in which the Jews lived.

Moishe having fallen into silence and the political events in Hungary beginning to exert pressure on the Jews, the father moves into the center of the son's narrative. Like Moishe he is characterized by the act of speaking and the effectiveness of his speech, which declines to the degree that Moishe's "foolish" speech becomes validated. As the narrative arrives in the spring of 1944, time speeds up. Both historic time and religious time are more intensely felt. The two worlds come into conflict, and one of them breaks and reveals itself as an illusion. The Jewish cocoon spun of intellect and imagination is shattered by physical violence.

After the Germans have occupied the town, Passover, the celebration of moving from bondage to freedom, arrives. The ritual observance of the holiday is experienced as a game of "pretend[ing]" (10) that is brought to a grotesque climax on the last day with the arrest of the Jewish leaders and the beginning of the captivity of the Jews, who are herded into ever-narrower cages (their own houses, the big ghetto, the little ghetto, a single synagogue, the boxcars). "The race toward death had begun" (10). The Jews adjust their lives to the new conditions, and "little by little life returned to 'normal' " (11). The narrator offers no explanation for this phenomenon, and the evidence in the text is too weak to argue that it is simply a reflex of exile: you accept the conditions you find and use faith as your compensatory loophole into another, better world. The narrator refers only in a summary way to "delusion" as ruling the ghetto (12).

The narrator is now preparing the climactic scene of chapter 1, which takes place "[s]ome two weeks before Shavuot" (12). The grim events in Sighet on Passover served merely as a preparation for what is to come, just as the Israelites' emergence from Egyptian bondage into the freedom of the desert was a preparation for receiving the Torah at Mount Sinai fifty days later, which is celebrated on Shavuot. The word *Shavuot* means "weeks" and marks the end of the seven-week period after Passover, during which each day was counted as the Israelites prepared themselves to receive the word of God. The festival is also known as *zman matan torah*, the season of the giving of the Torah. *Shavuot* also means "oaths," and Hasidim especially believe that at the giving of the Torah, God and his people exchanged oaths not to forsake each other. It is customary upon the arrival of Shavuot at sundown to stay up all night and study sections of the Torah. The custom is traditionally explained by the story that, at the time of the giving of the Torah at Mount Sinai, the Jews did not rise early in the day and that it was necessary for God himself to awaken the Jews. To compensate for their behavior, the Jews made it a custom to stay awake all night.

To readers familiar with the customs and the religious significance of Shavuot, the climactic scene of the first chapter, the annunciation of the deportations, during which the impotence of Eliezer's worldly father is exposed, reads like a bitter travesty of the traditional holiday.

As night falls, twenty people have gathered in the backyard of the narrator's house, as if for a traditional learning, known as *tikkun leil shavuot* ("repair of the world"). But with Eliezer's father as the central figure, the gathering is secular. "My father was sharing some anecdotes and holding forth on his opinion of the situation. He was a good story teller" (12). The father is shown here in full bloom as an effective talker. But this holding forth is brought to an abrupt end: "Suddenly, the gate opened, and Stern [. . .] took my father aside" (12). An expectation of those schooled in kabbalah is that on the first night of Shavuot the gates of the heavens open and all prayers offered at that moment will go straight to God. In Sighet the only evidence of heaven is the name of the emissary (*stern* means "star"). In a paragraph that is on par with the parodies of Kafka in *The Trial*, the celestially named emissary summons the father, an unwilling Moses, to come and receive the word of the law. "The story he had interrupted would remain unfinished" (12). It would never be finished, because when the father returns with the new commandment, the world has changed for the Jews. The father along with the Jews he spoke for will decline into weakness, speechlessness, and death.

During the father's conference with the new gods of Sighet, however, the Jews conduct their Shavuot vigil. "We were ready to wait as long as necessary. . . . We stood, waiting for the door to open. Neighbors, hearing the rumors, had joined us. [. . .] Time had slowed down" (13). When the father returns, the commandments he brings with him can be summed up in one word: "Transports" (13). One word has replaced all the father's anecdotes and explanations. Like the Israelites of old, the Jews of Sighet will now be on the move to the "land" that was "promised" them early on in Hitler's reign.

In the subsequent narrative of the preparation for the transports, the ironies abound. Rather than settle on one religious event as a foil for the unfolding historic events (as the narrator had done for the Passover and the Shavuot scenes), the narrative opens up and presents imagery that accommodates a host of associations with instances of the Israelites' breaking up camp and setting out for elsewhere. Most immediate is the replay of the exodus from Egypt. It is evoked by the hasty nighttime awakenings of Sighet's Jews and their admonition to prepare themselves for a journey and by the text's emphasis on food preparation, as the unwilling Moses runs back and forth to find out whether the authorities hadn't changed their minds. The journey's destination is a secret known only to the Jewish leadership, but reverberating as destiny in the text's allusions to both Passover and Shavuot is the idea of the Promised Land, which turns out to be certain death. Yet in another bitterly perverted allusion to Passover, whose ritual narrative (the Haggadah) is punctuated by admonitions never to forget the exodus from Egypt, the text repeats several times that those who had already been deported were quickly forgotten (6, 20).

Meanwhile the narrator has stepped into Moishe the Beadle's shoes and is going from house to house literally to awaken the Jews to their destiny (as Moishe had tried to do metaphorically). In the words he chooses to arouse the Jews we hear ironic echoes of the prophet Isaiah's "kumi, ori" ("arise, shine; for your light has come" [Isaiah 60.1]). When questioned what this madness means, the narrator, like any prophet who is a mouthpiece for rather than the source of information, experiences his first crisis of language: "My throat was dry and the words were choking me, paralyzing my lips. There was nothing else to say" (15).

As the Jews get ready to leave, they abandon their possessions. Their belongings lie on the ground, "pitiful relics that seemed never to have had a home. . . . They had ceased to matter" (15, 17). The scene recalls Thucydides's account of the plague of Athens in *The Peloponnesian War* that decimated the Athenians and made them for the short time of the natural disaster utterly indifferent to worldly goods and social distinctions.[5] The narrator's emphasis throughout on the hot sun and the brilliant blue sky accentuates the cruel indifference of nature. The juxtaposition of the summer's brilliance with the sorrow of the Jews harkens back to the beginning of one of the great Yiddish novels, Mendele Moykher Sforim's *Fishke the Lame*, in which the narrator points out that as summer sets in, the Jews begin their period of mourning.[6]

When the procession of the Jews moves out of the big ghetto of Sighet, the narrator's frame of reference shifts from religious to historic time. The refusal of the Germans to give water to the journeying Jews (16) integrates the Germans into a long line of *soyne Yisroel*, historic enemies of the Jews, who refused them water on the way to the Promised Land. What the narrator sees also reminds him of the Babylonian captivity and the Spanish Inquisition (17).[7] After the Jews have left, leaving their houses open and their possessions lying around for anyone to grab them, the narrator compares the scene to "an open tomb" (17). We may think at first of a robbed Egyptian tomb, but it's not a good fit. In this tomb the possessions are intact, but the body is gone. Wiesel's French Catholic readers may have been struck by this image as an allusion to the grave of the risen Christ. But what we have here is death without the redemption.[8] The body of Christ is being led to the slaughter.

In a final travesty that has sprung from the Nazis' brains rather than the narrator's, the remaining Jews of the little ghetto are herded into their synagogue on Shabbat. Among the Jews of the little ghetto "[t]here no longer was any distinction between rich and poor, notables and the others; we were all people condemned to the same fate—still unknown" (21). As they once stood together at Mount Sinai to receive the Torah, they are now assembled, squeezed together as one big mass into the space where they used to hear the word of God. But the skies do not open. In their great human need they are forced to soil their house of study and prayer. And the following morning they are marched to the station, and "[t]he cars were sealed" (22).

Although the French version of Wiesel's text was trimmed of both Yiddish sentiment and quotations from classic Jewish texts to prepare it for a non-Jewish readership, the editing out of these elements was not complete. Wiesel's literary device of using the Jewish religious narratives' promise of redemption as a foil against which to measure reality—a satiric device prominently used by the secular Yiddish masters Sholem Aleichem and Mendele Moykher Sforim in their most widely read novels—could not be removed without destroying the entire narrative structure of *Night*'s first chapter. Whereas in the Yiddish novels the satiric device puts the onus on God for not delivering on the promise, in Wiesel's text it is the Jews who are blamed for falling prey to a "dangerous illusion." In *Night*'s subsequent chapters, Wiesel is easier on the Jews and harder on God.

NOTES

[1] This organization was first discussed by Colin Davis (55).

[2] In the Yiddish text the description of Moishe is much more detailed. There we learn that he has a yellow beard, is a Kosever Hasid, and has a chronically sick wife and four or five children (*Un di velt* 9–10). Similarly, Sighet, which in the Yiddish memoir was a significant specific place with a specific history, is in the French text a vague shtetl with fuzzy contours that could stand for any Eastern European Jewish settlement.

[3] Compare with Nikolaus von Kues, *De coniecturis* (2:1.2). Jewish mysticism is more complicated in its concept of the restitution of the unity of the world. The concept of *tikkun* ("repair") in the thinking of Isaac Luria requires also a coincidence of opposites (see Scholem 273–76).

[4] At the beginning of *Un di velt hot geshvign*, the narrator points out the three elements that were the source of the Jews' misfortune: foolish faith, trust, and dangerous illusion (*geferlekhe illuzie* [7]).

[5] In the Yiddish version the indifference to worldly goods is given greater play and resembles Thucydides's description more clearly (*Un di velt* 34).

[6] In the Yiddish version the emphasis on nature's brilliance surrounding the suffering Jews is even stronger than in the French text (*Un di velt* 35).

[7] Wiesel is probably thinking of the expulsion of the Spanish Jews in 1492, a step taken by the Spanish monarchs in consequence of the Inquisition.

[8] Wiesel uses the image of an open grave (*an ofener kever*) for the open, abandoned houses of the Jews in the Yiddish text (34). It is preceded by a short, ironically modified quotation from the Aramaic invitation to the hungry and distressed that opens the Passover Haggadah: "kol dikhfin yetei vyekakh" ("all who are hungry enter and take," instead of the Haggadah's *yekhul* ["eat"]).

Night in the Contexts of Holocaust Memoirs

David Patterson

When teaching Holocaust memoirs in general and Elie Wiesel's *Night* in particular, one must bear in mind certain differences between the Holocaust memoir
and other autobiographical reflections on one's life. The Holocaust memoir is
not an account of a person's life; rather, it is the tale of one's own death. As
Moishe the Beadle, who survived the horror of a mass grave in Wiesel's *Night*,
states it, "I wanted to return to Sighet to describe to you my death" (7). And,
like other survivors, he faced the frustration of having to transmit a message
that could not be transmitted. The events related in the Holocaust memoir are
not events the survivor has lived through; they continue to live through him, as
he continues to live in the shadow of the kingdom of night. Commenting on the
corpse that stared back at him from the mirror, Wiesel ends his memoir by saying, "The look in his eyes as he gazed at me has never left me" (115). If the narrative of a life ordinarily provides it with some sense of meaning, Wiesel's character Gregor from *The Gates of the Forest* expresses the sentiment often
conveyed in the Holocaust memoir: if the event "has no meaning, then it's an
insult, and if it does have meaning, it's even more so" (197).

At the end of a series of "nevers," Wiesel cries out from the pages of *Night*,

> Never shall I forget those moments that murdered my God and my
> soul [. . .]
> Never shall I forget those things, even if I were condemned to live as
> long as God Himself.
> Never. (34)

This "never" is steeped in a forever that places the antiworld forever in the foreground of the survivor's consciousness. Having lived through his own death, the
survivor cannot die. That is the horror: the heart continues to beat when it
should have come to a stop. For it has been stripped of the sign that would seal
the tomb of the past. What is the sign that signifies such a closure? It is the
cemetery. But, as Wiesel has said, "my generation has been robbed of everything, even of our cemeteries" (*Legends* 9). One function of memory in *Night* is
to become such a sign. The one who has lived through his own death cannot die
away from the horror. For his death has been murdered in the obliteration of
the gravesites of Jewish mothers, fathers, and children.

Therefore, coming to the end of *Night*, Wiesel comes to no end. It is as
though he remains inside the sealed train and, like Mrs. Schächter, is shouting
to us, "Jews, listen to me, . . . I see a fire! I see flames, huge flames!" (25). And
yet this very shouting, this very testimony, might open up a path back to life.
And the fact that we hold Wiesel's memoir in our hands means that there is

something of value to be understood in this testimony, some matter of great urgency that must be transmitted.

What, then, might be gathered from Wiesel's choice to endure the ordeal of putting to paper the memory of this radical assault on his very soul? In this memoir, as in other Holocaust memoirs, recovery is the key to this question. And the word *recovery* is to be understood on at least two levels:

> The recovery of value and meaning in life through the testimony to its undoing. For Wiesel, this recovery entails some sort of recovery of the sacred teachings of the Jewish tradition.
>
> A recovery in the sense of recovering from the illness of a deaf and indifferent humanity that, through its indifference, lost its humanity. There is also a certain indifference that overcomes those who were abandoned by humanity.

These aspects of recovery are interwoven, and instructors should keep both in mind when teaching *Night*. For both go into a process of returning a trace of life to the corpse that stares into the eyes of Eliezer—and of the reader—at the end of the memoir.

The Recovery of Value and Meaning in Life

In Wiesel's memoir the recovery of value and meaning in life is tied to the recovery of Jewish teaching; the process of recovery is dialectically tied to the tale of this devastating loss. "There comes a time," Wiesel has said, "when only those who do believe in God will cry out to him in wrath and anguish" (*From the Kingdom* 20). His memoir is just such an outcry.

The process of recovering what was lost begins with his brief account of what was lost, as Wiesel describes his life as a Hasidic adolescent who studied Talmud during the day and at night would "weep over the destruction of the Temple" (3). In Wiesel's account of his passage from his Hasidic world into the Nazi antiworld, we see various dimensions of the Nazi assault on the sacred tradition that defined Eliezer's soul. In keeping with the Nazi practice of planning actions according to the Jewish holy calendar, we see that on the seventh day of Passover, a day of special observance and miraculous significance, the Germans arrested the Jewish leaders in Sighet (10); that they chose the Sabbath for the day of the Jews' expulsion (21–22); and that they made the period just following Rosh Hashanah into an occasion for mass selections (69). God had designated certain days when holiness would enter time, and the Nazis chose those days to erase the holy from time.

Just as the holiness of Jewish time comes under assault, the holiness of Jewish prayer unravels. When their transport arrives at Auschwitz, Eliezer and the others find themselves saying the Kaddish, the prayer for the dead, for themselves. "I don't know whether," says Eliezer, "during the history of the Jewish people, men have ever before recited Kaddish for themselves" (33). His rebellion against God manifests itself in a play on a Jewish prayer, when at Rosh Hashanah he wonders,

> How could I say to Him: Blessed be Thou, Almighty, Master of the Universe, who chose us among all nations to be tortured day and night, to watch as our fathers, our mothers, our brothers end up in the furnaces? (67)

And yet the prayer, which is itself a trace of the divine presence, has a life of its own. For when Eliezer sees that Rabbi Eliahu's son has abandoned his father, he remembers, "in spite of myself, a prayer formed inside me, a prayer to this God in whom I no longer believed" (91). It was a prayer that he should never abandon his own father, as Rabbi Eliahu's son had done.

To be sure, the memoir *Night* is itself a kind of prayer that Wiesel should never abandon his father—both the father he remembers in the memoir and the Father in whom he could no longer believe. For just as he remembers the Nazis' murder of his father, so does he remember the Nazis' murder of God. Indeed, the murder of God is a pivotal scene in the memoir: it happens when a child is hanged before the prisoners assembled at Buna. "For God's sake, where is God?" Eliezer hears a man behind him ask. "And from within me, I heard a voice answer: 'Where He is? This is where—hanging here from this gallows . . .' " (65). This memory of the murder of God harbors a testimony to what is at stake in the act of remembrance. The Talmud teaches that creation itself is sustained by the breath of children (Shabbat 119b). And, according to a Jewish tradition, only the prayers from our children reach God's ear, for their lips are untainted by sin (see Kitov 75–76). When children are silenced God grows deaf. Words lose their meaning, and human beings lose their humanity.

What is at stake in this memory of the murder of God, then, is the idea of a human being and the dearness of a human life. "At Auschwitz, not only man died, but also the idea of man," Elie Wiesel has said (*Legends* 190). That idea dies with the death of a Jewish teaching and tradition concerning the holiness of every human being. The loss of that sense of holiness underlies humanity's illness of indifference from which Wiesel seeks a recovery.

The Recovery from Humanity's Illness of Indifference

Like the memory of the loss of the divine presence, the memory of human indifference harbors both an indictment and a testimony. And, just as the memory of God's death is part of an effort to recover even a negative relation to God, the memory of this indifference is an attempt to reawaken the divine image in the human being. For that image lives precisely in the care and concern offered to other human beings, which is precisely what the Nazis set out to destroy. Indeed, the title of the Yiddish edition of *Night* conveys just such a testimony: *Un di velt hot geshvign* ("And the World Remained Silent").

Wiesel underscores this illness when he and his father enter Auschwitz, smell the odor of burning flesh, and see babies thrown alive into pits of flames. Eliezer says that he could not believe that humanity would tolerate such a horror, to which his father replies, "The world? The world is not interested in us. Today, everything is possible, even the crematoria . . ." (33). The Nazis relied on the world's indifference toward the torture and murder of the Jews. And, once they had the Jews locked into the concentrationary universe, they cultivated that indifference among the Jews themselves. This indifference was a key part of the assault on the soul.

Following selection after Rosh Hashanah, those marked for the gas chambers "were standing apart, abandoned by the whole world" (72). And when Eliezer tries to help his father, the head of a block tells him, "In this place, there is no such thing as father, brother, friend. Each of us lives and dies alone" (110). In this place designed to murder Jews, a Jew is not a Jew. For with this collapse of all human relation comes the complete collapse of the human being as a someone.

This imposed illness from which the survivor seeks recovery overwhelms Eliezer most profoundly on the death of his father. If the tale of his own death turns on a single moment, this is that moment. "His last word had been my name," he confesses. "He had called out to me and I had not answered" (112). It was as though he no longer knew his name or had a name. What began with having his name erased by the number A-7713 ended in this silence, into which was gathered a silencing of the human image and the divine spark that animates the human being. Three pages later the corpse is staring back at the survivor, with eyes that have never left him. But this "never" is tied to another dimension of the recovery at work in the memoir.

Night *in the Contexts of Other Memoirs*

To better understand these aspects of *Night* that distinguish it as a Holocaust memoir, we should note its similarities and differences with respect to other memoirs. To this end, I consider two other well-known memoirs of survivors from very different backgrounds: *Survival in Auschwitz: The Nazi Assault on Humanity*, by Primo Levi, and *Auschwitz: True Tales from a Grotesque Land*, by Sara Nomberg-Przytyk. Whereas Wiesel entered Auschwitz as a Hasidic Jew, Levi was a secular Jew; Nomberg-Przytyk was raised in a Hasidic family, but by the time she was sent to Auschwitz, she was a thoroughgoing Communist. There are other differences among these three: we have a teenager, a male adult, and a female adult, and we have a Hungarian, an Italian, and a Pole.

Nevertheless, the memoirs of all three share some defining characteristics of the Holocaust memoir, although they manifest those defining characteristics differently. Whereas a central image in Wiesel's memoir is the murder of God in the hanging of the child, in Levi's memoir a central image is "the demolition of a man" (26). To be sure, Levi's memoir is subtitled "The Nazi Assault on Humanity," which is an assault on what Wiesel refers to as "the idea of man." Thus in Levi's book we have a profound insight into a distinctively Nazi creation: the *Muselman*. These denizens of Auschwitz are

> the backbone of the camp, an anonymous mass, continually renewed and always identical, of non-men who march and labour in silence, the divine spark dead within them, already too empty to really suffer. One hesitates to call them living: one hesitates to call their death death.   (90)

With Levi, then, we have an additional insight into a defining feature of the concentrationary universe: death itself is obliterated.

The tension between language and silence in the tearing of word from meaning also characterizes both survivors' memoirs in different ways. Wiesel sees parallels between meaning in the word, meaning in prayer, and the relation between one human being and another. When a prisoner tells Eliezer and other new arrivals that there should be comradeship among them, Wiesel refers to these as "the first human words" (41). Joining human being to human being—these words are joined to meaning. With Levi we see that "our language lacks words to express this offence, the demolition of a man" (26), precisely because the demolition of a man happens on the demolition of the word, which is the demolition of human relation. Therefore he twice invokes the Tower of Babel (38, 73) to show the parallel between the confusion of tongues and the confusion over what a human being is.

In Levi's memoir one key illustration of the collapse of the link between word and meaning is that bread is not bread; it is "bread-Brot-Broid-chleb-pain-lechem-keynér," the "holy grey slab" (39) that is to be hoarded and not offered. It is the object of worship for one who, in Wiesel's words, was no longer a human being but merely "a famished stomach" (52). When bread is not bread, then, a human being is not a human being. When is bread bread? When it is offered to another human being. Therefore, in keeping with his emphasis on humanity, Levi relates that the first sign that the prisoners had regained some trace of their humanity after the Nazis had fled was when one person offered another something to eat (160).

Nomberg-Przytyk also sees the tearing of word from meaning and humanity from the human being as "the best evidence of the devastation that Auschwitz created in the psyche of every human being" (72). For her, however, the word torn from meaning in a tearing of humanity from human being is not *bread*; it is *Mama*. Listen:

> Suddenly, the stillness was broken by the screaming of children, . . . a scream repeated a thousand times in the single word, "Mama," a scream that increased in intensity every second, enveloping the whole camp and every inmate.

Our lips parted without our being conscious of what we were doing, and a scream of despair tore out of our throats . . . At the end everything was enveloped in death and silence.   (81)

In Wiesel's memoir we saw that in the camp there are "no fathers, no brothers"; in Nomberg-Przytyk's memoir we realize that in the camp there are no mothers, no children. Therefore there is no divine presence. For the Talmud teaches that only through our mothers does blessing come into our homes (Bava Metzia 59a). Indeed, it is through the mothers of Israel that the Torah comes into the world (see, e.g., Rashi's commentary on Exodus 19.3).

Thus whereas Wiesel associates the murder of the child with the murder of God, Nomberg-Przytyk associates this horror with the murder of the very origin, the murder of the mother. This point is made most starkly when she relates the horror of having to kill a mother's newborn infant in order to save the mother—who, then, is not a mother. "You can't give birth to a living baby," she explains to the new mother. "Otherwise, you will die with it" (70). If, according to the Nazis, the Jew's crime is being, then there is no criminal worse than the one who brings a Jew into being. For Jewish women, then, to give birth is to incur death. Thus the singular horror of having to kill an infant to save a mother. And with each infant slain to save a mother who is not a mother, a piece of the survivor's soul was obliterated.

In Wiesel's memoir we saw the devastation of the world's indifference and of how it crept into the prisoners in the camp. Nomberg-Przytyk experienced a similar isolation in her very first camp, in Stutthof, where the Jewish prisoners found themselves "in complete isolation" not only from the world but also from all the other prisoners in the camp (4). Further, just as prisoners selected for the gas in Wiesel's memoir were already as though removed from the world, Nomberg-Przytyk confesses her failure to speak to a woman selected for death (27). Subsequently, says Levi, in the antiworld of the *Lager* "everyone is desperately and ferociously alone" (88), isolated not only from one another but also from "civilians" such as the three German girls who work in the chemical laboratory in Buna: like the giggling German girls in Wiesel's memoir (46), they chat about how they are going to spend the holidays, with the scent of the chimneys all around them (143).

If in the antiworld every Jew is "ferociously alone," the one who is alone most ferociously is the one who is the most radically silent, most radically indifferent: the *Muselman*. Wiesel mentions the *Muselman* only once, where he comments that anyone found to be a *Muselman* would be sent to the crematory (70). Already consigned to "the other side," they were dead before they were dead—dead from indifference, both from without and from within. But, as already noted, Levi penetrates much more deeply into the meaning of the *Muselman*: he is, says Levi, the image of "all the evil of our time" (90). That symbol of Nazi evil is what human beings made of human beings in Auschwitz, beginning with the Jews, from whom we have the most ancient testimony to the holiness of the human being. That is why the corpse that stares back at Eliezer also stares back at us.

If the corpse that gazes back at him is to recover its humanity, then Eliezer must recover from the illness of indifference. And, because that look remains with him, the process of recovery and return is never ending. The problem of return, then, is tied to the problem of indifference, which includes the indifference of those to whom the survivor tells his tale. Whereas Moishe the Beadle met with indifference among the townspeople of Sighet, Levi relates the recurring nightmare of encountering indifference among members of his own family. Relating the nightmare that haunted his nights in the camp, he says, "I cannot help noticing that my listeners do not follow me. In fact, they are completely indifferent" (60). And, remembering her first day of "liberation," Nomberg-Przytyk recalls the absence of anyone to whom she might return: "I was alone, no one was waiting for me, there was no one to return to" (154).

Thus each survivor offers a different perspective on the problem of liberation. Some have no home to return to. Others return but cannot tell the tale or transmit the message. And all are unable to leave behind the assault on their souls that, in Wiesel's words, "has turned my life into one long night seven times sealed" (*Night* 34).

Teaching Night *in the Contexts of Holocaust Memoirs*

When teaching *Night* in the contexts of Holocaust memoirs, one should keep several points in mind. First are the various expressions of a defining feature of the Holocaust, namely the assault not only on human beings but on the notion of a human being. The Nazis understand the value of a human being to lie in an accident of nature, that is, in "race." Further, the Nazi sees in himself absolutely no connection to any other "race," so that he has no obligation to anyone. The Jew, on the other hand, represents the teaching that every human being is created in the image of the infinite one and that each of us stands in a divinely commanded, ethical relation to other human beings. When one teaches *Night* the Jew must not be forgotten.

Second, there is the multilayered issue of recovery and the effort to return to life through an act of testimony. Some survivors try to recover a sense of humanity; others try to recover a relation to the divinity. All struggle to recover a sense of meaning and value. And all are moved by a sense of urgency that would stir the world from the sleep of indifference. That we have these testimonies demonstrates the abiding trace of something infinitely precious, despite the Nazi attempt to annihilate it. The one who could not find a listener now asks us to listen. Therefore we become part of the Jew's project to return to life: we are transformed into messengers. This transformation too is an open-ended aspect of the survivor's recovery and return to life: those who receive the message transmitted in *Night* and other memoirs can receive it only by transmitting it in turn.

Finally, students who gaze into the mirror at the end of *Night* should be reminded that the aim of this study is not to succumb to despair or to be left in such a state. They must struggle to move, as Wiesel himself moved, from *Night* to *Dawn* to *Day* (the titles of his first three books). They must find a way to rejoice and give thanks—not for the evil of the Holocaust, certainly, but for the fact that it was evil. Which means there is something good and holy at stake in this study. For in this study something infinitely precious is placed in our care. Therefore we must answer the questions that the first murderer failed to answer: Where is your brother? And what have you done?

Strategies for Teaching Wiesel's *Night* with Levi's *Survival in Auschwitz*

Jonathan Druker

At a recent gathering of Holocaust scholars, a historian earnestly discussed whether, with space in a syllabus for a single canonical Nazi concentration camp memoir, one ought to teach Elie Wiesel's *Night* or Primo Levi's *Survival in Auschwitz*. Skeptical audience members called this a false choice, saying that the particular goals of different college courses ought to dictate the selection rather than one historian's assessment of the two books' relative historical value. Besides, the audience argued, the excellent memoirs to choose among number in the dozens, not just two. I had to agree with these cautions, and I had one other: the Nazi concentration camps constitute a range of phenomena so vast in historical, psychological, and ethical terms that no ten memoirs, let alone one, can encompass them wholly. Still, as I listened to the discussion, I reflected on the practical successes I have had teaching *Night* and *Survival in Auschwitz* together in a course on Holocaust literature and film that I designed for the general education curriculum at a large midwestern university where few students have a thorough knowledge of either the Holocaust or Judaism. I have concluded that teaching both of these Auschwitz memoirs rather than just one of them is more than twice as effective in pedagogical terms. Indeed, putting the two books in dialogue and exploiting the differences and similarities between them can produce a valuable classroom synergy.

This essay describes several crucial points of contact between the two texts and offers specific teaching strategies as well as writing assignments for helping students compare and contrast Wiesel's religious response with Levi's secular humanist response to the rupture the Holocaust left in its wake. In brief, the nature of Auschwitz in Wiesel's memoir, in its relentless slaughter of the innocent, threatens the very possibility of faith in God and, therefore, the basis of the Jewish religion and identity. In Levi's memoir, Auschwitz is understood as a dehumanizing machine that perverts the rational powers of the human mind for the express purpose of undermining the Enlightenment's exalted idea of humanity. Wiesel tends to focus on the particularity of the victims, European Jewry, and the damaged covenant between God and the Jewish people. Levi tries to repair the humanist concept of Man by reasserting the Enlightenment principle of universality (the idea that all human beings are essentially the same and must be accorded the same rights and freedoms) against Nazism's shocking determination that some among us are subhuman.

In the process of discovering that each author's impression of Auschwitz was shaped by his personal circumstances and beliefs, students begin to appreciate that historical events like the Holocaust have no inherent meanings but only those projected by writers (and readers) through the lens of specific cultural and ideological frames of reference. Simply put, students understand more fully the differences between Levi's and Wiesel's memoirs when they recognize that Levi writes as an atheist-moralist who returned to his Italian community after the war, and Wiesel writes as a devout Jew from a deeply religious community in Hungary that virtually ceased to exist as a result of the Holocaust. It is also helpful to know that the twenty-four-year-old Levi passed his year in Auschwitz without close family members. Conversely, Wiesel, in captivity at just fifteen, was both supported and burdened by the presence of his father and then deeply scarred by witnessing his father's demise. In later remarks about each other, the two memoirists confirm the impact of these dissimilarities. "I was lucky," Levi said in an interview. "When I returned to Italy, I found my home, I found my family. . . . [Wiesel] belonged to a religious family and he lost, along with his family, his faith, or at least endangered it" (Belpoliti and Gordon 27). Of Levi, Wiesel wrote, "we came from different milieus, and even in Auschwitz led different lives" (*All Rivers* 83).

What was Levi's milieu? His strongly secular values were typical among the well-educated bourgeois Jews of his native Turin, who were some of the most assimilated in Europe, having exchanged willingly a large share of their Jewish particularity (but not all) for Italian nationalism and the Enlightenment's promise of universal rights. In *Survival in Auschwitz*, a book whose original Italian title, *Se questo è un uomo*, is best translated as "If This Is a Man," Levi affirms both human dignity and the deep ethical bond between individuals. His text challenges Nazi ideology by showing that what we human beings have in common is far more important than what separates us. Fully identified with science and Italian culture, Levi drew on both Darwin and Dante in writing his survivor memoir in his native Italian. With a little prompting, students see that Levi's autobiographical narrator speaks first as a man, then as an Italian (and a Western European), then as a scientist (he was trained as a chemist). His scientific background is reflected in the detailed descriptions of the concentration camp and in the apparent objectivity of his even-toned narrative voice. While the Nazis believed that Levi's Jewish lineage was of fundamental importance, Levi testifies to the Holocaust as a citizen and rational human being whose particular ethnicity and religion ought to have no bearing in the public sphere. Indeed, Levi's memoir implies that to write about himself as a Jewish victim would have been a capitulation to Nazi essentializing and an admission that the Enlightenment had failed to deliver the emancipation and equality it promised to the Jews.

What was Wiesel's milieu before the Holocaust? Certainly, Enlightenment ideas made strong inroads among Eastern European Jewry in the decades before World War II, but in Jewish communities like Wiesel's Sighet, the desirability of individual rights did not overshadow the hope for group rights. The first chapter of *Night* shows that his community wished to coexist with its Hungarian neighbors, not so much as Hungarians as a relatively unassimilated minority with both rights and obligations to the nation. Students begin to understand what *unassimilated* means when they learn that Wiesel originally wrote his memoir not in Hungarian but in Yiddish. While *Survival in Auschwitz* does not represent Jews as a community unto themselves, *Night* consistently does. Wiesel even remarks on the feeling of safety and comfort when the Germans first established ghettos in Sighet. "We would no longer have to look at all those hostile faces [. . .] We would live among Jews, among brothers" (12). (Although I mainly compare the two books as concentration camp testimonies, teachers should not miss the occasion afforded by Wiesel's brief description of ghettoization to remind students that most Holocaust victims in Eastern Europe experienced this additional trauma while those of Western Europe mostly did not.)

If, in the aftermath of the Holocaust, Levi's chief concern is the reduced status of the undifferentiated person, "a man," Wiesel's is largely with the precarious fate of the Jews and Judaism. Having encountered their first horrors at Auschwitz and seeing no possibility for escape, the pious men and boys of Sighet say the Kaddish (the Jewish prayer for the dead) for themselves. As he hears this prayer, a blessing on the name of God, young Eliezer thinks, "Why should I sanctify His name? The Almighty, the eternal and terrible Master of the Universe, chose to be silent. What was there to thank Him for?" (33). The crucial question for Eliezer is whether he should understand the Holocaust as the greatest in a long list of catastrophes in Jewish history intended to test the Jews' faith or whether the unprecedented evil that unfolds in Auschwitz overturns the very idea of a covenant with a good and powerful God. One of the strengths of *Night* is that it avoids a premature resolution to this difficult question (although Wiesel's later writings affirm that his faith has survived even this challenge).

For the purposes of this essay, I have begun by sketching out the broad contrast between two types of Holocaust survivor memoirs, the religious and the secular. In the classroom, I recommend proceeding in just the opposite fashion: students ought to be trained to arrive at conclusions by starting with close readings. Thus when teaching the comparative approach I select pairs of passages that reveal how the texts under study converge and diverge. I have found it effective to compare Levi's epigraphic poem (11) with Wiesel's prose poem, "Never shall I forget that night" (34). Students notice that the two poems evoke themes central to their respective books and even occasion their titles (the original one in Levi's case). Levi's ethical agenda is brought to the fore by his verses, which command the reader surrounded by "friendly faces" to reflect on whether the dehumanized Holocaust victim, "who fights for a scrap of bread," is yet a human being for whom the reader is responsible: "Consider if this is a man" (11). The failure to recognize the victim's suffering will bring the curse articulated at the end of the poem: the reader's children will turn away their faces, will, in effect, deny the human recognition that he or she, now mimicking the position of the victim, certainly requires. The poem imitates but also varies a biblical passage that forms the key prayer in Judaism, the

Shema, which asserts the fundamental principle of monotheism (drawn from Deut. 6.4–9). (Untitled in *Survival*, the poem was titled "Shemà" when published in Levi's *Collected Poems*.) In keeping with Levi's secular humanism, his poem replaces the Jews' commitment to Yahweh with a fundamental commitment to the humanity of the other. Only in this way, Levi seems to suggest, can the damage of Nazism be undone.

Wiesel's prose poem purposefully interrupts the narrative progress of his memoir for a moment of reflection. Deploying visceral imagery and drumming repetition, his strongly rhythmical sentences are nothing short of poetry. Like Levi's, Wiesel's poem has a liturgical quality and even parodies biblical rhetoric with its "one long night seven times sealed." At the same time, it adopts a vocabulary not exploited in Levi's verses that marks Holocaust poetry in general ("smoke," "flame," "dust," "silence"). Wiesel does not use his poem to make an ethical demand on the reader; rather, he intones it as an oath to eternally memorialize the losses he has suffered at Auschwitz: his innocence (having seen the brutality inflicted on innocent children), his faith, and his God ("murdered," he writes). Indeed, just three pages later he describes himself as "a different person. The student of Talmud, the child I was, had been consumed by the flames" (37). In strong contrast to Levi's habitually detached style, "Never shall I forget that night" exemplifies the intense spirituality of Wiesel's adolescent narrator whose voice modulates between realism and a poetical surrealism, between an uninflected tone and an emotional one.

An even more direct point of comparison arises in the authors' diverse memories of and thoughts about the brutal hangings that they were forced to witness at Auschwitz. "The Last One," a chapter in *Survival in Auschwitz* that recounts the hanging of a defiant rebel, becomes a meditation on shame. (For a fuller engagement with the topic, students can also read Levi's short essay "Shame," found in *The Drowned and the Saved*.) The rebel represents an exception: he is the last "man" among the docile prisoners because he resists the camp's regime of dehumanization instead of waiting to die. But Levi and the other prisoners, "an abject flock" (149), have been deprived of agency and dignity. They may be able to satisfy "the daily ragings of hunger" and their other animal needs, but these accomplishments alone do not make them men again. They are "oppressed by shame" in Auschwitz, and if they survive, ashamed forever after. "To destroy a man is difficult," Levi writes. "But you Germans have succeeded" (150). What students ought to take from this passage is that, for Levi, Auschwitz does more than kill: it attacks fundamental assumptions about the dignity and worth of human life.

Wiesel describes two hangings. The defiant last words of the first victim, a vigorous boy accused of theft, seem to buoy Eliezer's spirits (62–63). Unlike Levi, he is not ashamed on account of someone else's manly courage. The second victim, a young boy Wiesel calls "the sad-eyed angel" (64), is punished for sabotage, and his hanging has a dramatically different effect on Eliezer and the other prisoners. At the sight of the boy's slow and agonizing death someone asks, "where is God?" Eliezer thinks, "Where He is? This is where—hanging here from this gallows . . ." (65). This scene, a second reference to Wiesel's murdered God, powerfully dramatizes a simple yet crucial idea: there can be no God, no force for order and good, in a world where evil rules and blameless children suffer. Comparing passages like the ones above shows students how both books document the same facts of Auschwitz but still draw different conclusions from the experience. (As an aside, many of my students are struck by the Christian imagery in the hanging of "the sad-eyed angel." While I do not insist on a single interpretation of the passage, I purpose that Wiesel might have had in mind the idea that antisemitism has produced a tragic number of Christ-like victims, that is, other Jews who died because their religious practice or cultural traditions did not gain the approval of the powerful, whether the ancient Romans or Christian societies over the centuries or Nazis.)

In advance of the class meeting when the hanging scenes will be discussed, I have students write three or four paragraphs about the similarities and differences in each book's treatment of the topic and encourage them to show how the two passages shed light on each other. These written responses not only enable students to discuss more effectively among themselves the diverse forms of loss engendered by the Holocaust, whether that of basic human dignity or of innocence or of faith, but also constitute a preliminary step toward completing formal comparison papers on *Night* and *Survival in Auschwitz*, an assignment to which I return at the end of this essay.

After presenting some general background on European Jewry, I ask my students to discuss the roles of nationality, religion, and language in each book and to support their claims with specific details and passages from the texts. Now they are ready to insert specific ideas drawn from close reading into a broad framework of distinctions between the largely assimilated Jews of Western Europe and the less assimilated ones of Eastern Europe. With little or no coaxing, students should be able to articulate certain dissimilarities. For example, unlike Wiesel, whose identity as a Jew owed little to the idea of national (Hungarian) citizenship, Levi finds nationality and national character useful categories for organizing his perceptions of Auschwitz. For him, nationality even became a valuable form of community and an avenue for survival: he was saved from almost certain death by the generosity of Lorenzo, a non-Jewish Italian civilian worker who risked his life to aid more than one Italian concentration camp inmate (119–22). For his part, Wiesel dwells on aspects of Jewish ritual performed inside the camps and on discussions, no doubt in Yiddish, about whether the Jews have been abandoned by God (45). Levi does not describe these rituals or discussions, of which he seemed largely unaware and, in any case, could not have easily understood because of the linguistic and cultural barriers that made the secular Italian Jews a distinct minority among the prisoners. Wiesel and his father suffered unimaginably in the camp, but at least they understood German and Yiddish, two of the three important languages there (Polish was the third). For Levi, the camp was "a perpetual Babel, in which everyone shouts orders and threats in languages never heard before, and woe betide whoever fails to grasp the meaning" (38). Levi was fortunate in knowing a bit of German; still, he felt linguistically marginalized, remarking that "even the Polish Jews despise [the Italian Jews] as they do not speak Yiddish" (49). By now, students will have grasped the key point: that each author's cultural formation and the languages he understood crucially shaped his impression of Auschwitz.

Once some of the ways in which the two memoirs differ have been discussed, it is important to exploit their similarities in the classroom. For students who possess little or no historical background, teachers may wish to draw parallels between the texts to reinforce basic facts about Auschwitz and also explain discrepancies. For example, both authors suffer an almost unbearable thirst during deportation as they ride in painfully crowded boxcars to a place, Auschwitz, whose name means nothing to them (*Survival* 16–18; *Night* 23–27). While Levi describes his arrival in February 1944 as steeped in an eerie silence punctuated by moments of violence (19–20), Wiesel, arriving in May, recounts the unimaginable sight of burning babies and children (32). Students need to understand that Wiesel's hellish testimony is plausible since, as the Soviet offensive advanced in the late spring and early summer of 1944, the Germans increased exterminations at Auschwitz far beyond planned capacity.

There are a great many other shared details. Both men have numbers tattooed on their bodies and, in effect, lose their names (*Night* 42; *Survival* 27–28). Both men were lucky enough to be transferred to a smaller satellite work camp known as Auschwitz-Monowitz, or Buna, where chances for survival were marginally better (*Night* 46–47; *Survival* 25), although they have no recollection of having met there. Both stories end in liberation, but the circumstances are different. Levi happened to be ill just before the Russians arrived in January 1945 and was not evacuated, unlike his friend Alberto and thousands of other unlucky prisoners. "Perhaps someone will write their story one day" (155), Levi muses. Wiesel has. He and his father were marched west toward Germany on what is now known as the death march, arriving at Buchenwald after great suffering that, in turn, led to his father's death. There may be no better dramatization of survivor guilt than Wiesel's recollection of what he felt about his father's end (104–12).

On the idea that moral guilt is the price of survival, the two memoirs usefully complement each other: where Levi's is abstract, Wiesel's is concrete. According to Levi, Auschwitz is a Darwinian realm governed by "a pitiless process of natural selection" where "the struggle to survive is without respite, because everyone is desperately and ferociously alone" (88–89). With the total breakdown of community among the prisoners, each is compelled to disregard the humanity of the others. Indeed, Levi remarked on the rarity of survival "without renunciation of any part of one's own moral world" (92). (He later elaborated on this dilemma in his accessible essay "The Gray Zone," found in *The Drowned and the Saved*.) In *Night*, Eliezer is repelled, and also partially convinced, by the amoral idea that he should look to his own survival now that his father is beyond help (110–11). But who can survive intact under the weight of such guilt? "His last word had been my name. He had called out to me and I had not answered" (112). The last two sentences of Eliezer's story convey the survivor's traumatic sensation of being both dead and alive, of having lost so much—not only family and community but also God—yet fated to go on living in an impaired state (115). Meanwhile, Levi's story ends on a quiet note of optimism about the fate of human dignity and the renewal of ethical obligations after the Holocaust. Now that the Germans have fled the camp and the Darwinian law of Auschwitz has ended, a new sense of community among the victims marks the point at which "we who had not died slowly changed from [prisoners] to men again" (160). (It should be noted that Levi's later works describe the post-Holocaust world in bleaker terms.)

To return to the broader concerns of this essay, a comparative approach to survivor testimony, whether using *Night* and *Survival in Auschwitz* or other texts, is one effective strategy among many for teaching the Holocaust. By presenting diverse responses to genocide, educators can overcome the shallow understanding and premature closure promoted by popular Holocaust representations that our students often absorb uncritically. Regardless of whether the teacher embraces a religious outlook or a humanist one or neither, a nonpartisan stance in the classroom has advantages. In setting forth without prejudice the religious and secular responses to the Holocaust, the instructor not only introduces two significant worldviews that have been used to situate the Holocaust in the present but also enacts an open-ended pedagogy that encourages students to think for themselves and to write with conviction.

Students in my course must write a short formal paper about Holocaust survivor testimony. If they choose to compare and contrast *Night* and *Survival in Auschwitz*, I ask them to discuss how the authors' personal circumstances and beliefs shaped their respective descriptions of and responses to Auschwitz. I invite students to address questions like the following: What are the authors' respective assumptions about God and humanity, and how are those assumptions challenged by Auschwitz? What is the crisis of belief at the center of each book? If both books describe loss and rupture, what generalizations might one make about the Holocaust and representations of it? Before taking on the comparison essay, students should be cautioned that an effective analysis of contrasts also requires the essayist to establish the common ground shared by the two texts.

I conclude this essay, as I do my classroom presentation of *Night* and *Survival in Auschwitz*, by suggesting that there is indeed a crisis of belief at the center of each book and that Levi and Wiesel are engaged in a shared struggle to sustain their pre-Holocaust worldviews in a traumatic, post-Holocaust world that threatens to render those views obsolete. If the enormous suffering of the Jewish people served no divine purpose, the efficacy of Wiesel's theodicy, his carefully considered faith in the goodness of God despite the existence of evil, is called into question. In a sense, *Night* is a day-by-day account of how the young Wiesel reckons with this intractable problem. As for Levi, even in his atheism, his faith in the power of reason and science to legitimate human rights and guarantee social progress constitutes a kind of theodicy in which humanity's rational faculty is vindicated despite its potential to oppress people. Auschwitz calls this faith into question. To be sure, Levi uses reason as a tool of resistance against Nazism's attempt to reduce him to an unthinking "non-man" (90). In his memoir, he tries to comprehend the victims' profound suffering and to understand its purpose in the workings of xenophobia, totalitarianism, and social Darwinism. Yet Levi must also contend with the fact that in Auschwitz, a facility designed for the rational administration of pain, suffering was not just a means but an end in itself. And, worse still, this suffering probably had no redeemable purpose and cannot be justified by any coherent system of belief. Finally, what the two memoirs share is the courage to face the genuine crisis of faith provoked by the Holocaust, a crisis that affects both religion and the Enlightenment project, and to do so without offering perfunctory solutions or surrendering altogether to despair.

Seeing Atrocity:
Night and the Limits of Witnessing

Michael Bernard-Donals

> My gaze remained fixed on someone who, eyes wide
> open, stared into space. His colorless face was covered
> with a layer of frost and snow.
>
> —Elie Wiesel, *Night*

Night is a horrifyingly straightforward book: it presents what one witness to the Holocaust—Elie Wiesel—saw over the course of a year, part of which he spent in Auschwitz. But because the book's strength depends so much on what Wiesel saw and how he manages to tell his readers what he saw, it's worth paying close attention to what might be called the language of witnessing. How does Wiesel not just tell his readers what he saw but also make them act as witnesses themselves? Are there some events that are simply so horrifying that Wiesel can't bring himself to tell them? And are there events that Wiesel tries to make us see but, because of the language he has at his disposal, fails to make readers witness? Questions like these have less to do with the object of the book—the Holocaust, the details of what happened to Wiesel—than with how the Holocaust both allows and prevents one of its premier witnesses to tell his story and to tell it in such a way that his readers, in turn, bear witness. I have taught *Night* and books like it in undergraduate classrooms by asking my students one simple but theoretically rich question: how does focusing on the language of seeing help us understand not just the Holocaust but also those—like Etty Hillesum, diarists from the ghettos like Abraham Lewin, or witnesses to other atrocities (see, e.g., Gross)—whose writing bears the pressure of events that seem beyond language and even beyond experience itself? My students quickly begin to see that *Night* is very much an instrument of witnessing: it allows them to see. This fact is ironic, because though on the surface *Night* seems to be an endless series of horrifying scenes as seen through the eyes of Wiesel, the book is at least as much about where Wiesel fails to see the horror of the Holocaust, and it's that failure to see that his readers see. I argue here that one can teach *Night* as a book that shows the limits of seeing in the face of atrocity. It's worth asking not just of *Night* but also of other memoirs: how does the language of the eyewitness function, what does it allow its readers to see, what are its limits—why, for example, does the canon of law as far back as Deuteronomy insist on two eyewitnesses to corroborate each other?—and how do the events of the Holocaust pose special problems, if any, to the act of witnessing?

There are three principal pedagogical issues that are important to confront when one teaches Wiesel's book in such a context. (I mean by "pedagogical" not how a person teaches the book but how the book itself teaches, or divulges, aspects of its ostensible subject.) First is the problem of witnessing itself: how does the epistemology of witness function, and how does it manifest itself in *Night*? The problem of witnessing also involves a corollary problem of memory, for to report what one saw, the witness must recall it from memory, which is itself a fraught conceptual instrument. Second is what, for the narrator of *Night*, is a problem of theodicy—how to reconcile the outrageous injustices perpetrated upon Jews during the Holocaust with divine justice—and what in secular terms could be called the question of the sublime. There are some experiences that seem beyond expression, that remain unspeakable, but that also appear—because of their enormity—to compel expression. The problem of the sublime is related to the problem of trauma: how does the victim of a disaster, which seems to debilitate that victim (in this instance, the author of *Night*), express pain and describe the event that caused it? Finally, there is the problem of history: if it is true that the events of the Holocaust are so horrifying as to defy description, what means are left to the historian and to the writer to make clear the events that form the core of what we know as the Holocaust? The novelist Aharon Appelfeld has gone so far as to say, with reference to writing about the event, "one does not look directly into the sun" (qtd. in Lang, *Writing* 8). But if the witness's gaze is diverted, what, then, does the witness see?

The problem of witnessing can be approached from two directions. Lawrence Langer's book *Holocaust Testimonies* was the result of research at the Yale Fortunoff archive of video testimonies of Holocaust survivors. Langer's conclusions are useful to see *Night* as a testimony. There is an impasse between what one sees and what one can say about what was seen. Langer sometimes calls this impasse a conflict of selves—the self that was involved in the events and the self describing those events—over the telling of the testimony. One could see this conflict as a conflict between conceptual faculties: what the person sees, particularly in events like those described in books like *Night*, follows no logical pattern and does not proceed as a narrative, with a beginning, a middle, and an end; and what the person says, following the conventions of language and narrative, orders events and necessarily displaces and substitutes that narrative for what happened. The act of witnessing and the act of testifying, then, are not coincident, so what Langer describes as a conflict of selves is in fact an impasse between two related but different acts.

The witness forgets the difficult events and substitutes for them other, more readily remembered events. Cathy Caruth ("Unclaimed Experience") and Shoshana Felman ("Education in Crisis"), among others, also understand that there's an epistemological distinction between witnessing and testifying—that seeing and saying are distinct acts—but suggest that in the case of trauma (such as events described by Wiesel and other survivors of the Shoah), the event itself is blotted out or lost to understanding altogether. This isn't to say that, for Wiesel or for other eyewitnesses, the event didn't occur; far from it. The event's extremity stands in the way of the witness's capacity to describe or represent it.

The event isn't so much forgotten as it is absent from consciousness altogether.

The second issue, the problem of the sublime, is a difficult one in Holocaust studies. Dominick LaCapra, among others, has made clear why it may be inappropriate to use the term in connection with the events of the Holocaust (see especially *Representing the Holocaust*). In Kant's formulation of the sublime, phenomena that the mind was unable to grasp through reason produced feelings of both pleasure and pain: pain because of the mind's recognition that it was confronted with something out of its range, pleasure because the mind was able nonetheless to recognize its limits. For LaCapra, to say that the Holocaust, as a sublime event, could produce pleasure is to admit that Theodor Adorno was right: Holocaust representation is an abomination if the depiction of unimaginable suffering produces pleasure. But I argue that the sublime is a useful category when paying attention to Holocaust representations, particularly to testimonies, because it gives students a way to understand what happens when one is confronted by something that is otherwise unnamable or unspeakable. Kant suggested that in apprehending the sublime, time and space collapse—that the viewers lose track of where they are or of the passage of time—and that this collapse is reflected in the language used to portray the object of the sublime. One way to explain the difficulty the eyewitness faces when trying to describe feelings of hunger or torture or deprivation is through just such a collapse: the conceptual tools available under normal circumstances, tools that would adequately convey the sense of what was happening, simply fail, and what the witness is left with is a kind of discursive void. The stutters and ellipses, the incongruities in images and phrases in written and oral testimonies, suggest just such a void.

For Kant, the sublime was also associated with a notion of the divine, and this connection is another reason why the category poses such a problem for Holocaust studies. To associate the unspeakable events of the Holocaust with the unspeakability of the divine name is to come close to blasphemy. And yet it is just such an association that becomes clear in Wiesel's book. Like Appelfeld's injunction against looking at the sun—against directly representing the events of the Holocaust—the second commandment (which Kant called "the most sublime law" in the Jewish canon [185]) prohibits idolatry; as a *bilderverbot*, an injunction against direct representation, it can be read as the traditional ban not only against graven images but also against direct representations of that which seems abominable—murder, rape, and other forms of violence and taboo.

It's because of the problem of the sublime that writers—from the philosopher Jean-François Lyotard (*The Differend*) and the writer Maurice Blanchot (*The Writing of the Disaster*) to the historians Hayden White ("Historical Emplotment") and Yosef Yerushalmi (*Zakhor*), all of whose work I've used in classes on Holocaust representation with much success—have suggested that they may need to find some other language to describe the Holocaust. Historians may have to pass the torch to novelists: it may be through means contrived by the verbal artist rather than the apparently clear language of history that the events of the Shoah are most successfully indicated. Even the least artistic testimonial accounts—those like Lewin's diary, Hillesum's diaries and letters, and the oral testimonies found in the Fortunoff and other video archives—are full of instances where the witness struggles for words and finds that there are some things best left unspoken.

How, then, are these issues—witnessing versus testimony, the sublime, the limits of history—made manifest in *Night*, and how does a teacher go about making these difficult issues available to students?

Let me draw attention to two instances of witnessing, instances that on the face of it are pretty clear representations of what Wiesel saw. The first is a pair of hangings that appear near the middle of the book: the first person to be hanged, a young Pole, was accused of stealing during an Allied raid on the Buna rubber works adjacent to Auschwitz. Wiesel writes that, as the man stands on the gallows, "[t]he thousands of people who died daily in Auschwitz and Birkenau, in the crematoria, no longer troubled me. But this boy, leaning against his gallows, upset me deeply" (62). The question to ask is, Why? One answer, the most obvious, is that the death of an individual may affect Wiesel more than the deaths of thousands, whose individuality is suppressed by the machinery of death, because its singularity makes it matter more. And then, "the entire camp, block after block, filed past the hanged boy and stared at his extinguished eyes, the tongue hanging from his gaping mouth. The Kapos forced everyone to look him squarely in the face" (62–63). But this episode is not the last hanging—Wiesel reports that he witnessed others—and the chapter ends with the hanging of a *pipel*, a young boy whose associate was accused of sabotage and who had the face of a "sad-eyed angel" (64). Not unlike the language used for the earlier one, the results of the second hanging are described this way:

> And so he remained for more than half an hour, lingering between life and death, writhing before our eyes. And we were forced to look at him at close range. He was still alive when I passed him. His tongue was still red, his eyes not yet extinguished.   (65)

Each scene of hanging is punctuated with a report on the taste of that evening's soup. Of the first, Wiesel reports "I remember that on that evening, the soup tasted better than ever" (63); of the second, "[t]hat night, the soup tasted of corpses" (65).

This pair of scenes is at least as important for what Wiesel doesn't report as for what he does. In both scenes, the writer reports what he saw, and in both scenes what the writer saw is not all that different: in each a young man is hanged, but in the second scene it is a child who does not die immediately. The most significant aspect of the detail Wiesel gives the reader has nothing to do with what he saw. Or maybe more to the point, while the writer saw what happened, the language he uses to tell his readers about it seems to point out something that he saw but was unwilling, or unable, to present. This substitution is typical of testimonies of trauma: during one interview of a Holocaust survivor in Saint Louis, a woman, on being asked to recall what it was like to live through her mother's death of starvation and disease in the Lodz ghetto, said, "it was hard, terrible . . ." and then after a long silence said, "terrible. Eleven million died in the war, six million Jews, and of that number a million and a half children" (Mary R.). In that silence, the survivor obviously saw something, but the language she uses to describe what she saw doesn't describe it at all. In fact, the language after the pause stands in and substitutes for what the survivor saw, almost as if she couldn't bring herself to say it or couldn't find the language with which to do so. Wiesel demonstrates the same feeling in this pair of scenes. What looks like the language of seeing turns out to be at least in part language that marks an absence of seeing. Here what marks the absence of what is seen is Wiesel's comment about the soup: in one of the memoir's most arresting images, the uncanny relation between the taste of the soup and that of corpses (clearly not a taste that Wiesel could claim to know) is an image not of witnessing but of what stands in for what the witness saw. The event itself, like the survivor's memory of her mother's death in Lodz, is blotted out (if not for the witness then certainly for the reader), substituted by a figural displacement: taste for sight; disgust for satiety; death for life. As in another figural displacement for the event remembered—Wiesel describes the child Meir fighting his father to the death for a scrap of bread thrown into a crowded train car, concluding not with a description of what he saw but with the sentence, "I was sixteen" (102)—it is as if the horror of what was seen overwhelms the witness; but the result of the blotting out of the event, and the language that marks it, is precisely the instrument through which the reader sees (though what the reader sees is not necessarily what Wiesel saw). It is in these places in the book—and not those in which description is most artfully rendered—where language substitutes most obviously for memory, that the reader acts as a witness.

But a witness to what? If the reader can't recall what Wiesel saw because the reader was not there and if Wiesel's descriptions don't render the event but only its (forgetful) effect on memory, what is the object of witness? One could argue that what Wiesel focuses his attention on in scenes like the ones described above is the void of memory rather than memory's object. In one of the most figurally dense passages in *Night*, Wiesel writes:

> Never shall I forget that night, the first night in camp, that turned my life into one long night seven times sealed.
> Never shall I forget that smoke.
> Never shall I forget the small faces of the children whose bodies I saw transformed into smoke under a silent sky. [. . .]
> Never shall I forget the nocturnal silence that deprived me for all eternity of the desire to live.   (34)

The images here, which Wiesel does not witness so much as indicate as absent objects of witness, are precisely that—incorporeal: wreaths of smoke take the place of the bodies of the children; day is replaced by the absence of light; the absence of sound takes the place not only of sound but also of the desire to live. It's through the image of displacement—of one memory for another, of one object for another, of incorporeality for the present-ness of the objects of memory—that Wiesel points the reader not to what he remembers but to what the reader is enjoined to remember.

Instead of remembering the fact of the Holocaust or the events that compose it, readers remember what they themselves make of it. The book begins with another act of witnessing: that of Moishe the Beadle, the kabbalist in Wiesel's Sighet with whom the author studied mysticism in secret. Moishe explained to the young Wiesel that

> every question possessed a power that was lost in the answer . . .
> Man comes closer to God through the questions he asks Him, he liked to say. Therein lies true dialogue. Man asks and God replies. But we don't understand His replies. (5)

Because he was a Jew from outside Hungary, Moishe was deported at the beginning of the war and quickly forgotten. On his return some time later, however, he speaks nothing of kabbalah and instead tells of what had happened to him in the camps. Again, the most obvious question to ask about the opening of the book is why the people of Sighet refuse to believe him or even to listen to him. One reply is that his stories were plainly unbelievable: the mass killing of Jews, given the relatively untroubled existence of the rural Jews of this part of Hungary (their systematic destruction did not begin until early 1944), seemed too unreasonable and beyond the ken of the residents' experience to be believed. So in one sense, by beginning with Moishe, Wiesel tells a parable of the failure of witnessing: here we have someone who saw but whose stories are so unbelievable that they fail to induce witnessing on the part of those to whom he speaks.

But there's another way of looking at the beginning of *Night*, one that links the problem of witnessing with the problem of memory and of sublimity's relation to trauma. One approach is to begin with the poem that opens Primo Levi's *Survival in Auschwitz*. Entitled "Shema," it invokes the Hebrew prayer, the recitation of the requirement to recall God's oneness at various points throughout the day and to wear fringed garments and tefillin as aide-mémoire. The strength of Levi's poem resides in the substitution of the enormity of the Holocaust for the oneness of God: what Jews are commanded to remember, on the pain of death, is another sort of tremendum, the events of the Shoah that—like God—are not only beyond language but also (for those who weren't there) beyond direct experience and hence memory. What Moishe seems to indicate, on his return to Sighet, is a similar substitution: "He no longer mentioned either God or Kabbalah. He spoke only of what he had seen" (7). It's as if the questions he once asked are now answered, not by the incomprehensible utterances of God but by the equally—if not more—incomprehensible horrors called to mind by the eyewitness. Again, what matters here is that what Moishe saw, like what Wiesel reports throughout *Night*, is often left unreported or, when reported—the story "of Malka, the young girl who lay dying for three days, and that of Tobie, the tailor who begged to die before his sons were killed" (7)—do not contain the detail one expects from the witness. In effect, Moishe himself becomes the aide-mémoire: he acts as a reminder of that which can't be seen, let alone remembered, but which haunts the residents of Sighet before their deportation. The central scene of the hanged child functions in the same way. The most obvious reading of this scene is that here, finally, Wiesel has lost his faith, but I suggest another reading: it is here, finally, that Wiesel becomes the eyewitness. Now the divine is replaced by the horror of the Holocaust, and it is this horror that, perhaps for the first time, he sees fully. Yet what he says—the testimony he provides—represents not the object of witness but its absence: "Where [God] is? This is where—hanging here from this gallows" (65), as if the nearly lifeless child hanging from a rope could substitute for God or for the "thousands of people who died daily in Auschwitz and Birkenau" (62).

The absence of the object of witness is a function of the traumatic. Consistent with reports supplied by Caruth and Felman and Dori Laub (*Testimony*), along with the countless testimonies in the Fortunoff archive described so eloquently by Langer in *Holocaust Testimonies*, here the terrible event itself is blotted out and remains unreported, and yet the language that the survivor has at his disposal is troubled, interrupted, and strained by the absent event. It's as if in the fabric of the eyewitnesses' testimonies there remains an imperfection in the cloth, an imperfection that catches the sharp edges of memory and stops the story from proceeding seamlessly; as if the horror could be replaced by the child; as if, in another episode, the memory of the kindness of a young woman could substitute for Wiesel's anger at his father. In a warehouse in the Buna camp, where Wiesel worked for a time, a French-speaking woman tended to his wounds after he was beaten savagely by a *Kapo*. Thinking she spoke no German, he was surprised when, as she tended to him and gave him bread, she told him, "in almost perfect German: 'Bite your lips, little brother . . . Don't cry. Keep your anger, your hate, for another day, for later' " (53; ellipses in orig). Wiesel goes on to say that many years later, in Paris, he recognized the woman on the Métro, and they talked for an hour, remembering the time in the camp. It is a strange episode—it comes directly after Wiesel describes his fear that he would lose a gold crown to a crooked camp dentist and just before he describes the beating his father received for some perceived transgression by the ruthless *Kapo* Idek: "if I felt anger at that moment, it was not directed at the Kapo but at my father. Why couldn't he have avoided Idek's wrath? That was what life in a concentration camp had made of me . . ." (54). The question to ask one's students is just how these episodes, so oddly unconnected to one another, function together: to what do they testify? It is conceivable that they don't testify to their object—their object is, after all, unclear—but stand in for absent memory, blotted out by the ugliness of their occurrence at the time. "That was what life in a concentration camp had made of me": just what is the *that* of the statement?

Half a dozen pages later, Wiesel describes an air raid on the camp during which a prisoner, apparently half crazed, throws himself toward a cauldron of piping hot soup, an act that leads to his being shot and killed. After the raid, Wiesel writes, "In the very center of the camp lay the body of the man with soup stains on his face, the only victim. The cauldrons were carried back to the kitchen" (60–61). The body left to lie in the middle of the camp, like the memory of the kindness of the French woman and their meeting years later, seems to function as an image that stands in and substitutes for what happened and for that which can't be told as a story. These episodes, incongruous with the scheme of the narrative—with its chronological march through the year during which Wiesel and his father lived through the hell of Auschwitz and the death march to Buchenwald—are a sign, like the imperfection in the fabric of testimony, of something that may not be available to memory, or to language, at all.

In fact, one could argue that it is this point—about what happens to language and to knowledge in the face of the horrifying event—that *Night* makes most directly. The book seems to work against the *bilderverbot*, the injunction against idolatry, because it insists that, while the event may not be available to memory or language, memory and language are all we have. It's no coincidence that the book is punctuated by explicit references to the failure of language and narrative in the face of events: from the story Wiesel's father does not finish early in the book (because he is called to a meeting of the Jewish council just before Sighet's ghetto is liquidated) to Mrs. Schächter's failure to make those in the boxcar on its way to Auschwitz see the fire that only she can see (until they reach the camp and see it themselves), the book isn't a testimony or a memoir so much as it is a document that shows the limits of language and memory when confronted by events. Or, more precisely, *Night* makes clear what happens when one substitutes images, language, and memories of the ready-at-hand for what is impossible to recall or to relate to others.

Through the inevitable failure of his stories—it's through his inability to testify to what he saw and through the marks this horror leaves on his writing in the form of hesitations, failures of seeing, incongruities, and the disbelief with which the witness seems to describe even those things he saw—Wiesel most clearly succeeds not in witnessing himself but in providing an instrument for his readers to witness. Though we and our students may not see the horrors Wiesel saw, we are able to glimpse the limits of witnessing and how language both does and doesn't represent the atrocity of the Shoah.

NOTE

The epigraph is from page 98 of *Night*.

Night and Critical Thinking

Paul Eisenstein

For several years now, I have been teaching *Night* in a junior-level composition and literature course, The Dilemma of Human Existence. Required of all students, this course is a staple of our core curriculum and is charged primarily with the task of improving communication and critical thinking skills. As at many liberal arts colleges, such a course is structured on a kind of "great books" model and thus involves readings ranging from antiquity to the present. The pedagogical direction pursued by such courses, however, is not primarily historicist—not only because there is not the time to contextualize works with any rigor, but also because the course has a bigger fish to hook. I refer here to those students majoring in fields outside the humanities who are more likely to see the significance and vitality of literature for their own lives and value systems when every work is treated as if it were their contemporary. Those of us entrusted with a course of the kind I am talking about, then, teach particular literary works not so much for how they reflect or participate in the discourse of their day as for the way they stage for our students difficult encounters with their own ideas or beliefs. In my course, in the attempt to catalyze a critical dialogue about divine justice and our memorial obligations to the dead, I begin usually with Sophocles's *Oedipus* plays, Dante's *Inferno*, and then Shakespeare's *Hamlet*. These texts present characters who struggle with the unfairness of the world, the justness of theodicy, and the problem of doing right by the dead—matters that *Night* so powerfully and forcefully foregrounds.

I think it is fair to say, however, that Wiesel's memoir takes the opportunity for—and practice of—critical thinking a step beyond the level that writers of tragedies like Sophocles, Dante, and Shakespeare get us to inhabit. The tragic story told in *Night* differs in significant ways. First, Sophocles, Dante, and Shakespeare invite us, to greater or lesser degrees, to regard the suffering they present as warranted—caused or prolonged either by tragic character flaws or manifestly sinful conduct. Second, Sophocles, Dante, and Shakespeare dramatize a suffering that is, for their protagonists (and audiences), unmistakably ennobling—part of some meaningfully cathartic, divinely inspired, pedagogical design. The fate Sophocles gives his tragic hero in *Oedipus the King* does, in the end, ratify the integrity of oracular knowledge (a fact noted by the play's chorus), and in *Oedipus at Colonus*, an aged Oedipus is granted a sanctuary and a miraculous death. Dante is repeatedly moved to remark on the moral lesson his journey through hell is designed to teach him, and it is, after all, a journey that will eventually take him to heaven and his angelic beloved Beatrice. Shakespeare does, by play's end, affirm a providential heroism in his hero's conduct. Finally, the stories of Oedipus, Dante, and Hamlet include scenes in which suffering or death is recognized and memorialized by a wider public. These are scenes in which it appears that certain obligations to the casualties of violence are being met: the place of Oedipus's death is designated sacred by the gods and protected as such by the Athenian king, Theseus; Dante consistently asks the sinners he meets for their stories so that, as he says at one point, "your memory / In men's minds in the former world won't fade / But live on under many suns" (29.110–12); and Hamlet has, in the end, done right by his murdered father by fulfilling his father's ghost's command to avenge his death—an act commemorated by Fortinbras in the play's final lines, which announce a ceremony meant to bear witness to Hamlet's essential royalty.

All these features suggest that literary renderings of tragic occurrences operate under a kind of mandate to disclose the larger, affirmative horizon to which such occurrences (ostensibly) belong. Wiesel's book, however, forcefully repudiates this mandate: in *Night*, no characterological flaw or sin is ever described or invoked as a warrant for what the book's narrator experiences. There is, moreover, no way to see Jewish suffering or death as heroic or ennobling. And finally, there is no certainty that what has transpired will be (or is even capable of being) suitably memorialized. If the authors of *Oedipus the King* and *Oedipus at Colonus*, *The Inferno*, and *Hamlet* have given us ways to understand and resolve the suffering and death their works depict, the author of *Night* has written a book replete instead with moments of interpretive crisis that find no satisfactory resolution. To read *Night* is, for this reason, to be forced to think critically, since such moments of crisis suspend (and thereby render inadequate) all the traditional ways we give meaning to our world and to our lives. Indeed, so many of the traumatic scenes and images in Wiesel's memoir—spare and unadorned in their description—stand implicitly as calls to see the truth or viability of cherished ideas and beliefs as entirely contingent, as dependent on location and circumstance and thus without any claim to stand as absolute or immutable, apart from the catastrophe of history. For me, the sine qua non of any class devoted to critical thinking is the capacity to see knowledge and belief as fundamentally conditioned and thus as capable of crisis. Herein, moreover, lies the ethical importance of critical thinking, since to see truth and belief as conditioned for or capable of crisis is to lose the certitude that often motivates the commission of violence against those who do not share the same truth or belief. Bereft of such certitude, critical thinkers begin to see that traditional codes of ethical conduct are not always singular and not always clear.

So that students are ready to see themselves addressed by the difficult scenes and images of Wiesel's book, I assign (and we discuss) his essay "The Holocaust as Literary Inspiration" before our consideration of *Night*. Invoking the Holocaust's "magnitude and its ontological nature," Wiesel suggests that all our ways of being at home in the world need now to be set against the background of "that faraway kingdom of darkness." According to Wiesel, "all that can be obtained through knowledge has to be recalled into question. . . . [M]an's relationship to his creator, to society, to politics, to literature, to his fellow man and to himself has to be reexamined" (6). In claims such as these, Wiesel enjoins us to see critical thinking as one primary, ethical legacy of the Holocaust, to see the challenge bequeathed to us by it: since virtually every facet of organized society was complicit in the crime (or ineffectual in trying to stop it), every facet must now be reexamined to prevent its repetition. Wiesel sounds a similar theme later in his essay when he claims that if we are to understand the Holocaust, we will have to understand "why all the killers were Christians, bad Christians surely, but Christians" and "why so many killers were intellectuals, academicians, college professors, lawyers, engineers, physicians, theologians" (17).

These claims exempt nothing from critical scrutiny, and we talk here about how Wiesel's remarks bridge the gap between the extreme and the ordinary, about how our ordinary occupations and belief systems are perhaps always just a stone's throw from an extreme that we do not see as extreme or as relevant to us. Thinking about this proximity can get us to recognize how easily our ordinary occupations and belief systems might involve us implicitly in the commission of violence or how our own pursuits might be suddenly halted by the extreme acts of others. Indeed, I try to point out how the very terms *ordinary* and *extreme* already imply a certain perspective or subject position, since during the Holocaust (and even today) the proximity or conflation of the two were experienced in radically different ways depending on how much power, privilege, and comfort one enjoyed. I sometimes write the words *ordinary* and *extreme* on the chalkboard and solicit general impressions of what experiential features might constitute each category. Our reading of the first ten or so stories of Ida Fink's short story volume *Traces* helps with this exercise, since the stories are fundamentally concerned with the threshold—one story in this set is titled "The Threshold" and the word appears in several others—that separates the ordinary (e.g., musical concerts, first romantic loves, schooling plans, enjoyment of nature) from the extreme (e.g., terror, violence, separation, loss). Sometimes I depict the categories as columns and write them intentionally as far apart on the chalkboard as I can. This setup allows me, when we have finished our data collection, to pose a question about the distance, in our heads, between these two concepts. At other times I write *ordinary* and collect its features at the top half of one board and write *extreme* and collect its features on the bottom half of the same board: this format allows us to consider that perhaps the extreme lies beneath the ordinary and is capable, at a moment's notice, of erupting into it. Either way, the stage is thereby set for a discussion of how Wiesel's goal is to ward off the conflation of the two terms by asking us constantly to remember when they were indistinguishable. At one point in his essay, Wiesel writes that "[a]nyone who does not actively, constantly engage in remembering and in making others remember is an accomplice of the enemy" (16). What this line shares with all the lines I have so far cited from "The Holocaust as Literary Inspiration" is Wiesel's insistence on the Holocaust's universal implications—his belief that everyone has a stake in thinking about the lasting consequences of what happened. Elsewhere in the essay, Wiesel suggests that the victims "did not die alone, for something in all of us died with them" (7) and that although he sees everything "through that event . . . it would be wrong to assume that it means something only to us Jews" (17).

While I have had students who begin spontaneously to think about the connection between their own ordinary academic disciplines and the commission of extreme (Nazi) violence, my teaching of *Night* aims to use the traumatic scenes to train a critical eye on two of the more general items in Wiesel's list of things in need of reexamination: traditional religious belief and the faith we place in our fellow human beings (especially parental figures). Let me begin with traditional religious belief, because it is the issue that occupies two of the three eighty-minute sessions I give to the book. Here, Wiesel's concern is to document the corrosive effects of Auschwitz on a young boy's piety—his deteriorating belief in a God endowed with traditional attributes, capable of intervening (on his own or at the behest of prayer) in history. Sometimes I hand out a simple, twenty-minute writing prompt that reads:

> How does Wiesel *change* over the course of the first sixty-five pages of *Night*? Introduce and discuss two scenes that you see capturing this change.

At other times I ask questions like, What kind of boy is Wiesel at the beginning of the book? Why do you suppose Wiesel elected to begin with the figure of Moishe the Beadle? In eliciting responses to these sorts of questions, I aim to begin to establish that Wiesel's belief—his daily devotion to prayer and his ardent desire to study the Talmud—is genuine (in anticipation of those students who, after Wiesel loses his faith at Auschwitz, will claim that it must not have been all that strong in the first place). I want also to chart carefully the deterioration of his religious belief, so that we can see Wiesel's eventual loss of faith as a process, as the outcome of a struggle. On the morning of their deportation,

Wiesel wakes at dawn because he "wanted to have time to pray before leaving" (18), and when they arrive at the ghetto, he invokes a prayer that refers to God's "infinite compassion" (20). At the last stop on the way to Auschwitz, when the deportees are told that they are being taken to a labor camp, Wiesel reports that "[we] gave thanks to God" (27). Even after the traumatic first night of Auschwitz—when Wiesel reacts angrily to his father's recital of the Kaddish, when he sees the smokestacks, which he states "murdered my God and my soul" (34), and when he claims that the student of the Talmud whom he had once been "had been consumed by the flames" (37)—Wiesel still evinces a belief in God's power and the efficacy of prayer. When his new pair of shoes is hidden by mud, he thanks God in an "improvised prayer" (38), and when he hears men in his barrack lending a religious meaning to their experience, he doubts not God's existence but his absolute justice (45). Later in the book, he even offers up a prayer "to this God in whom I no longer believed" (91).

A close reading of passages such as these can help deepen a consideration of later scenes that dramatize Wiesel's disbelief in God's traditional attributes and the efficacy of prayer. I refer here not just to the death of the *pipel* (whose body on the gallows, Wiesel claims, is God incarnate [65]) but also to the scenes that follow that death, when the other prisoners are able to pray in observance of Rosh Hashanah and Yom Kippur (66–69). To these scenes one might add Wiesel's portraits of Akiba Drumer and the rabbi "from a small town in Poland" (76), both of whom remain believers for a long time in Auschwitz but, at the end, break under the strain. Students are moved by these scenes, and some try to argue that Wiesel does not lose his religious faith entirely if we take seriously Moishe the Beadle's claim early in the book that "Man comes closer to God through the questions he asks Him" (5). There is an interesting discussion to be had regarding the status of Wiesel's faith, but, ultimately, it ought not to stop us from asking what is the implication of Wiesel's instances of disbelief for students' own religious beliefs and for religious belief more generally. To pursue this line of inquiry, I have sometimes collected on the chalkboard a set of religious propositions ordinarily regarded to be absolutely true. These range from the claim that "All creation bears witness to the greatness of God" to bumper sticker formulations such as "Never Underestimate the Power of God" or "Prayer Works!" We end up talking about the extent to which the Holocaust forces us to qualify or dismiss altogether such maxims. To get at the provisional nature of truths many regard as eternally self-evident, I ask questions along the following lines: How are we to regard assertions whose truth appears a function of the distance between the extreme and the ordinary? Eliminate this distance—as, indeed, it was eliminated for a Jewish boy like Wiesel—and what are you left with? What would you say about an actual bumper sticker in a death camp announcing the power of prayer?

The power of *Night*'s ability to catalyze critical thinking about traditional religious belief and the efficacy of prayer exists not only at the level of the narrative but also in the form of the book. I refer here to the inclusion of François

Mauriac's foreword. In this foreword, Mauriac (the Nobel Prize–winning French Catholic author whose work is consistently occupied with the religious themes of grace and redemption) recounts his first meeting with Wiesel in Paris after the war and recalls wanting to provide the Jewish survivor with the redemptive and loving message of the Christian gospel. Mauriac cites the lines in *Night* that seal Wiesel's absolute estrangement from the God he once adored and in response writes:

> And I, who believe that God is love, what answer was there to give my young interlocutor whose dark eyes still held the reflection of that angelic sadness that had appeared one day on the face of a hanged child? What did I say to him? Did I speak to him of that other Jew, this crucified brother who perhaps resembled him and whose cross conquered the world? Did I explain to him that what had been a stumbling block for *his* faith had become the cornerstone for *mine*? And that the connection between the cross and human suffering remains, in my view, the key to the unfathomable mystery in which the faith of his childhood was lost? And yet, Zion has risen up again out of the crematoria and the slaughterhouses. The Jewish nation has been resurrected from among its thousands of dead. It is they who have given it new life. We do not know the worth of one single drop of blood, one single tear. All is grace. If the Almighty is the Almighty, the last word for each of us belongs to Him. That is what I should have said to the Jewish child. But all I could do was embrace him and weep. (xxi)

This passage is remarkably powerful and should be read aloud in class. Some instructors may elect to assign the foreword as an afterword; my inclination is to teach it before *Night*, but either way it works to clarify the impasse between Christianity as a progressive (and redemptive) philosophy of history and the Holocaust survivor who will reject the consolations offered by it. Mauriac's peroration is rhetorically complex, and there is much to be said not only about his suggestion that Israel's creation means that the story of the Jewish people remains a story of progress (a view that may need to be sketched out for students unfamiliar with the history of Israel's creation) but also the fact that Mauriac cannot say directly to Wiesel what he feels that he should have said. Does this reaction mean that when faced in person with someone whose experiences confirm Nietzsche's cry that God is dead, a Christian can say nothing? Or does Mauriac, by publishing the foreword (no doubt with Wiesel's consent), in fact say that the Holocaust was part of a divine plan, the necessity of which is bound up in a grace we cannot fathom? But if he can say it in print, why cannot he say it in person? And why did Wiesel allow Mauriac to say it in print when Mauriac could not say it in person? Does Holocaust testimony turn interfaith encounters into speechless embraces and restrict religious doctrinal disputes to print?

The second feature of Wiesel's memoir that I take as an occasion for critical thinking is the book's turn from religious belief to what might be called a kind of humanism—*Night*'s replacement of (as a source of sustenance) the divine father with the flesh and blood one. Here, I sometimes write on the chalkboard a line of testimony recorded in Robert Kraft's *Memory Perceived* (a study of the Fortunoff Video Archive at Yale University that is a valuable teaching resource, since it is full of powerful and discussion-catalyzing transcriptions of oral testimony given by Holocaust survivors). The line is uttered by Edith P.: "I don't pray to God, [she] says, I pray to my father" (130). Building on this idea, many undergraduate readers will speak of noticing and being drawn to Wiesel's growing reliance on (and intimacy with) his father as his belief in God wanes. As a pious boy, Wiesel is not at all close to his father, who is described early on as a "cultured man, rather unsentimental. He [. . .] was more involved with the welfare of others than with that of his own kin" (4). And yet from the moment the Nazis arrive in Sighet, a bond forms between the two of them. This bond becomes most pronounced at Auschwitz, and *Night* invites readers to believe that the bond between a parent and child in adverse circumstances is unbreakable. Wiesel's one thought on the ramp at Auschwitz is not to lose his father (30). Near the end of the book, when the prisoners learn that they will be evacuated, Wiesel thinks only of not being separated from his father. During the march to Gleiwitz, the presence of his father is the only thing that sustains him (86), and when they finally arrive at Buchenwald, Wiesel writes, "I tightened my grip on my father's hand. The old, familiar fear: not to lose him" (104). A case can be made, however, that the invitation implicit in such scenes is given only so that later it can be violently retracted. Students will notice, for instance, how Wiesel—in the Rabbi Eliahu episode (90–91)—foreshadows his own struggle with his father (another instance of failed prayer, since Wiesel had prayed never to become like Rabbi Eliahu's son). And in the scene of his father's death, Wiesel is forced to confess to feeling a sense of liberation (112).

I elicit the material I have just discussed by giving another in-class writing prompt:

> What do you see *Night* saying about fellowship, the human spirit, or human nature in extreme situations? Introduce and discuss two scenes in your answer.

As with the scenes of religious belief, students are moved by the scenes that reveal the disintegration of Wiesel's regard even for his father, but they must be pushed a bit to consider the wider implications for our notions of familial love. Here again, students must reckon with the way a truth's apparent immutability is a function of the distance between the ordinary and the extreme, between, say, nourishment and deprivation. Is a belief in familial love's inviolability entirely dependent on our own relative comforts? What does it mean when a *Blockälteste* says to Wiesel, "In this place, there is no such thing as father, brother, friend" (110)? Is the goodness of human nature in fact something that exists only in environments where basic needs are being met? Are there environments that put to rest any and all consideration of a triumphant human spirit? These questions are entertained with more complexity in *Night* than might first appear. Students notice, for instance, the extent to which Wiesel is beset by feelings of guilt and shame even as he entertains the notion of taking his father's rations. In the end, however, Wiesel believes himself "[f]ree at last" after his father has died (112). The book's final image is one that forces us to think critically about what it means to be human. Bereft of all cherished relationships—with God and with his father—Wiesel faces the mirror (and our students) as a living corpse. Students thus encounter a person whose very existence stands as a kind of dark spot on the ideas and beliefs we might want to believe are timeless and transcendent. And because *Night*'s final line leaves us with the clear sense that Wiesel is still this corpse, there is no way to cement anew an inviolable foundation for such ideas and beliefs—without appearing either to ignore the textual details of the book or to impose by fiat a meaning the book will not support. Our foundations shaken, Wiesel thus challenges us to linger with and concede the Holocaust's irremediable trauma. Getting us to see the contingency of any and all values, *Night* works ethically to create critical thinkers who are ready to endure the destabilization of their unshakable truths, who are capable of seeing their cherished ideas and beliefs less as absolute or self-evident truths and more as difficult, opaque, and in some cases insoluble problems. In their absolute or fixed form, such ideas and beliefs often animate or sanction the commission of violence, underwriting in the process an understanding of history and experience as essentially progressive and redemptive. In the form in which Wiesel gets us to consider them, however, such ideas and beliefs become provisional and plural, requiring debate and dialogue and remembrance of those events in history that cannot be redeemed. Here, perhaps, is the insuperable value of teaching a book like *Night* in a class devoted to critical thinking.

Negotiating the Distance:
Collaborative Learning and Teaching *Night*

Phyllis Lassner

Night has become a canonical text, not only for Holocaust scholars and university courses on Holocaust representation, but also for many younger readers. As my undergraduate students at Northwestern University tell me, the ubiquity of *Night* on high school reading lists relates to its enduring stature as testimony and its emotive narrative power as well as to its appeal to teenage readers. This appeal is based on the assumption that students' own adolescent growing pains provide an emotional bridge across the void that separates them from the wrenching psychological and moral experiences faced by young people during the Holocaust. For this reason, despite their obvious differences in context, experience, and form, *Night* is often paired with that other iconic Holocaust testimony, *The Diary of Anne Frank*. Trusting the stability of students' identification and empathy, high school teachers often engage their young readers by asking how they might react in a similar situation or by having them draw a picture, create an interview, or keep a journal to show their feelings about an incident in the text and to create a pathway of relatedness with the Holocaust character. Such activities represent a pedagogical challenge. For if we agree that experiences within the Holocaust universe remain inconceivable and unimaginable to those who escaped its claws, then how do we teach testimonies of adolescent experience that defy the possibility of bridging the chasm to relatedness or identification?

This question has shaped the development of my course Representing the Holocaust in Literature and Film, where the identities and knowledge base of the students create another tension. The course is designed as an upper-level undergraduate seminar; its enrollment limit of sixteen students ensures concentrated time and attention devoted to their individual and collective attempts to express anxious and exploratory responses to disturbing and disorienting readings and films. Although Jewish students usually have some Holocaust education through their congregations and trips to various museums and even to Auschwitz and some students have learned about the Holocaust through other means, neither they nor the uninitiated are prepared for issues raised by the testimony of Elie Wiesel, Charlotte Delbo, and Primo Levi and by ongoing Holocaust criticism: the paradoxical imperatives of silence and filling its void with testimony, the loss of ethical consciousness to survival instincts, and the limits of representation. Though these issues remain vexed even for seasoned scholars, they also provide a template that leads them and students to analyze and interpret not only Holocaust texts but also their own responses. Daniel Schwarz's chapter "The Ethics of Reading Elie Wiesel's *Night*" is a case in point, where he examines the ethical components of "acknowledging who we are and what are our biases and interests" while attending to "moral issues generated by events described within an imagined world" (46).

Compounding the ethics of one's reading position is another result of students' search and struggle to find pathways for creating meanings from the world of Holocaust experience. Students discover the social and cultural differences among themselves that shape their individual responses. Emphasizing the rhetorical and affective implications of their own language use invites students to address these multiple but related divisions as they work together. In turn, as students' discussion engages their differences, they form a group negotiation with the import and affect of the language of Holocaust texts. A crisis point for this negotiation occurs when the students actively confront limits of representation that most critics agree should not be violated. Critics continue to caution us about ethical concerns—fears of distorting, travestying, or denying the austere ghastliness to which victims were subjected—and about glosses of sentimentality, glamorized or eroticized sensationalism, and uplifting messages. Although my course addresses this last problem most directly, through recent Holocaust fictions and films, Wiesel's *Night* offers many narrative occasions for students to confront these distances and limits and to establish critical criteria of their own for the purposes of interpreting other texts and films. In turn these critical criteria allow us to review our previous texts and to address a key question raised early on—whether an empathetic relationship to the characters and events of Holocaust narratives is even possible. In fact, as a final opportunity to challenge the students' conclusions, I assign Cynthia Ozick's polemical essay "The Rights of History and the Rights of Imagination," in which she condemns the manipulative and exploitative sentimentality associated with the various adaptations of Anne Frank's diary. By the end of the course, when we read a novel like Bernhard Schlink's *The Reader* or Sherri Szeman's *The Kommandant's Mistress* and see the film *Life Is Beautiful*, the range of students' identities and cultural values, as well as their reading relations with texts and with one another, has developed into a multifaceted relation with Holocaust reading. Among these facets are new questions evolving from old ones that in concert most often bring students to the open-ended conclusion that even as writers and readers are constrained by the limits imposed by selective memory and the inadequacies of language, we have much to learn about the Holocaust from its imaginative reconstructions and constructions.

These classroom experiences are based on a collaborative approach to teaching and learning that activates the representational and ethical limits of the language we use to constitute our analyses and interpretations. I borrow assumptions about the benefits of collaborative learning from feminist pedagogy, which developed methods to ameliorate the inhibiting effects on women students of highly competitive, often male-dominated classes. Feminist pedagogy encourages all students to feel confident about articulating their views while showing respect for and acknowledging the importance of other views for their own critical thinking. Having originated in women's studies programs, such precepts are now part of mainstream teaching. In my experience both in women's studies courses and in Holocaust courses, collaborative learning can translate highly contentious issues into sources of productive contemplation and discussion. One such issue that benefits greatly from this translation is students' responses to the historical and psychological distances between themselves and young people victimized by the Holocaust. As students struggle to find the language and rhetorical strategies through which to represent their responses to Holocaust texts, their written and spoken work dramatizes the emotional distance not only between their safe positions and the perils of the Holocaust but also between students' adolescent angst and that of young Holocaust victims.

Having students work together in pairs or groups of three creates a cooperative relationship that enables them to assuage their anxieties about giving oral presentations and sharing written work, even as the experience creates tensions in understanding their different approaches. An example of such cooperation and collaboration is researching aspects of the contexts of *Night*. A pair of students would share the work of defining the shtetl as a social, historical, and cultural community and provide illustrations from Poland, the Pale of Settlement, and Hungary. Another pair or group of three would discuss the particular history and fate of Hungarian Jews as they were rounded up in 1944. As each group or pair decides how to divide the tasks that build toward its presentation, students assume and share responsibility for the work and in the process get to know, trust, and rely on one another for supportive criticism.

I realize that this statement could easily produce mistrust in its pedagogical romantic optimism. Indeed, a couple examples expose the difficulties of negotiating opposing views and solutions respectful of the students and the source. On one occasion, in offering illustrations of shtetl life, a student in a small group wanted to show a film clip from *Fiddler on the Roof*, and another criticized its distorting sentimentality. The impasse was solved by the movie fan's insistent commitment to the value of popular entertainment in Holocaust education. Looking for confirmation of the movie's underlying authenticity, she researched its source and found and then distributed photocopies of a section from Sholem Aleichem's Tevye stories, and her colleagues in the group offered a brief summary of shtetl life and history accompanied by a short reading from Eva Hoffman's elegant book *Shtetl*.

The intensity of emotion produced by reading the extreme experiences Wiesel narrates in *Night* could easily develop into tension, misunderstanding, competition for righteousness, and discord. I want to emphasize, however, that by collaboration I do not mean working toward a consensus of ideas, which can often be an exercise in coercion, reinforcing feelings of inadequacy. Instead, collaborative work activates both critical and supportive perspectives. Students are encouraged to bring their individual responses to the group and to test them by actively listening to the others' positions, by viewing them as critical questions for their own perspective. In terms of teaching Holocaust representation, this critical collaboration negotiates the difficulties of finding precise and appropriate language through which to describe or interpret Holocaust texts, as well as the intense and often intimidating arguments about representation.

An example of the difficulties of bridging the experiential divide between Wiesel's character and students is in the recognition of the divide itself, as illustrated by a word I hear and read too often, despite my interventions: "relatable." Regardless of historical distance or differences in religious or cultural identity, students will claim to find Holocaust characters relatable if their interpersonal relationships produce responses they recognize as normative. With *Night*, students have little or no difficulty understanding the narrator's estrangement from adult reactions to crisis or impending doom. To test students' ease with the text, I ask for two pairs of students to contrast their responses to one such relatable scene and to a scene in Auschwitz. In this instance, instead of working out these issues within one small group, the two pairs bring their responses to be mediated by the larger seminar group. The results have been instructively different. In one instance, a combination of anxious and comforting laughter erupted at the emerging inadequacy of "relatable," while in another, the seminar found different responses between Jewish and non-Jewish students emerging as an issue that would take several days to resolve. Here collaboration assumed the complexion of conflict until one non-Jewish student implored, "If I have no way of relating to Jewish Holocaust victims, or to Gypsies, homosexuals, or the handicapped, why is this course being taught to all Northwestern undergraduates?"

A reading of Wiesel's essay "A Plea for the Dead" sets the tone for this tense collaboration with its paradoxical voices and messages and therefore its invitation for various interpretations. Just as the essay inveighs against banal and insensitive interpretations of Holocaust experience and representation, it demonstrates the necessity of asking questions. As a teaching instrument, the essay demands close textual analysis of voice, language, and rhetorical strategies, all of which in turn invite discussion and debate about its implications for students' own expressed responses. This analysis and discussion takes place as a relation that mirrors one Wiesel sets up by deploying alternating and juxtaposed voices. As he veers between "I" and "we," students enter the fray by reading sentences aloud in pairs, deciphering and discussing who these voices might represent and addressing how Wiesel's "we" may involve them as readers and partners in his polemic. This collaborative negotiation creates a critical context that extends from the history of Wiesel's immediate purpose to its meanings for them as students of Holocaust representation. Wiesel leads readers to confront the different meanings suggested by his use of "I" as well as that of the "I" of a friend of his who was also incarcerated at Auschwitz. The gap between their impressions of an experience universally accepted as an absolute horror is telling, for in opposition to Wiesel's portrait of its relentless and putrescent brutality, the friend depicts the death camp as "a spectacle of terrifying beauty" (176). What this exchange teaches us is that we who wish to visualize and know what Auschwitz was like are barred from doing so by two interlocking systems.

First, the camp was designed to create disorientation by such means as a cacophony of languages and seemingly benign questions from guards that often brought about brutal beatings or murder. And second, these disorienting conditions in turn produced neither a lens nor a language that is capable of transmitting its realities to our own frameworks for understanding.

Reading *Night* through the conundrums of "A Plea for the Dead" offers a method of constructing questions. This also follows Wiesel's narrative approach in *Night*, where at the very beginning, Moishe the Beadle becomes a mentor to the twelve-year-old protagonist:

> "Why do you cry when you pray?" he asked, as though he knew me well.
> "I don't know," I answered, troubled. [. . .]
> "Why do you pray?" he asked after a moment.
> Why did I pray? Strange question. Why did I live? Why did I breathe? . . . He explained to me, with great emphasis, that every question possessed a power that was lost in the answer . . .   (4–5)

For Wiesel, this response has become the hallmark of his career after writing his Holocaust trilogy. As he speaks and teaches, his method has become increasingly immersed in a midrashic discourse of questions and commentary that lead to more questions. For students, the power of questions as a heuristic replaces responses that "A Plea for the Dead" warns us against: reliance on narrative themes that offer such uplifting messages as the power of self-discovery and the power that accompanies gaining knowledge of the world. Moishe the Beadle offers his own warning: that neither hallowed texts nor the embrace of mystery could initiate Eliezer into the experience he would have to discover for himself. Only with that unchosen immersion would he then discover "that time when question and answer would become ONE" (5; emphasis in orig.).

After students have been initiated into this approach to studying *Night*, we engage the memoir as they work in pairs or in threes to construct questions and responses. Immersion in the text bridges several divides. Made aware that *Night* in an English edition is a translation twice over, students then perform their own translation. They grapple with the narrative's voices, forms of address, and ironies and translate dialogue, narration, and drama into questions. Analyzing their own questions, students then discover that their resulting inversions of textual statements also construct commentaries and interpretation. This analysis creates a dialogue not only among themselves but also with the relation between "A Plea for the Dead" and *Night*. A particularly telling point is the movement from Eliezer's recognition of question and answer becoming one to the historical statement, "And then, one day all foreign Jews were expelled from Sighet. And Moishe the Beadle was a foreigner" (6). Instead of an articulated transition between these lines, Wiesel implants a space. No mere convenience, the space can also be studied as begging a question of its own, as students have remarked: What is the relation between Eliezer's epiphany and the historical statement that follows?

Returning to "A Plea for the Dead" as a guide, students find answers in the question they have devised and the metaphoric associations they develop from it. The relation they question consists of a definitive space—a fissure—between the historically documented Nazi atrocities and the students' perplexity about what the Allies and their constituencies might have done to help the victims. Once one pair of students has recognized this space as a text, others pick up the cue and begin to read it by making associations with the accusatory voice of Wiesel's essay. And so even if they are being denied the possibility of relatedness or empathy with Wiesel's position, they can support him by reading the empty space as signifying the devastating silences of the world's indifference, of its insistence on innocent ignorance. As students return to *Night*, this gash is figured even further. They might first notice the empty space between Eliezer's declaration of not knowing, the emotional denial of the Sighet community, and the history that would engulf them all. Beginning with the expulsion of foreign Jews, this history proceeds through the story of deportation, incarceration, and death, the trajectory of which is also figured emotionally and theologically as an incantatory refrain in such passages as that beginning "Never shall I forget that night" (34). Coupled with the final lines of *Night*, this passage confronts readers with an image of death in life. Regardless of their differing responses, what stares back at readers are the Holocaust's silences and emptiness, all of which are encapsulated in the title, *Night*, with its connotations of infinite void through which no voice can travel or be heard and the obliteration of light and perhaps the possibility that language is capable of carrying Holocaust meaning. As Sara Horowitz notes, "it is not only the inadequacy of language that silences survivors. For what is one to do with this chilling and discordant knowledge of self and world?" (*Voicing* 112).

As students work their way into this darkness and discordance, they also try to determine what they might do to negotiate its silences and emptiness. It is at this point that I refer them to contextual historical reading. Of all the histories and historical reflections available, we follow Wiesel's lead and read history as debate instead of presenting the historical narrative as a seamless or transparent chronology. Serving this purpose well is Donald Niewyk's book *The Holocaust: Problems and Perspectives of Interpretation*, which presents its history as a series of issues, each of which is represented by different investigators. The chapter "The Holocaust Experience" juxtaposes Bruno Bettelheim's theory of "Helpless Victims" with Terrence Des Pres's "The Will to Survive," Richard Glazer's testimony "Surviving Extermination Camp Treblinka," and Alexander Donat's "Surviving Slave Labor at Maidanek." Choosing one point of difference between two selections, student pairs can create critical questions of each selection in the light of the other. As they reconvene and share their responses in the larger group, additional questions are raised, as is the possibility of constructing a complex interpretation that reflects a synthesis of all their work. Reading *Night* in these contextual frameworks, students can then examine it through the lens of their developing questions and interpretations, testing each through the others.

As part of this construction of a synthetic interpretation, what students accomplish in their negotiations with texts and with one another is the recognition of the many varieties of irony that inform the voices of so many Holocaust narratives. While some critics insist that *Night* in particular "resists irony . . . as it enacts the power of language" (D. Schwarz 54), this very power is often a feature of an ironic juxtaposition that serves as a kind of shorthand or terse reminder of circumstances or emotional responses that at the time of their production precluded the possibility of more discursive narration. Perhaps nowhere is this irony more apparent than in Tadeusz Borowski's story, "This Way for the Gas, Ladies and Gentlemen." We begin our discussion of irony early in the course with a viewing of the documentary film *Memory of the Camps*, based on footage shot by the Allied army as it entered Dachau, Bergen-Belsen, and other camps. Its voice-over narration by the renowned actor Trevor Howard never fails to disturb students who worry about the direction of his ironic tone. As we discuss the propagandist purposes of the film as a context for understanding its ironic voice, students are led to view irony as a trope representing various forms of reading distances. Irony leads us to recognize the affective implications of these distances: between our contextual knowledge and characters' innocent or willful ignorance, between the narrator and characters, between characters, and between the firsthand experience of Holocaust victims and survivors and our secondhand knowledge, which prevents us from ever knowing enough to fully understand. With its kaleidoscopic, shifting perspectives, irony complicates and even unsettles the learning relation to Holocaust narratives. With *Night*, Alan Rosen reminds us of "the irony that underlies the fact that the Jews of Sighet had never heard of Auschwitz until they arrived there" (1318).

As with attempting to chart the trajectory of a character's development within the concentration camp universe, studying irony leads to further questions about the limits of generalizing about the characters and characteristics of Holocaust narrative strategies and effects. Wiesel's description and assessment of Sighet's first encounters with German soldiers suspends judgment as Wiesel catalogs various Jewish responses, some quite favorable. Yet his final line of the passage reeks with the sense of the doom Wiesel knows we already know and about which Sighet has been warned by Moishe the Beadle but has chosen to deny: "The Germans were already in our town, the Fascists were already in power, the verdict was already out—and the Jews of Sighet were still smiling" (10). In addition to our own hindsight, what creates the irony in this passage is the negotiation Wiesel is asking us to conduct with his own voice and with the character of the Jews who would not heed Moishe the Beadle's warning. We must first interpret the narrative position of Wiesel's voice and its relation to the emotional tenor of its irony. Learning from the prefaces that *Night* was written ten years after the events it dramatizes and then revised and translated into English even later leads us to reflect on the affective direction of the older Wiesel toward the people who occupy his past and toward readers of succeeding generations. Is his irony condemnatory or accepting, or could it express a weary or affectionate sadness?

As the memoir unfolds and the horrors of the camps are recounted, students can return to this early passage to see its ironic connection to Wiesel's narrative of suffering. From the position of hindsight, they might ask whether Wiesel has established the town's defensive denial as implicated in the fate that awaits him. But this positioning of the reader also begs the question, Can we judge Sighet's Jews as deficient without assuming ourselves to be superior? If we were to do so, we would be creating our own irrevocable distance from them. Students can be put off by this possibility, but they can also see how Wiesel encourages them otherwise. Before the announcement of the ghetto's liquidation and the Jews' deportation, he writes, "The story he [Eliezer's father, Shlomo Wiesel] had interrupted would remain unfinished" (12). In his narration of the deportation itself Wiesel comments, "It was like a page torn from a book, a historical novel, perhaps, dealing with the captivity in Babylon or the Spanish Inquisition" (17). In the light of what follows and the memoir's final mirroring image of silence and emptiness, these comments can be taught as tropes not only for the narrative structure of *Night* but also for the unending and unsettling relation between all Holocaust survivor narratives and their readers. The overdetermined suggestiveness of Wiesel's comments invites students to work with it as a conversation, weaving its possibilities together into complex interpretations but in the process becoming aware that the memoir's structure may draw them in with its self-reflexive comments and that it also confronts them with a lack of resolution.

An unfinished story, like a torn page, suggests both open-endedness and the impossibility of closure or resolution. The effects of this interpretation may be seen as a rupture filled with the haunting of Wiesel's consciousness by events that remain inconceivable even as knowledge accumulates. At this point of our study, I ask students to approach this haunted space by writing a paper that develops their paired reflections into their own individual interpretations. Inevitably, it seems, they find that they must wrestle with the anxieties and even fears that connect the memoir's final ghostly image to that of the torn page. If the idea of an unfinished story is seen as an invitation to complete it with students' growing knowledge, those whose imaginations are seized by the images of captivity and the Spanish Inquisition wonder if Wiesel is implying an unending history of Jewish persecution. Clearly, this conclusion is a heavy burden to bear, but it does not have to be definitive. Wiesel's continuous writing and speaking testifies to the resilient determination that has characterized the survival history of Jews and Jewish culture. As students' collaborations with one another have demonstrated, rather than remain passive receptors of information gathering, they too have borne witness. On the last day of class, my students agreed that it is now time for us to take responsibility and to continue to make sure that the events of the Holocaust are not forgotten.

Interdisciplinary *Night*:
An Integrative Approach

Christopher J. Frost

We enter Elie Wiesel's *Night* at Sighet, "the little town in Transylvania" (3) where Wiesel spent his childhood. By the time we have concluded the auto-biographical tale, we must confront a question parallel to the question Wiesel asks himself. Wiesel, staring into a mirror, is faced with the indeterminacy of the image reflected back. As a reader who has now traveled from a village in Romania to the concentration camp, I am compelled by the power of the journey to turn my gaze back onto myself and my world and ask what it is that I now see. For me, the image I see as I move from *Night* to the world at present is all too clear, all too tangible, and unbelievably ironic: I see the face of an orphan, the little face of a baby boy, staring back at me from within a tiny village in Romania.

It was the summer of 1999. My wife and I were living in Romania and were spending a substantial amount of time in Romanian orphanages. Our journey began with a trip to the largest orphanage in the country, one that housed approximately five hundred children ranging in age from a few days to five years. We were led first to a building on the grounds, "home" to about sixty children, the youngest never having known another facility save the hospital where they were born and abandoned. Our first glimpse of the children came when we entered a room of about twenty children—some strapped to a metal cage ("crib" by another name) to prevent a fall or jump onto the concrete floor. We saw other children so crippled by their isolation that they incessantly banged their heads against a stone wall just to experience some feeling—any feeling—and still others so resigned to confinement that they simply stared blankly into the empty distance. As our time in Romania marched on, we learned that the scene before us was not just an unfortunate lapse in an otherwise full and interactive day. Rather, these orphans spent every hour of every day in this state of neglect and monotony, the quick and rudimentary diaper changes and noninteractive feeding sessions the only salve.

Kathryn and I have always thought (and hoped) that, had we lived during the Holocaust, we would have been among those who risked their lives to save others in need. Now here we were: a moral morass staring us directly (and literally) in the face. Were the images we witnessed real? How could this be, at a time heralded as modern and enlightened (or postmodern and postenlightened)? Fifty-five years had passed since the opening scene of Wiesel's *Night*, and here we were living a moral tale that also began in a small town in Transylvania.

From that day forward, sharing my experiences in the orphanages of Romania (Wiesel's birthplace) provides an entrée into *Night*. Wiesel's life and work has profoundly affected my life experience and defined many of my life questions; the linkages between text and life are explicit and multiple. Such a union is important, because students thrive on explicit, integrative links between knowledge and life but seem to have little experience making such connections themselves. Carnegie Foundation reports on teaching and learning confirm what I have learned in two decades of life and teaching: students routinely fail to make connections between knowledge learned in one academic discipline and knowledge learned in another and between knowledge gained in the classroom and challenges faced in life (home, community, or workplace). To offer *Night* to students simply as a history text or simply as another contribution to Holocaust literature may take students only so far in connecting text to reality.

Making connections between knowledge and life becomes meaningful and explicit when instructors learn to draw on the many disciplines integral to the encompassing questions that Wiesel's text suggests. I teach *Night* as one of eight texts in an interdisciplinary course entitled Science, Religion, and the Quest for Meaning. The other works are rooted in science, literature, philosophy, existentialism, and existential psychology and include a book on science as a way of life (Dawkins), a book of essays on science and the future (Brockman), the *Tao Te Ching* (Lao-tzu), Tom Robbins's popular novel *Jitterbug Perfume*, Erich Fromm's *Escape from Freedom*, and a book on the life and work of Simone Weil (Frost and Bell-Metereau). In this course, we address a number of imposing questions: How are we to assess the damage done to religious faith by science in general and social science in particular? Are we consigned to a choice between naive acceptance of religious tradition, with the risk of living a healthy illusion, and total rejection of any system of meaning that extends beyond confirmation of sensory experience, with the risk of living with an uneasy sense that there must be more to life than this? Has science led us to a more progressive epoch in terms of the good life, or does the historical record of the twentieth century suggest a continuous (or accelerating) record of an inhumane way of life? How do we account for the continuing record of inhumanity, and how does one achieve a rich sense of life meaning in its midst?

One can readily see that no single discipline can claim sole proprietorship of such knotted questions. As we undertake a reading of Wiesel's *Night*, then, we intentionally bring multiple lenses with which to see what is there.

Identity: Personal Grounding of the Interdisciplinary Motif

We cross the threshold of Wiesel's *Night* at the opening sentence: "They called him Moishe the Beadle, as if his entire life he had never had a surname"(3). With no surname, Moishe's identity is in question, especially in the context of Judaism, where one's surname and lineage are of great importance. We discuss the founding and naming of the twelve tribes and the theme of the Torah and its laws that the sins of the father are visited on the third generation but good deeds may bring blessings forever. The link between parents and lineage or identity can also be seen in the cultural context of *naches*, the notion that parents derive pleasure from their children's accomplishments. In the final analysis, a Jew's identity flows entirely from the surname, and, theoretically, all Jews are related by way of shared ancestry. To be devoid of a surname is to lack an identity.

Only one sentence into the book, then, and already it is as if Moishe—like Wiesel and the countless other children of *Night* who became orphans—has no identity. As Wiesel later writes in *Legends of Our Time*, "My first friend was an orphan. . . . [Now I know] we all belong to a generation of orphans. . . . Sometimes I wonder if he [the orphan] did not have my face, my fate perhaps, and if he was not already what I was about to become" (35, 37). Recognizing Wiesel's penchant for linking the first sentence of a work to the last, I invite students to juxtapose *Night*'s opening words with the two concluding sentences: "From the depths of the mirror, a corpse was contemplating me. The look in his eyes as he gazed at me has never left me" (115). A major theme has been introduced: the drama of identity as it plays itself out through a lived story. And another connection to Judaism has been made: the Torah also often connects the first and last sentences (or at least the first and last ideas), connoting a timelessness, a sense that there is no before or after.

The infusion of the identity theme at the outset of the course is not accidental. The theme crosses multiple intellectual disciplines and perspectives and thus begs to be viewed through multiple lenses. Simultaneously, the concept of identity connects the central course theme, meaning, to the individual that seeks meaning. A sense of personal identity and a perception of life meaning are knotted together, as I demonstrate by sharing my experiences in Romanian orphanages. When we consider that many students are struggling with issues of personal identity, the introduction of this theme is even more compelling. *Night* recounts the experience of a teenager, and the lived story may gain power when read by those who can relate to that life chapter.

We enter *Night* at the end (just as much of the world learned of Auschwitz and other camps only after their liberation). I ask students first to note that it is a corpse that looks back. Does this image mean that Wiesel sees a part of himself (perhaps the most noble part) as dead? What part of one's self, one's identity, can die? Under what circumstances? With what consequences for life thereafter and with what impact on one's quest for meaning in life? Is there a scientific, an empirical, solution to the puzzle? Or does one unravel such matters by a more intangible path of value—framed by faith?

As complex as these questions are, the issue becomes knottier when students consider another version of the ending that Wiesel might have chosen: the impulse to shatter the mirror.[1] This alternative rendering would put other enigmas before us. Were Wiesel to act on the impulse, is it the mirror that is shattered? Or is it the image in the mirror that is shattered? Must an identity that has been externally (artificially) forced on a person by the Nazis be shattered to reconstruct the pieces into a (real) whole? In deciding between these interpretive readings of the text, we need to confront directly the elusive issue of identity.

The Puzzle of Identity and the Jigsaw Classroom

At this point I bring an interdisciplinary frame to bear by using the jigsaw technique. The class is broken into four or five smaller groups. Each group is responsible for researching one piece of the identity puzzle from a particular disciplinary perspective, employing the essential concepts of that discipline. Each group then gives a fifteen- to twenty-minute presentation. After each presentation we attempt to put together the conceptual pieces and arrive at a patterned whole.

A wide range of disciplines may contribute to assembling the puzzle and understanding the pattern, although with *Night* I generally rely on a particular few. First, one group examines the religious component in general and Hasidism in particular. Because I try to use concise, succinct sources (the class reading load is a heavy one), a simple but adequate choice is the "Hasidism" entry in the *Encyclopedia Judaica*: "[B]asic Hasidic philosophy is [characterized by] *hitlahavut*, 'burning enthusiasm,' in which the soul is aflame with ardor for God *whose presence is everywhere*" (1405; emphasis added). I encourage students to explore Hasidism in terms of its distinguishing features—charismatic leadership, ecstatic prayer, and panentheism—and in the broader context of Jewish mysticism (see Scholem). In his seminar Literature of Memory, taught at Boston University, Wiesel acknowledged that "*Night* is actually a work in Kabbalistic literature."

A second group takes on a literary perspective, examining dimensions of Wiesel's identity either by exploring the role that a particular body of Judaic literature plays in defining Hasidism—speculative literature, expository pamphlets, and, most important, tales and legends—or by examining the issue of identity in literature as a whole. The group then brings this literary perspective to bear on *Night*. Wiesel said in the seminar that *Night* is also "a story of the son sacrificing the father," a reversal of the biblical story of Abraham sacrificing Isaac. Both literary paths lead to a common destination: providing a crucial puzzle piece awaiting correct fitting into the (identity) whole. And both paths can be connected to Wiesel's identifying himself as a storyteller.

A third group explores the historical and political dimensions essential to understanding *Night*. Students may pragmatically narrow the focus to the conclusion of World War I, the Treaty of Versailles, and the interval between the world wars. They often analyze the historical literature that attempts to document the escalation of Nazi persecution from the organized gang violence of Kristallnacht to Hitler's final solution. In pursuing this line of investigation, the historical group begins at a crucial focal point, Wiesel's title for the original version, "And the World Remained Silent." Wiesel refers to the world's indifference in *Night*: "How was it possible that men, women, and children were being burned and that the world kept silent? No. All this could not be real" (32).

I also share with this group a historical incident and a statement from another of Wiesel's works:

> At the risk of offending, it must be emphasized that the victims suffered more, and more profoundly, from the indifference of the onlookers than from the brutality of the executioner. The cruelty of the enemy would have been incapable of breaking the prisoner; it was the silence of those he believed to be his friends—cruelty more cowardly, more subtle—which broke his heart.   (*Legends* 189)

The statement stems from a visit to the White House in the late 1970s, when President Carter offered some reconnaissance photos of the concentration camps to Wiesel as a gift. Wiesel turned the photographs over and saw that their dates preceded the Nazi's 1944 incursions into Hungary and into Wiesel's town of Sighet. Wiesel declined to accept the photographs, explaining that he and his community really needed to see the photographs in late 1943 or early 1944. (The Nazis did not enter Sighet until spring 1944.) Heartbroken, Wiesel asked President Carter why the Allied forces, incontrovertible proof of the camps in hand, did not simply bomb the railroad tracks leading to the camps. Questions of this sort link the past and the present to the original title of the work.

Some students have connected this theme to other historical events in which the indifferent onlookers played a part. Martin Luther King, Jr., wrote of the "regrettable conclusion" at which he arrived while confined to his Birmingham jail cell: it was "not the White Citizen's Counciler or the Ku Klux Klanner" that stood in the way of the progress for blacks; rather, it was the general public, concerned with maintaining the status quo, who served as the grossest stumbling block. Students begin to see clearly how these historical patterns continue to thrive in various epochs and to consider the impact of such behavior on issues of identity and meaning. And lest there be any doubt concerning human myopia, we return to our discussion of the Romanian orphanages, existing now, in the twenty-first century; to the condition of millions of children around the world, now; to the Sudan, now.

A fourth group explores the psychological dimensions of identity, drawing on the rich, extensive literature on the development of the self. Though there are numerous angles to explore in this dimension, I introduce one with which I—and many of our students—am familiar: loss. How does intense suffering ensuing from loss affect one's sense of identity, one's sense of self, and one's quest for meaning in life? In attempting to isolate why experiences of loss hurt, psychologists often resort to a homeostatic explanation: loss—whether personal, tangible, or symbolic—creates a gap between what persons have, want, or expect in life and what they now (at the perceptual moment of loss) get out of life. To perceive oneself as helpless in the face of events is to perceive a gap between the challenges of life and one's abilities and resources to meet those challenges successfully. A major problem with congruity models, however, is that they assume that a person can always return to a balanced state. Is this assumption correct? To explore congruity models in reference to Wiesel and *Night* is incredibly illuminating. A psychological reading of *Night* conveys that certain life events occur such that balance may never be completely restored. In such circumstances, melancholy (an accurate, though saddening, perception of a life domain) may be the only appropriate response with a view to survival. The greater the gap between perceived opposites (like Hasidic fervor and friendship versus Holocaust horror), the more intense the struggle with melancholy.

The concentration camp shows that incongruity is not merely a cognitive dilemma or cognitive distortion in need of correction or amenable to simple restoration of personal balance. While psychologists generally consider incongruity a negative state of being inevitably in need of correction, the life and writing of Wiesel suggest that there are certain life experiences that are both tragic and incongruous. In such cases, an authentic and accurate perception (and indelible memory) of the event is required even though it means sustaining the very incongruity that psychologists maintain must be avoided; that is, even though it entails melancholy.

Because identity psychologists such as Erik Erikson recognized the crucial role of life context in the formation of identity, students from this fourth group see that information from the religious, literary, and historical and political groups will inform their work as well. And yet that is precisely the point. When the groups are later brought together to communicate their particular pieces of the puzzle, the excitement that is created as the pieces begin to mesh into a more integrated whole is palpable. Before assembling the puzzle, however, students must fully realize the importance and role of each individual piece. Just as the breadth of disciplines selected can be tailored according to the instructor and to the course (we could add sociology, philosophy, theology, economics, technology, and more in approaching *Night*), so can the depth.

As we see in *Night*, to avoid melancholy by giving way to false optimism can be a dangerous path: "At daybreak, the gloom had lifted. The mood was more confident. There were those who said: 'Who knows, they may be sending us away for our own good'" (21). By the end of the story, however, we learn that we must be willing to look into the mirror and see accurately what is reflected therein. As Wiesel writes later, "[T]ruth . . . must be sought. That's all. Assuming it is concealed in melancholy, is that any reason to seek elsewhere?" (*Souls* 240).

Assembling the Pieces: Coherence of a Gestalt

The often misquoted gestalt psychologists did not argue that the whole is greater than the sum of its parts; they argued that the whole is *different from* the sum of its parts. These researchers were trying to bring us an understanding of the qualitative dimensions of human perception, a critical distinction as well for the interdisciplinary inquirer and instructor. You can have students hear a lecture from multiple perspectives or read assignments from different disciplines, but those multidisciplinary sources do not come together on their own. For integration to occur, we must bring those pieces together and struggle to arrange them until a pattern begins to emerge—until the pieces cohere with such elegance that individual components are scarcely noticed.

How is this coherence achieved? In my view, we integrate pieces by way of honest and open-ended exploration, dialogue, and debate. Freud provides an apt metaphor that might clarify here. He argued that the relationship between patient and analyst (and, by analogy, student and teacher) is similar to that between a mountaineering guide and an explorer. When exploring a previously unknown place, the guide—though never having been to these exact mountains or faced these exact challenges—nonetheless brings his expertise to bear in such a way as to increase the likelihood of a successful expedition. The explorer determines the place to be explored and the nature of the expedition. The two together, by combining their willingness and expertise on a shared quest, discover something previously unknown to either.

In the classroom, no one, including the teacher, knows what pattern will finally emerge or when; no algorithm for coherence (or meaning) in life exists. The best pedagogical method I have found is to follow the group presentation series with a discussion of the unifying theme (identity, in this instance) and to move as carefully and critically as possible among the group insights and *Night*. Even the form of the group insights cannot be specified in advance: although the use of language, of discourse, is the most common form, I have witnessed presentations that incorporate art, music, graphic imagery, film, and poetry to astonishing effect.

In addition to seminar exploration, I make use of course journals and thought papers, in which students are asked to reflect on the core texts in terms of their own lives (just as I do by way of my experiences in the orphanage). Thus while working in jigsaw groups from a specific frame, students are also required to reflect on how the insights gained from *Night* (and subsequent dialogue) have informed their understandings of identity. In this way, students explicitly integrate knowledge and their own lives. By the time that we search for some common understandings (tentative though they may be), we are engaged in an intricate conversational interplay among the text, the jigsaw presentations, and personal explorations stimulated by journal writing.

As our conversation deepens and we progressively refine our understanding of the theme of identity embedded in *Night*, I also strive (as instructor) to connect this discussion to broader course issues: the nexus of religious faith and identity in juxtaposition to natural and social scientific portraits of who we are, the knotty question of what constitutes faith versus illusion or truth versus meaning and the basis on which we are to make such distinctions, and the overarching question of paths to a life of meaning. After having explored only the initial theme, I can already report that students who participate in this class, in the reading of the text and journal writing, in the jigsaw groups, and in the integrative dialogue emerge changed. Having begun with the question of who was Moishe the Beadle and who was looking into (and from) the mirror, we reach the point of reasking, Who am I? (with a more seamless integration of the religious, literary, historical and political, and psychological ingredients that define *self*).

Night *in Intellectual Context: Additional Texts in the Course*

In the course Science, Religion, and the Quest for Meaning, we rely not only on the multiple lenses of varying disciplines (including variant perspectives and concepts) but also on multiple texts. While some of the texts cut across terrain not so far astray from *Night* (Frankl; Fromm; Frost and Bell-Metereau), the readings that veer in a decidedly different direction are those that view humanity through the prism of science (Dawkins; Brockman).

To begin, try this thought experiment for yourself and then suggest that students do the same. Ask anyone how the world might be better in fifty years, one hundred years, five hundred years, or another millennium and ask that person to elaborate on his or her answers. Almost assuredly, the answers somehow revolve around expected technological advances—almost never around imminent moral, social, or psychological improvements. It is after reading and reflecting on these scientific essays, watching the science fiction film *Gattaca* (1997), and viewing life through the scientific prism as carefully as possible that we turn to Wiesel and his memory of that first night.

Why is Wiesel's text so effective? First, and simply, because the text is real: students engage with a slice of life from which there is no escape and to which they immediately and naively respond with questions. How and why could the events depicted in *Night* have occurred? How am I, situated afar in time and space, to understand the Holocaust? The asking of these questions unveils the need to approach the work from multiple perspectives. Once confronted with questions of why, students naturally set sights on multiple intellectual domains—historical, sociological, religious, political, psychological, philosophical, and more—as they ask questions and probe for answers to those questions. A second reason for the power of the text, then, is that it inherently requires readers to move beyond a one-dimensional frame.

Third, the text sustains the voice of its author. As we strive for understanding, we cannot take refuge in abstract pronouncements but must continually ground our search in the concrete reality of a single human being. The potential for integration increases as we attempt intellectually to combine insights gleaned from a variety of perspectives and seek to combine those insights into some pattern or configuration that makes sense, that coheres, particularly from the vantage of the author. Thus we are inevitably engaged in the task of connecting the concrete reality of a life with abstract ideas from multiple perspectives. The task of integration literally stares us in the face, so much so that we might reword the conclusion of *Night* as a conclusion for this essay: "From the depths of the mirror, a corpse was contemplating [Wiesel]" (115). Having now read and studied the text, can we identify what it was that Wiesel saw? And as I—concluding *Night*—turn my gaze back on myself and my world, what do I now see?

For me, the image that I see as I move from *Night* to the world at present is the face of an orphan, the face of a baby that never made it out of the darkness and into the light. He died on 7 June 1999, in a little town in Transylvania (Frost and Frost).

NOTE

[1] As the Yiddish account shows, Wiesel eventually did act on the impulse (*All Rivers* 319–20).

Night and Spiritual Autobiography

Kevin Lewis

Undergraduates at the state university in the South where I teach enroll in my course Spiritual Autobiography because they share my interest in exploring what it is that makes people of substance and accomplishment tick. In particular, we share an interest in how others at different times and in different places absorb religion early and then work and rework it as their experience of the outer world evolves. I assume that my students keep this interest in mind when they read and respond to texts like *Night*, and my experience justifies this assumption. I ask them to respond to each text individually. I use no particular linking themes. I assign *Night* along with other works of life writing to enrich the common project of evolving and strengthening identity that goes forward in each of us, in part by reading our own life into that of others and that of others into our own. Sharing this personal project with my students, I want them to respect but also to challenge the impossibility of identifying fully with the disrupting otherness of the life of a Holocaust survivor.

The course is an ongoing experimental workshop that mixes kinds of life writing and kinds of writers. It does not pause to address academic distinctions drawn between the religious and the spiritual. The list of readings has changed over time. I like poetry, and *Song of Myself* (1855) is a staple. Emily Dickinson, Anne Sexton (*The Book of Folly* [1973]), and Basil Bunting (*Briggflatts* [1965]) have made appearances, as have Ben Franklin, Frederick Douglass, James Baldwin (*Go Tell It on the Mountain* [1953]), and Yukio Mishima (*Sun and Steel* [1970]). Stretching the definition of life writing, last year I included Lillian Smith's anatomy of the South (and, arguably, of herself), *Killers of the Dream* (1949). Augustine's *Confessions* and Jung's *Memory, Dreams, Reflection* (1961) lasted awhile before being retired for their excessively demanding length. With *Black Elk Speaks* (1932), James Joyce's *Portrait of the Artist as a Young Man* (1916), and Simone Weil's always provocative *Waiting for God* (1951), *Night* has consistently held a place of honor on my list. Its unmitigated darkness consorts nicely with these other texts to shock my students, I hope, even if only briefly, away from complacent assumptions about advanced Western civilization. Instead of exams, I ask students to write short papers on each writer on topics of their choice, usually conceived as a result of class discussion.

As a teacher of religion I am still influenced by the existentialist approaches to questions of meaning and truth I encountered as a college student years ago. I start the course by observing that religious belief effectively remains abstract until taken up into the life of an individual and of a community. We read spiritual autobiographies to glimpse what it is that religion, whether of strict or loose definition, can do in the life of a person. How is religious belief and feeling planted, grown, and tested in a single life? Answers shed light on our own life experiences with faiths and practices inherited and new-blown. Wiesel's text opens a window on a childhood shaped in a world of luminous religious belief, a world abruptly destroyed by the war—to be reconstructed later in contexts altered by impinging forces of modernity and postmodernity. Very few of my students are Jewish. I pass around a collection of Roman Vishniac's photo images of the vanished world of Eastern European Jewry. The comparativist in me urges students to grasp as much as they can in class of the traditional Jewish worldview at the heart of Wiesel's Sighet. I tell them what little I know of the Hasidic movement to renew Judaism in the eighteenth century. I recall the impact on me of the television production of Wiesel's drama *Zalman; or, the Madness of God* years ago when we note the role of Moishe the Beadle. I remind them of my department's watchword, echoing the early professional comparativist Max Muller: "He who knows only one religion knows none." *Night* and the other "foreign" texts in the course help me introduce in some students and reinforce in others the civilizing awareness of the contingency and the relativity of all cultural formations.

The world of Wiesel's childhood was replaced by the horrifying misery of the death camp experience at Auschwitz, the most productive site of the Holocaust extermination project. Multitudes shared his fate, as Wiesel persistently reminds us. Many high school students in South Carolina are now reading *Night* in a Holocaust education segment of an updated curriculum. Like *The Diary of Anne Frank*, it has justifiably become a sacred text bearing witness to a people's destruction. As a longtime Holocaust educator, I am familiar with useful, contextualizing documentaries. In this course I have time for only one. My current choice is the English army footage of Bergen-Belsen being liberated in 1945, *Memory of the Camps*. Its rawness, the long silences on the sound track (irritating to ears trained to expect continuous narration), and the aloofness of the actor Trevor Howard's voice (as though fighting off tedium—a bystander who might have preferred to turn away) strike the right note for me. It works for my students.

But here I face a pedagogical challenge. To an extent clearly appropriate for this autobiography course, focused as it is on individual life trajectories, I juggle *Night* as iconic Holocaust testimony with *Night* in its dimension as existentialist life writing. I want not to lose the former for the latter but rather to guide students through the horror of the Shoah to the particulars of Wiesel's interpretation of his own passage within it. As a teacher of life writing, I reach beyond (or within) *Night*'s important function as a compelling chronicle of genocide to hold up Wiesel himself.

The nature of religion compels people of faith to distinguish, perhaps not without struggle and even if only for themselves, the true from the false. But there is no disputing the truth of the lives we encounter in the well-made autobiographical lives produced by the writers on our list. Young people brought up in or influenced by faith traditions other than Wiesel's respond to his gripping personal truth, and the passion in the writing ensures it. Young people rent by spiritual conflict can be sympathetic to his honest account of the revolt against

God rising up in Wiesel "[f]or the first time" (33) as he discovers what Auschwitz is about. The closing passage describing the futility, despair, and guilt he felt when unable to help his dying father proves especially recognizable and moving: "Listen to me, kid. [. . .] In this place, there is no such thing as father, brother, friend" (110).

But I urge students to read below the surface of the text. I want them to query what is known already or can be discovered through a probing of the historical life to which the writer responds in the autobiographical life created in the text. This life will always bear a problematic hence interesting, question-begging relation to the actual life of the writer. I want my students to take interest in the writer of the assigned text and in the function of the creation of the text in the life of the writer, who crafts the autobiographical life for a purpose or purposes. Teaching religious studies may explain this double focus on the writer as well as on the projected version of himself or herself by which the writer bids to be known. In the Judeo-Christian-Islamic tradition, we encounter the belief that the creator God knows each of us more thoroughly than we can ever hope to know ourselves, hard as we may try. Thus our true identity is never thoroughly knowable—it is not only dynamic and fluid but also mysterious. Throughout life, we remain tantalizingly out of our own reach.

But far from suppressing the effort to know oneself, in the belief that we cannot know so should not try, this religious teaching does just the opposite. Western culture, shaped profoundly by the ideal of individuality, has encouraged the enterprise of fashioning selves strategically to meet the needs of disparate settings and audiences throughout life.[1] We may not be able to know our life as God would, but we command the resources (and feel the pressure) to come forward with a life—or more than one, more than several, if need be—on demand, whether explicitly in life writing or implicitly on a daily basis.

I approach discussion of *Night* with this understanding of the fluidity of identity in mind. I also remind my students of the need to be critical as well as appreciative of texts, like this one, that have won canonical status for good reasons. Teaching the importance of the interpretive and rhetorical choices writers make in carrying out their discernible or guessable goals—teaching the writer's selectivity, conscious and unconscious—is made easier by Wiesel himself. He famously writes elsewhere of the problem of adequately telling the truth of his experience: "One cannot write about the Holocaust. Not if you are a writer" ("Holocaust" 9). Precisely. So what exactly do writers do when they write? What is it to craft and control a piece of writing on this subject—what is the inherent frustration? the inherent opportunity?—if the writer was caught up in the maelstrom of Auschwitz? How can a writer write about the Holocaust? Likewise what is life writing generally? Can a writer write an autobiography—if this is to mean a youthful representation of the actual life in all its messiness?

Wiesel functions for me as a great teaching example, perhaps an extreme example, of the person who, growing up indelibly formed in a strong religious tradition, must then struggle with the inevitable distress encountered on moving into the larger world, the world of the increasingly secularized, salad bar religious culture of the West and its default skepticism. Few of us are wrenched from our roots as dramatically as he was in 1944, at age fifteen. I ask my students to contemplate the observation and its supporting arguments that the Holocaust was a unique evil in the history of humanity. Despite that uniqueness and the unfathomable mystery of evil, *Night* makes Wiesel's experience vividly available to our common humanity. It holds challenging symbolic personal truth for my students here in the South, where evangelical Protestantism runs deep and where a university education and especially a university course in religious studies can still shock and destabilize.

Night is not a classic autobiography, that is, not a retrospective account of almost a whole life. I follow early writers on theory of autobiography in adhering to this guideline, writers like Roy Pascal, Karl Weintraub, and Barrett John Mandel. Weintraub tells us that young people are simply unable to produce the sweep of an autobiographical life—for, of course, they are young, and they lack the achievement of a well-earned and tested integrated perspective applied to a significant length of experience. (In his foreword to *Night*, François Mauriac writes tellingly, "The child who tells us his story here was one of God's chosen" [xix].) But *Night* does not purport to be a classic autobiography. It does not need to be. I suggest students read it rather as an act of self-reclamation on the part of a man too young for an autobiography but in desperate need of integrating the shattered fragments of his self-understanding after losing his identity (and his faith?). We consider its dimensions as a therapeutic antibildungsroman: an account of a youth propelled involuntarily through a series of "plotted" incidents, the cumulative effect of which is to leave him unprepared to face the daylight after his rending night, to face not a life but a death (see the corpse in the mirror at the close of the novel [115]). We consider it a venting cry of the paradoxically positive kind that my teacher in college years ago, Paul Tillich, would have described (as he described Picasso's *Guernica*) as a dialectical gesture of "redemption in spite of."

I urge students to think about what sort of project Wiesel in his early twenties set for himself when he began writing about his Holocaust experience. I guide them beyond the boundaries of the text and report what I know of Wiesel from other, later life writings. I remind them that the Wiesel who endured the terrible privations of *Night* did come through his ordeal to lead a productive, remarkably restabilized adult life. That gaunt face in the often reproduced photograph in the barracks at Buchenwald took flesh again. He came alive again, a man gifted with strengthened faith, robust humanity, creative talent, and resolve to inspire countless readers and audiences. Wiesel went on to produce work more closely resembling official autobiography over four decades after *Night*, in two parts: *All Rivers Run to the Sea* (1995) and *And the Sea Is Never Full* (1999). I have not yet read these works, but I am aided immensely by "Recalling Swallowed-Up Worlds," an essay Wiesel wrote for the 27 May 1981 issue of the liberal Protestant weekly the *Christian Century* as part of a series of contributions entitled How My Mind Has Changed. I do not ask students to read it, but I make use of it in class.

In the essay, Wiesel writes that at Auschwitz, he did not change as a person. Rather, he "[a]trophied, . . . evolved passively, accepting events without questioning them" (610). Only afterward, the experience over, did he change, decisively leaving behind the child of Sighet. I press students to imagine undergoing a prolonged crisis of belief and identity, despairing of both humanity and God, nursing loss and continuing anger. Wiesel lived and traveled alone for "months and months, for years" (610), his spiritual wound festering:

> I mistrusted my fellow humans: I suspected them. I no longer believed in the word as a vehicle of thought and life; I shunned love, aspiring only to silence and madness. Disgusted with the West, I turned toward the East. I was attracted by Hindu mysticism; I was interested in Sufism; I even began to explore the occult domains of marginal sects here and there in Europe. It's simple: I was looking for something else. I was anxious to venture to the other side of reality, of what constituted the basis of civilization. Meditation counted more for me than action; I drowned myself in contemplation. The appearance of things repulsed me, that of people even more.   (610)

We have learned over the years to recognize the Holocaust survivor syndrome. (*The Pawnbroker* [1965], featuring Rod Steiger as a Holocaust survivor weighed down unbearably by his wartime suffering and losses, remains a staple of another course I offer, which devotes a full semester to Holocaust literature and film.) But with immense effort, drawing upon remarkable resources of spirit and intellect, Wiesel the wandering refugee searching for beliefs found what he needed to overcome despair and come back to life. I want my students to identify with this voyage, though, of course, they have experienced nothing like the Holocaust. I query them for incidents or periods in their lives when they or others they knew responded similarly to great hurt. Psychological language comes to our aid. (Psychology is the favorite major in my university's college of liberal arts.) We discuss the theory of reaction formations after trauma and what the involuntary erection of defenses against unrelenting threats to one's person would feel like during and after an extended stay at Auschwitz (the conditions there are aptly conveyed in Tim Blake Nelson's film *The Grey Zone*, set in 1944 during the months when transports delivered the Hungarian Jews to the camp).

I teach religious studies as a specialist in culture and the arts. Much of my work in the classroom is comparativist in spirit, but I am not trained in any of the non-Western traditions. By inclination I maintain a preferential option for the West, for its diverse cultures and dialectical complexity. And so in pointing my students to Wiesel's wandering quest for self-reclamation after Auschwitz, haunted as the author was by despair for the plight of the Jews and by rationally unwarranted guilt at his father's death (I cite Bruno Bettleheim's "Surviving," on the fundamental humanity of this sort of debilitating guilt), I emphasize his considered rejection of India and Hinduism as a possible life-support alternative. I do so to lift up Western culture without apology. I acknowledge my personal bias. A teacher should liberate students, and my special charge is to liberate students from narrowed, uninformed, hastily dismissive misappropriations of the Western philosophical and religious traditions. Again, I acknowledge early influence by Tillich—his departing advice in his last course lecture was to seek more deeply in our own tradition adaptable means of resolving purpose and method for present need. I, also, want my students to discover the promising ambiguities of our own rich cultural tradition, its heritage of diverse religious options as well as its alternative spiritual paths. I describe to them what the sociologist Thomas Luckmann in *The Invisible Religion* calls the work of individualized bricolage (choosing and blending elements to forge one's own philosophy of life) effectively prescribed for each of us in the pluralistic West.

But my students do not read *Night* as an anguished promissory note of recommitment to the mystical and ecstatic rhetorical elements of Judaism and to Western culture until I tell them what Wiesel writes in "Recalling" of resisting temptation "to settle in an ashram somewhere in India" as a solution to his personal quest:

> I had seen, under the incandescent sky of India, an immeasurable, unnamable suffering. I couldn't bear it. In the face of this suffering, the problem of evil imposed itself on me with a destructive force. I could choose to steel myself to it or flee. Now I was not anxious to be an accomplice. Hindu friends would cross the street stepping over a crowd of mutilated and sick bodies without even looking at them. I couldn't. I looked and I felt guilty.   (610)

He tells us that, unlike these local friends, he cannot accept the destiny of the street beggars "in their place, in their name, for them and even against them—or at least like them." Not to notice, not to protest, was to acquiesce, and he found this response unbearable. "I refused to understand that certain situations couldn't be changed" (610–11).

He returned to the West, recommitting himself "to its necessary ambiguities, which confer to thought its brilliance, if not its vigor." (He speaks to my bias!) He returned to Paris, holed up with his books, and found sanctuary in a gnomic kabbalistic notion of creation "moved from its center in order to exile itself" (611). There, struggling daily against a sense of defeat both personal and collective, in "a room which was much like a prison cell," I imagine him preparing to write *Night*. How are we to understand evil? How are we to reformulate his shaken faith? In *Night* he quotes his father at Birkenau: "The world? The world is not interested in us. Today, everything is possible, even the crematoria . . ."

(33). I remind my students of the words Fyodor Dostoyevsky gives to the cynical Ivan Karamazov: "All is permitted" (50).

I urge my students to imagine Wiesel in that room seeking words commensurate with his pain and need and finding them deep within his own tradition, deep within the treasury of his lost childhood. I remind them of the writer's strategic use of Moishe the Beadle in the first chapter, of Moishe's liberalism as a prescient kabbalist dreamer. In that room Wiesel found for himself the enabling truth of Moishe's words:

> There are a thousand and one gates allowing entry into the orchard of mystical truth. Every human being has his own gate. He must not err and wish to enter the orchard through a gate other than his own.   (5)

Wiesel found through those words the redeeming, revelatory character of his own awful experience. Auschwitz had provided a path to illumination. I illustrate with the apocalyptic poetry of the much quoted passage in *Night* describing the first glimpse of Auschwitz as the transport pulls alongside the platform inside Birkenau at night: "Never shall I forget that night, the first night in camp" (34). Having walked it as a tourist on several occasions, I re-create for the students the geography: crematoriums 2 and 3 (and 4 and 5 through the woods) busy with the incredible, hallucinatory work of destruction.

Night proves powerful in my classroom—every year. I cannot imagine tiring of it, as a teacher and as an inquirer into the depths of the evil Wiesel addresses. Many of my students and, of course, much of the Bible Belt is acquainted with the Calvinist rhetorical insistence on original sin, or total depravity. Wiesel bears witness to a deadly, historical depravity of an unimaginable order, which I challenge my students to imagine. As a liberal, postmodernist Calvinist myself, I suggest the claim of that incalculable evil on all of us—even as it claimed Wiesel, and for which he found an appropriate image in the corpse's head returning his gaze into the mirror. For all its writerly strategizing (and because of it), the reduced self-portrait of an unbearable personal truth in the text brings us up short, especially because we can gather from testimony born in other Wiesel texts how it was that *Night* represents a palpable triumph after prolonged, heroic struggle. The extraordinary humanity in his fierce determination not to remain a victim is compelling. My autobiography course needs this text. It needs this story of a gifted young man challenged by the "vigor" and "brilliance" of Western civilization, despite its "ambiguities," to recover from the childhood wrested away from him the moral, visionary key to his own remaking.

NOTE

[1] On this view of Western culture in relation to autobiography, see Weintraub.

Night and Video Testimony

Jan Darsa

Years ago, a teacher asked me if I would help him think about how to teach Elie Wiesel's "novel" *Night*. This request was made by a seasoned literature teacher visiting the United States from England and working at a prestigious high school in the Boston area. Not only was I struck by his use of the word *novel*, but I wondered how many others might mislabel this memoir as a novel, a work of fiction. When I explored bookstore shelves and local libraries, I was again surprised at how many of these locales had placed *Night* in the fiction section. Why was *Night*, clearly a memoir of the author's terrifying experiences as a young boy during the Holocaust, placed with works of fiction? Why were literature teachers, trained to recognize fiction from memoir, placing this book in the wrong category? Was the truth of the story, a story of unimaginable cruelty, horror, and death, too hard to fathom? Was the eloquence of the author's writing, his poetic and lyrical style, too easy to dismiss as fiction? Whatever the reason, I wanted to approach the teaching of *Night* so that students would not make that mistake.

As I reread *Night*, the voices of the video testimonies I had been watching as part of another project began to echo in my head. Conceived by the staff of Facing History and Ourselves, where I was and still am working, and guided by the literary scholar Lawrence Langer, the project involved exploring the use of video testimonies as a teaching tool to accompany the history and the literature of the Holocaust.[1] We had been viewing and piloting with our teachers testimonies available from the Fortunoff Video Archives at Yale University. I had watched over one hundred video interviews of survivors of the Holocaust, and I realized how many of their voices mirrored Wiesel's in *Night*. What an opportunity, I thought, for teachers to bring these voices into their classrooms in conjunction with teaching *Night*.[2]

The combination of literary and video testimonies provides a valuable teaching tool for teachers attempting to help students understand the history of the Holocaust beyond the facts. It lends the human and ethical dimension to the specific historical events and allows teachers and students to ponder some of the deeper philosophical questions that arise out of a study of this history. It felt like an antidote to the problem of placing *Night* in the realm of fiction. Combining *Night* with testimony makes the numbers imaginatively available to students. It also provides them with a way to access the implications and magnitude of this event as well as a glimmer of what was lost and the irreversibility of that loss. Since much of the documentation used to teach the history was done by the perpetrators, *Night* and other victim testimony afford the learner a chance to look at this history through another lens. As Terrence Des Pres writes:

> Survivors do not bear witness to guilt, neither theirs nor ours, but to objective conditions of evil. In the literature of survival we find an image of

things so grim, so heartbreaking, so starkly unbearable, that inevitably the survivor's scream begins to be our own.   (54)

Survivor accounts like *Night* and video testimony can help bring us closer to the experience and, with the important context of historical documentation, give us a more personal and complete picture.

Facing History staff members and teachers created a video montage that is a compilation of voices that corroborates the voice of Wiesel while giving the teacher an opportunity to delve deeply into some frequently asked questions about the Holocaust. This videotape, *Challenge of Memory,* and the study guide that accompanies it (Johnson and Strom) are available through the Facing History and Ourselves Resource Center in Brookline, Massachusetts, for teachers in our network. Teachers using *Night* can borrow the video while they teach the book. Middle and high school teachers usually begin with the first excerpt on the video to introduce students to the book and the author and then use clips as they relate to the previous day's reading since each five- to seven-minute video excerpt is paired with a segment of *Night*. There are a total of seven excerpts of survivor and witness testimonies, and it usually takes about five to six class sessions to show them all and discuss each one with the students' daily reading assignments. Students can also read together in class. At the college level, where teachers only see their students one to three times a week but have longer class sessions and where students often read the book in one sitting, one or two class sessions would probably be enough time to discuss the book and the testimonies.

In the opening tape excerpt, Wiesel himself speaks to a group of Boston-area high school students who have read *Night*. Instead of speaking about his own experiences, which is what the students were expecting, he calls on his friend the rabbi Joseph Polak, Hillel director at Boston University, to tell a story. Polak, caught off guard, struggles at first to think about what he might say and gradually begins to relate a story of his own childhood in the camp of Bergen-Belsen. Wiesel returns to the podium and connects Polak's story to the message he wants to convey to the students. He says, "These stories are to sensitize people—to make you more sensitive . . . because whatever happens today is directly related to what happened then [during the Holocaust]." The clip offers a chance for the teacher to introduce the author and to ask students if Wiesel is correct in saying that hearing these stories will indeed sensitize people to others' pain. Or students could be asked to identify the purpose of reading these stories and studying this history, or any history for that matter, beyond the rationale that it happened. The teacher could ask students what Wiesel means when he says that whatever happens today is directly related to what happened then.

In the next excerpt, the survivor Shari B. tells of a man her father brought home from the synagogue in Hungary in 1944. The man was a Polish Jew who had escaped from a concentration camp. He began telling her family what was happening to the Jews in the concentration camps in Poland. Shari tells us this was the first time she heard of a plan to eliminate the Jews. She listened to this man's stories, as did her father and his friends, and she says no one could believe them. "The Germans are such a cultured people it was impossible to believe." This testimony reminds us of the scene in *Night* when Moishe the Beadle returns to Wiesel's hometown, Sighet, and warns the Jews of what awaits them:

> But people not only refused to believe his tales, they refused to listen. Some even insinuated that he only wanted their pity, that he was imagining things. Others flatly said that he had gone mad.   (7)

Sometimes when students read this section of *Night* they are upset, puzzled, and even angry that the people of Sighet responded this way to Moishe's warning. Hearing Shari's voice with Moishe's and with teacher guidance, students can begin to understand how difficult it was to assimilate such devastating information—information that at first seems so preposterous that it defies both experience and imagination. The Holocaust historian Yehuda Bauer speaks about the difference between knowing and internalizing knowledge. The video testimony corroborates this incident in *Night*, but it also enables students to better comprehend the reluctance of Sighet's Jews to recognize the impending danger. Because there was no historical precedent for this event—even in the horrors of earlier pogroms, many died, but many were spared, and the danger passed—Jews were often unable to see the potential deadliness of the Nazi regime. They fell victim to their faith in humanity.

These two stories help address the question students so often ask: Why didn't the Jews leave? Aside from the obvious difficulties of living during a world war, such as needing visas and having doors closed to them around the world, Jews were unable to grasp the fact that the world turned a blind eye to their impending fate and, even if they could get out, were unwilling to leave loved ones behind in a time of danger. Many lived with the belief that the war would turn around and at any moment the Nazis would be defeated and the Jews would be safe. It is easy to look back now and think, I would have left. But a teacher might ask students to think about what it means to leave—to go to a place where you don't speak the language, can't practice your profession, and have none of the supporting structures of the surrounding society in which you grew up.

In a third clip, Edith P. describes a transport in a boxcar traveling from Auschwitz to a labor camp in northern Germany. It is dark, and the other women in the boxcar tell her to look out of the wooden slats at the top of the boxcar and describe what she sees. She is too weak to climb up, so they suggest that she stand on someone else's shoulders. She does, and she sees life—normal life—and stares in disbelief. "Paradise must look like this," she tells the other women in the boxcar. "We saw the sun in Auschwitz," she says, "but it was never beautiful. It was just the beginning of another terrible day." She continues to tell the women as she looks out the window of the boxcar, "Girls, it is so beautiful, and there is a woman kissing her baby—is there such a thing as love?" In *Night* Wiesel talks about the beautiful spring day just after he has described the Nazis beating some of the prisoners walking from their workplace back to Auschwitz. He draws on the image of two universes, one inside the camp experience and the other outside. The world outside seems to him to go on routinely. The sun shines, the flowers bloom, and all these occurrences seem indifferent to the suffering of those inside the concentration camp experience. Like Wiesel, Edith is struck by the normality of the world outside, and her account mirrors not only the content of Wiesel's description but also his voice. She speaks in a manner that is similar to the way he writes, with poetic eloquence.

Both testimonies confront the reader or listener. Neither allows us to skirt the central issue of indifference—the indifference of both human beings and the natural world and divine presence—to the suffering of the victims. It is with these testimonies, both oral and written, that we are brought closer to the experience. We are at risk of penetrating people's defense mechanisms and creating cognitive dissonance, but this risk may be a necessary part of the learning experience. The clinical psychologist Israel Charney said when writing about the teaching of the Holocaust:

> We also have so much evidence to suggest that learning, even of simple factual material of an impersonal sort, takes place best under conditions of optimal anxiety, and not, as popularly thought, when students are entirely relaxed. . . . It therefore behooves us in considering teaching issues such as violence to strive to create a learning atmosphere in which there will be significant experience of anxiety, but not overwhelming terror. To leave sterile facts of our history books as the only thing we teach our children is to fail to encourage an emotionally meaningful or anxiety-responsive experience. (22)

In her testimony, Edith uses the words "mother," "baby," "sun," and "love." These words are part of our everyday discourse, but for her they are unattainable visions. Even the sun is not normal. She claims elsewhere in her testimony that the sun was black in Auschwitz. There is a sense of ultimate despair as she witnesses these normal occurrences that she and her sister and other women friends are being deprived of, just as Wiesel and his father are deprived of all that is available in that other universe that is closed off to them.

In the fourth and fifth clips, survivors relate incidents bearing on the cost of resistance and the extremity of hunger—issues at the center of *Night* as well. But the sixth clip is different from those that precede it. Leon Bass, an American soldier who witnessed the liberation of Buchenwald, the camp from which Wiesel was liberated, says that because he lacked a frame of reference, he had difficulty absorbing what he was seeing. He tells what he saw when he entered Buchenwald a few days after the liberation: people who were starved and sick

and who had so many sores on their hands that their fingers were webbed together by scabs. These people weren't speaking, they were just making guttural
sounds. Some of them looked like "walking dead." He asks himself, "What did
these people do? What was their crime that they should be treated this way?
You see, I had no frame of reference, I was only nineteen years old." He was
there. How difficult is it for those of us who weren't there to comprehend?

Bass's testimony parallels Wiesel's description of himself at liberation. Wiesel
says that when he looked in the mirror he saw a corpse gazing back at him and
that the look in his eyes has never left him. The juxtaposition of Wiesel's view of
himself and Bass's description of those he saw on that day in Buchenwald is
powerful. Two human beings were standing in the same place at the same time,
coming from two entirely different vantage points yet describing the scene in
closely linked ways. Bass, an African American who experienced discrimination
while in the army as well as after the war, says it was this moment that helped
him understand that suffering was universal and not just relegated to him or his
people. He has spoken publicly for many years around the United States in an
attempt to counter apathy and denial. Wiesel too has made a lifelong commitment to protecting the human rights of others around the world, and he was
awarded the Nobel Peace Prize in 1986 for his efforts.

Bass and Wiesel thus share a moment in time and a response to that moment
that connect someone who has lived through the experience of the Holocaust
to someone who witnessed it from the outside. That union of voices helps bring
us closer as well, but the abyss that exists between those who were there and
those who weren't will never be completely bridged.

The existence of such an abyss is powerfully dramatized in the final clip,
filmed in April 1985 for ABC News, when Wiesel went back to Auschwitz with
Peter Jennings at the fortieth anniversary of the camp's liberation. It is clear as
we watch these two men standing together in the bleak and snow-covered site
of Auschwitz that they are truly dwelling in two different realms, their conversation taking place on two entirely different planes. Wiesel is back forty years
ago, hearing the mothers crying and the children howling. He is in his memory
while Jennings stands there as a news anchorman, clearly moved by the experience yet removed from it. Wiesel is bearing witness, and Jennings is asking the
questions of a journalist. Closing Night with this excerpt offers students the vi-
sual image of Auschwitz today, and for many students this video clip is the most
powerful of the seven. It helps us understand that, although we are looking at
an event that took place sixty years ago in a world that may seem far removed
from the world where our students live, the memory of the experience has
never left those who lived through it.

Teaching Night in conjunction with video testimony engenders thought and
discussion on major themes of Holocaust history: the dichotomy between existing in the abnormal world of Auschwitz and living in the world outside
Auschwitz, modes of resistance and response living in the Third Reich, and
coping with memories and atrocities that occurred six decades ago. For many

survivors of the Holocaust and other mass atrocities, there is a real fear that as time moves us further from the event, the possibility grows that people might consider these accounts to be fiction. Hearing these voices and seeing these testimonies while reading *Night* help guide the reader to the conclusion that such testimony is true.

By adding video testimony to the teaching of *Night*, the story becomes yet more comprehensive and adds a unique dimension to the study of history. These testimonies allow students to hear a variety of voices speaking about different events and themes, thus reducing the inclination to generalize, find simple answers to complex questions, and doubt the authenticity of the memoir.

Teaching the Holocaust is clearly challenging. What responses do we want from our students? How do we elicit those responses? Teaching *Night* with the video testimonies brings our students and us closer to the experience. And at the heart of the experience are the voices of those who were there. They have chosen to reenter their painful pasts to leave their voices with us and therefore we have the privilege and obligation to listen.

NOTES

[1] Facing History and Ourselves (www.facinghistory.org) offers an interdisciplinary approach to citizenship education that connects the history of the Holocaust and other genocides to the moral questions young people face in their own lives. It provides middle school, high school, and university teachers with tools for teaching history and ethics.

[2] I particularly wanted to bring these voices together with Wiesel's to penetrate the denial mechanism that may operate for some readers of *Night*.

The Real Questions:
Using *Night* in Teaching the Holocaust

John K. Roth

Elie Wiesel says that *Night*, the foundation for all his subsequent work, was written for Holocaust survivors. It was written to show that there are no words that are fully adequate for testimony but that somehow language had to be found to bear witness. "I knew the story had to be told," he says. "Not to transmit an experience is to betray it. . . . But how to do this?" ("Why I Write" 201). Words, reports Wiesel, had to be searing, but they all seemed "inadequate, worn, foolish, lifeless." Still, the effort to transform them had to be made to wrench the victims from oblivion and to keep death from having the final say. Writing and teaching, too, are ways to bear witness, ways to remain faithful, provided one takes responsibility, Wiesel has emphasized, not only for what one says but also for what one does not say ("Why I Write" 201–02; *Oath* 154). Those convictions may help explain why *Night* begins by introducing one of Wiesel's teachers, Moishe. Although the year was 1941 and the Holocaust was well under way, it had not yet reached Wiesel's hometown. One day, the young Wiesel asked his teacher why he prayed. Moishe replied, "I pray to the God within me for the strength to ask Him the real questions." Wiesel adds, "We spoke that way almost every evening" (*Night* 5).

One needs to consider what some of "the real questions" might be when studying and teaching *Night*. I ask my students to read the memoir in two ways: all the way through in one sitting and in shorter segments, taking time to ponder each one. In both readings, I encourage them to reflect on questions that fall into three areas.

First, the real questions ought to include historical inquiries. It is important to be clear about what is actually happening in Wiesel's account and how his narrative fits into the larger context that forms overall what is now called the Holocaust. This part of the inquiry requires wrestling with some of Wiesel's silences. *Night* begins in 1941 but in a very few pages skips to the spring of 1944. Wiesel says almost nothing about the years 1942 and 1943, but it is worth asking what happened then. Consider 1942, which was the most deadly year in Jewish history. By that year's end, nearly four million European Jews had perished in what the Germans called the final solution. Of that four million, approximately two-thirds (about 2.6 million) died in 1942 alone. By the end of 1943, another 600,000 would be added to the total. As the spring of 1944 approached, the largest remaining Jewish population in Europe (approximately 725,000) was located in Hungary. When the Germans occupied the territory of their faltering ally on 19 March 1944, the fate of the Hungarian Jews, including Wiesel's family and the other Jews residing in Sighet, was sealed. In less than three months during the spring and summer of 1944, about 435,000 Hungarian Jews were deported, almost all to Auschwitz. (Here it should be noted that

Wiesel's *Night* describes briefly, but in some detail nonetheless, the process that the Germans had used many times before in other countries to ghettoize the Jews, expropriate their property, and deport them. Wiesel is not primarily a historian, but *Night's* succinct account of the destruction process in Sighet is significant.)

Second, the real questions unavoidably include interpretive questions that focus on the text and *Night's* possible meanings, the testimony that Wiesel wants to share, and the witness that he is intent on bearing. As one reads his memoir, it is important to ask, What is he emphasizing? Why? How has he crafted this communication? Two factors stand out as I think about such questions.

First, Wiesel is describing a process of destruction and the struggle to survive in the midst of it. His description emphasizes particular experiences and details. His book is not a history of the Holocaust, and yet with attention to the detail of his own experience it does document what happened to him and to people he knew. He writes to testify, and he intensifies memory so that the Holocaust will not be forgotten.

Next, I believe that Wiesel wrote *Night* more to raise questions than to answer them. *Night*, in fact, is a book of questions; it aims more to provoke inquiry than to settle opinion. The questions are not only about how the Holocaust happened but also about why it happened and about what this event means and implies, which includes exploring what it does not and must not mean and imply. A key question is, Where was and is God? It is highlighted in the memorable description of the hangings that Wiesel witnessed at Auschwitz, including the hanging of a child, which led Wiesel to think, "Where He is? This is where—hanging here from this gallows" (65).

Another question, equally important and implied by the one about God, is, Where was and is humanity? "At Auschwitz," Wiesel declares, "not only man died, but also the idea of man. . . . It was its own heart the world incinerated at Auschwitz" (*Legends* 190). But that conclusion is not the end of the matter, for Wiesel has also said that the most important words in his vocabulary are "and yet—and yet" ("Exile" 183). The anticipation of those words can be sensed in *Night*, for despite the corpse that stares back at Wiesel from the mirror at the book's end, life continues after Auschwitz, and writing and testimony follow. Although Wiesel wrote *Night* for the survivors, it can also be said that he wrote for anyone and everyone who cares enough to read the book and to hear its warnings, its protests, its sense that the forces of hate and destruction that created the Holocaust must not be allowed to prevail. *Night* is dark, but its witness, especially when the text is placed in the broader context of Wiesel's subsequent authorship, encourages sensitivity that could help to mend the world.

Thus a third kind of question must be included in the real questions that *Night* raises. These can be called reaction questions. They can and should be asked before, during, and after the historical and interpretive questions are explored. Some of the lines of reflection and sharing that might be explored are, How do we feel as we read and reread *Night*? What specific parts of the book affect us the most? What is the book's overall effect on us? What parts puzzle us the most? What would we have to know to respond well to the puzzlement? What would we have to do to make the world a place where what happened to Wiesel and his family will happen no more? To read *Night* and let it affect us is indeed an awesome experience and an immense responsibility that we shirk at our peril.

It is significant that much of Wiesel's experience and work has taken place in European and American cultures that embody Christian traditions, beliefs, and practices. Nearly everywhere he goes, Wiesel meets Christians and Christianity. Many of my students and I are among the large number of Christians who read *Night* and his many other books, attend his lectures, listen to his public pronouncements, and visit the United States Holocaust Memorial Museum, which he did so much to get built. For decades, Wiesel's writings—including the two-volume autobiography *All Rivers Run to the Sea* and *And the Sea Is Never Full*—indicate that Christians and Christianity are on his mind with some frequency. How could they not be? For in often devastating and therefore enduring ways, the Christian tradition has affected the Jewish tradition into which Wiesel was born. Without Christianity and its centuries of hostility toward Judaism and Jews, the Holocaust would scarcely have been conceivable. That reality accounts for one of Wiesel's most provocative judgments: "In Auschwitz all the Jews were victims, all the killers were Christian" (*Jew* 11). In *A Jew Today*, he added, "It is a painful statement to make, but we cannot ignore it: as surely as the victims are a problem for the Jews, the killers are a problem for the Christians" (12). That claim complicates how one reads *Night*, and light can be shed on that complexity by considering reflections that Wiesel offers in *All Rivers Run to the Sea* regarding some of the times and places, persons and events that help to construct and contextualize *Night*'s speech and silence.

As a Christian who has known Wiesel for many years and who has learned a vast amount from his teachings, I am convinced that his reflections about and appraisals of Christianity have an immensely important part to play in my tradition, for Wiesel correctly says that "Christians have to try to understand what has happened to the Christian tradition" (qtd. in Schuster and Boschert-Kimmig 100). To understand oneself is never easy and is often painful, but if Christianity is to be true to its core identity as a religion of love, then Wiesel is right: we Christians must ask, What happened to love? Together with *Night*, Wiesel's more recently published memoirs contain impressive moments that invite such reflection.

One day when he was eight years old, Wiesel accompanied his mother, Sarah, when she went to see the rabbi Israel of Wizhnitz. After speaking to her in the boy's presence, Israel spent time with him alone. What was he learning about Judaism? the old man wanted to know. After the young Wiesel responded, Israel spoke to Sarah again—this time privately. When Sarah emerged from that encounter, she was sobbing. Try as he might, her son never persuaded her to say why. Twenty-five years later, and almost by chance, he learned the reason for his mother's tears. Anshel Feig, a relative in whom Wiesel's mother had confided on that day, told him that Elie's mother had heard the old rabbi say, "Sarah, know that your son will become a *gadol b'Israel*, a great man in Israel, but neither you nor I will live to see the day. That's why I'm telling you now" (*All Rivers* 13).

Wiesel tells this story early in the first volume of his autobiography. It reveals much about him and sets the tone for the book. For Wiesel, stories are important because they raise questions. Wiesel's questions, in turn, lead not so much to answers as to other stories. Typically, autobiographies settle issues; memoirs put matters to rest. Wiesel, however, has a different plan for his memoirs, *Night* included. His storytelling invites readers to share his questions, but the questions his stories provoke do not produce indifference and despair. Instead they lead to more stories and to further questions that encourage protest against those conditions. And so it is that Wiesel acknowledges that as a boy he "knew nothing of the Christian religion." True, he had Christian classmates at school, but their religious tradition, he says, "inspired in me no curiosity, only fear." Yet Wiesel has not forgotten a Christian boy named Pishta, who was different from the others. He even helped Wiesel after the Germans established the ghetto in Sighet before deporting its Jews to Auschwitz in May 1944 (*All Rivers* 23).

What happened to love? Wiesel's life makes him wonder—sometimes in anger, frequently in awe, often in sadness, but always in ways that intensify memory so that bitterness can be avoided, hatred resisted, truth defended, and justice served. The stories within Wiesel's story can affect his Christian readers in the same way. If few solutions to his questions follow, greater moral and spiritual sensitivity can be aroused.

Israel was right about Wiesel. The shy, religious Jewish boy grew up to become an acclaimed author, a charismatic speaker, and a dedicated humanitarian who in 1986 received the Nobel Peace Prize. In his particularity as a Jew—it includes dedicated compassion for Jews who suffered under Soviet rule and passionate loyalty to Israel—as well as in his universality as a human being, Wiesel qualifies as a great man.

The rabbi was also right about Sarah. Neither she nor Israel nor Wiesel's beloved father, Shlomo, lived to see Wiesel's major accomplishments. Refusing to lighten the darkness of *Night*, Wiesel insists that none of his success is worth the violence unleashed, the losses incurred, the innocence demolished in a lifetime measured not simply by past, present, and future but through time broken before, during, and after Auschwitz. He would be the first to say that it would have been better if his cherished little sister, Tzipora, had lived and all his books had gone unwritten, for then the Holocaust might not have happened. Wiesel's honors, including the widespread popularity of *Night*, weigh heavily on him. They are inseparable from a question that will not go away: How can I justify my survival when my family and my world were destroyed?

Christianity alone did not cause the Holocaust, but it is not credible to think that Auschwitz would have existed if Christian love had included Jews, not by trying to Christianize them when they preferred their Jewish ways, but by honoring and defending their humanity and by helping them when they were in need. A version of Wiesel's question is important for post-Holocaust Christians. How are we to justify our tradition after Auschwitz? Wiesel responds to that question through his recollection of a Christian woman who is briefly mentioned in *Night* (20) but without the detail that Wiesel later provided (*All Rivers* 68–70). He says that his family's housekeeper Maria was "part of the family." As the Nazi threat came closer, she offered safety in her family's mountain cabin. She slipped through ghetto barricades to bring food and friendship to the family she served. Wiesel massively understates the case when he says, "Dear Maria. If other Christians had acted like her, the trains rolling toward the unknown would have been less crowded. . . . It was a simple and devout Christian woman," Wiesel adds, "who saved her town's honor" (*All Rivers* 69–70). Perhaps Maria saved some of Christianity's honor, too, or at least her example shows Christians how they might try to repair their tradition in the Holocaust's wake. And so does Wiesel's Jewish example, as Christians think about where it leads and calls.

Wiesel did not expect to survive the Holocaust. To this day, he wonders how and why he did. At the same time, his Jewish tradition and his own experience underscore that events never happen purely by accident. And yet, and especially where the Holocaust is concerned, the fact that events are linked by more than chance does not mean that everything can be explained or understood, at least not completely. Only by testifying about what happened in the Holocaust, only by bearing witness as truthfully and persistently as possible about what was lost, does Wiesel find that his survival makes sense. But the sense that it makes can never be enough to remove the scarring question marks that the Holocaust has burned forever into humanity's history and God's creation.

Wiesel's later memoirs are not triumphal vindications. Like *Night*, they are drenched in sadness and melancholy. But sadness and melancholy, and the despair to which they might yield, are not their last words. Out of them, out of *Night*, Wiesel forges something much more affirmative. Optimism, faith, hope—these words are too facile to contain his outlook. Defiance, resistance, protest—these terms come closer, but even they have to be supplemented by an emphasis on friendship, dialogue, reaching out to others, helping people in need, working to make people free, and striving to mend the world.

From *Night* to his two-volume autobiography, the greatest contributions of Wiesel's memoirs are ethical and spiritual. With *Night* as his authorship's foundational word, his memoirs show how Wiesel found ways to transform his suffering into sharing, his pain into caring. These transformations do not mean that Wiesel forgives any more than he forgets. The Holocaust was too immense, too devastating, to be redeemed by forgiveness that God or anyone else can give. But because the world has been shattered so severely, Wiesel believes that the moral imperative is to do all that one can do to repair it. Post-Holocaust Christians who study *Night* and Wiesel's other writings can help reclaim their tradition by affirming their own versions of Wiesel's Jewish perspective.

In 1964 Wiesel revisited his hometown. For more than one reason, his return to Sighet—that place in Eastern Europe where his mother and the rabbi had their fateful conversation—was anything but easy. After his liberation from Buchenwald in April 1945, Wiesel went to France, where he eventually became a reporter for an Israeli newspaper. Years later, his journalistic work took him to New York, where he became an American citizen, an event celebrated in his 2004 Fourth of July essay in *Parade*.

Sighet was far away. The distance, however, did not involve mileage alone. Once part of Romania, then annexed by Hungary, and once more under Romanian control, Sighet stood behind the iron curtain in the 1960s. Cold-war politics made the journey difficult and dangerous. Nevertheless, Wiesel was determined to go back to Sighet, "the town beyond the wall," as the title of one of his novels calls it.

Memory drew him there, even though Wiesel already knew what his visit would confirm: Sighet no longer existed—at least not as it was when he was born there, in 1928, or as he had known the place until he left it at fifteen, in 1944. More than time had passed. People had come and gone, but that fact only began to tell Sighet's story. Those things happen everywhere, but the way they happened in Sighet, the particularity and enormity of what happened there and in thousands of places like it, made Sighet's disappearance so devastating that the world itself could never again be what it was before.

Sighet vanished in the Holocaust's night and fog. Only traces remained of what once had been. Sighet's streets looked familiar to Wiesel in 1964, although one called the Street of Jews contained apartments that seemed as modest as they now were empty. His boyhood eyes, Wiesel realized, must have been unaware of the poverty that many of Sighet's Jews experienced. The movie theater still stood. So did the family house. It had not been sold but taken; strangers occupied it. Wiesel found the Jewish cemetery. He lit candles at his grandfather's grave. Elsewhere, Sighet was filled with living people, but Wiesel's hometown was gone. As the Germans liked to say twenty years before, Sighet had become *judenrein*.

Wiesel and his two older sisters, Hilda and Bea, survived the Holocaust, but most of Sighet's Jews did not. Few survivors went back there after the Nazis surrendered in May 1945. Poignantly, Wiesel reflects on all that was lost as he describes his visit to one of the few synagogues that was still open two decades later. Stacked inside were hundreds of books—Wiesel calls them "holy books"—that had been taken from abandoned Jewish homes and stored there. Wiesel began to look through them. He discovered some that had belonged to him. Tucked inside one, he writes, were "some yellowed, withered sheets of paper in a book of Bible commentaries." Wiesel recognized the handwriting they contained. It was his. Summing up his sadness, his memoirs observe that finding those pages is "a commentary on the commentaries I had written at the age of thirteen or fourteen" (*All Rivers* 360).

This story, the existence of yellow, withered sheets of paper, a boy's reflections on the Bible—all are part of a world that disappeared in *Night*. Wiesel seeks to make it live again through memory, testimony, and writing. The episodes he records spark more questions: Why did the Allies refuse to bomb the railways to Auschwitz? Why did Wiesel's family not accept the help of their housekeeper, Maria? Why was the world so indifferent to Jewish suffering? Where was God? What happened to love?

Wiesel's narratives of his life do not follow a simple or strict chronological form. His story does not fit the usual style of beginning, middle, end. The memories of his life circle around one another too much for that. From time to time, Wiesel breaks his commentary on himself even further by reflecting on his dreams. In one of them, the Wiesel family has gathered for a holiday celebration. Elie is asked to sing, but he cannot remember the traditional songs. He is asked for a story, but the stories have been forgotten too. *"Grandfather,"* Wiesel calls out in his dream, *"help me, help me find my memory!"* Astonished, Wiesel's grandfather looks back at him. *"But you're not a child anymore,"* he says. *"You're almost as old as I am"* (*All Rivers* 360).

As *Night* reminds us, Wiesel has lived for a long time. He has experienced and remembered more than most people, but he worries profoundly about forgetting. If we stop remembering, he warns, we stop being. Wiesel is older now than most of his extended family was when they were murdered during the Holocaust. He lives with the dead as well as with the living. Wiesel takes the titles of his two-volume autobiography from the biblical book of Ecclesiastes, which Christians share with Jews. It speaks of how generations come and go and of how the eye is not satisfied with seeing nor the ear filled with hearing.

Wiesel sounds a characteristically mystical note as he considers how all rivers run to the sea. Beginning in obscurity, streams of experience and memory rush forth. As they grow and merge, life's currents become a flood that eventually pours into the ocean's awesome depth. Like *Night* and Wiesel's more recent memoirs, the sea does not yield all its secrets. Instead its storms rage, its waves crash, its tides ebb and flow, and there are moments of beauty, calm, and silence too. Through it all, the sea endures, which is not an answer but an invitation to more stories and to their questions. The writings that follow *Night* shed light on that masterful Holocaust testimony—not by removing any of *Night*'s darkness, which must remain, but by supplementing and contextualizing that text in ways that show how *Night*'s greatest significance is found in the moral and spiritual challenges that it creates for humanity's future.

NOTES ON CONTRIBUTORS

Michael Berenbaum is director of the Sigi Ziering Institute: Exploring the Ethical and Theological Implications of the Holocaust and professor of theology at the University of Judaism in Los Angeles. The first of his sixteen books was *Elie Wiesel: God, the Holocaust, and the Children of Israel*.

Alan L. Berger occupies the Raddock Family Eminent Scholar Chair for Holocaust Studies and is professor of Judaic studies at Florida Atlantic University. Among his books are *Crisis and Covenant: The Holocaust in American Jewish Fiction*, *Second Generation Voices: Reflections by Children of Holocaust Survivors and Perpetrators* (ed. with his wife, Naomi), and *Children of Job: American Second-Generation Witnesses to the Holocaust*.

Michael Bernard-Donals is Nancy Hoefs Professor of English at the University of Wisconsin, Madison. He is the author of *An Introduction to Holocaust Studies: History, Memory, Representation*.

Jan Darsa is director of the Jewish education program Facing History and Ourselves in Brookline, Massachusetts. She is the coauthor of *Facing History and Ourselves: The Jews of Poland* and has been a Jerusalem Fellow as well as a scholar in residence at the Hertzilia Day School in Cape Town, South Africa.

Jonathan Druker teaches Italian and Holocaust literature at Illinois State University. He has contributed essays to *The Legacy of Primo Levi* (ed. Stanislao Pugliese), *Teaching the Representation of the Holocaust* (ed. Marianne Hirsch and Irene Kacandes), and *Clio*. He is now completing a book, *Primo Levi and Humanism after Auschwitz*.

Paul Eisenstein is associate professor in the Department of English at Otterbein College. He is the author of *Traumatic Encounters: Holocaust Representation and the Hegelian Subject* and is at work on a book treating counterfactual or nonmimetic representations of the Holocaust.

Christopher J. Frost is professor of religious studies and associate dean of undergraduate studies at San Diego State University. His books include *Religious Melancholy or Psychological Depression?*; *Simone Weil: On Politics, Religion, and Society* (coauthored); and *Moral Cruelty: A meaning and the Justification of Harm* (coauthored). He is the recipient of the Presidential Award for Excellence in Teaching.

Simone Gigliotti is lecturer in the history program at Victoria University of Wellington, New Zealand, and fellow of the Department of History at the University of Melbourne, Australia. Recent publications include *The Holocaust: A Reader*, coedited with Berel Lang.

Rita Horváth was a 2005–06 research fellow at the International Institute for Holocaust Research, Yad Vashem. She is the author of *A Deportáltakat Gondozó Országos Bizottság története, 1944–1952* ("The History of the National Relief Committee for Deportees, 1944–1952") and *"Never Asking Why Build, Only Asking Which Tools": Confessional Poetry and the Construction of the Self*. She is working on a book concerning Hungarian Jewish family novels.

Susanne Klingenstein, a literary scholar and journalist, directs the communication curriculum at the Harvard-MIT Division of Health Sciences and Technology and writes for *Frankfurter Allgemeine Zeitung*. She is the author of *Jews in the American Academy, 1900–1940: The Dynamics of Intellectual Assimilation* and *Enlarging America: The Cultural Work of Jewish Literary Scholars, 1930–1990*.

Phyllis Lassner teaches at Northwestern University. She is the author of two books on Elizabeth Bowen, *British Women Writers of World War II*, many articles on interwar and wartime women writers, and *Colonial Strangers: Women Writing the End of the British Empire*.

Kevin Lewis is associate professor of religious studies at the University of South Carolina, Columbia. He has contributed articles on Auden, Kosinski, Sexton, Thoreau, Weil, and Whitman to the fourth edition of *Die Religion in Geschichte und Gegenwart: Handwortenbuch fur Theologie und Religionwissenschaft*.

David Patterson holds the Bornblum Chair in Judaic Studies at the University of Memphis and is director of the university's Bornblum Judaic Studies Program. A winner of the Koret Jewish Book Award, he has published more than two dozen books. His most recent book is *Open Wounds: The Crsis of Jewish Thought in the Aftermath of Auschwitz*.

Nehemia Polen is professor of Jewish thought and director of the Hasidic Text Institute at Boston's Hebrew College. He is the author of *The Holy Fire: The Teachings of Rabbi Kalonymus Kalman Shapira, the Rebbe of the Warsaw Ghetto*; *The Rebbe's Daughter*; and, with Lawrence Kushner, *Filling Words with Light: Hasidic and Mystical Reflections on Jewish Prayer*.

Alan Rosen was a 2005–06 fellow at the International Institute for Holocaust Research, Yad Vashem. His books include *Sounds of Defiance: The Holocaust, Multilingualism, and the Problem of English* and *Obliged by Memory: Literature, Ethics, and Religion*, edited with Steven Katz. His current project is a book on Holocaust testimony.

John K. Roth is Edward J. Sexton Professor of Philosophy and director of the Center for the Study of the Holocaust, Genocide, and Human Rights at Claremont McKenna College. He is the author of *A Consuming Fire: Encounters with Elie Wiesel and the Holocaust*; *After-Words: Post-Holocaust Struggles with Forgiveness, Reconciliation, Justice* (ed. with David Patterson); and *Ethics during and after the Holocaust: In the Shadow of Birkenau*.

Judith Clark Schaneman is professor of French at Westminster College (Missouri). Her dissertation was entitled "The Force of Memory in Elie Wiesel's Novels."

Jan Schwarz is senior lecturer in the Department of Germanic Studies and Committee on Jewish Studies, University of Chicago. He is the author of *Imagining Lives: Autobiographical Fiction of Yiddish Writers*. His articles on Yiddish writers' responses to the Holocaust have appeared in *Polin: Studies in Polish Jewry* and *Eastern European Jewish Affairs*. His Danish translation of the Yiddish poet Abraham Sutzkever's *Green Aquarium* is forthcoming.

SURVEY PARTICIPANTS

Alan L. Berger, *Florida Atlantic University*
Pascale Bos, *University of Texas, Austin*
Andrew Davis
Jonathan Druker, *Illinois State University*
Carole Eisner, *University of Michigan*
Paul Eisenstein, *Ottobein University*
Robert Franciosi, *Grand Valley State University*
Christopher J. Frost, *San Diego State University*
Myrna Goldenberg, *Montgomery College, Rockville*
Nan Hackett, *Concordia University, Saint Paul*
Stephen Haynes, *Rhodes College*
Nels Highberg, *University of Illinois, Chicago*
Donald M. Kartiganer, *University of Mississippi*
Susanne Klingenstein
Phyllis Lassner, *Northwestern University*
Kevin Lewis, *University of South Carolina, Columbia*
James Moore, *Valparaiso University*
David Patterson, *Memphis State University*
John K. Roth, *Claremont McKenna College*
Daniel Schwartz, *Cornell University*
Jan Schwarz, *University of Chicago*
Eric Sterling, *Auburn University*
Ernesto Verdeja, *New School University*

WORKS CITED

Abrahamson, Irving, ed. *Against Silence: The Voice and Vision of Elie Wiesel*. 3 vols. New York: Holocaust Lib., 1985.

Abramowitz, Molly, ed. *Elie Wiesel: A Bibliography*. Metuchen: Scarecrow, 1974.

Adorno, Theodor. *Prisms*. Trans. Samuel Weber and Shierry Weber. Cambridge: MIT P, 1981.

Agamben, Giorgio. *Remnants of Auschwitz: The Witness and the Archive*. Trans. D. Heller-Roazen. New York: Zone, 1999.

Alfassi, Yitzhak, Eli Netzer, and Anna Szalai, eds. *The Heart Remembers Jewish Sziget*. Matan: Assn. of Former Szigetians in Israel, 2003.

Alter, Robert. "The Apocalyptic Temper." *After the Tradition: Essays on Modern Jewish Writing*. New York: Dutton, 1969. 46–60.

———. "Elie Wiesel: Between Hangmen and Victim." Cargas, *Responses* 83–92.

Alvarez, A. *Beyond All This Fiddle: Essays, 1955–1967*. London: Lane-Penguin, 1968.

Avni, Ora. "Beyond Psychoanalysis: Elie Wiesel's *Night* in Historical Perspective." Kritzman 203–18.

Bauer, Yehuda. *A History of the Holocaust*. Rev. ed. New York: Watts, 2001.

Belpoliti, Marco, and Robert Gordon, eds. *The Voice of Memory: Interviews, 1961–1987: Primo Levi*. Trans. Gordon. New York: New Press, 2001.

Berenbaum, Michael. *The Vision of the Void: Theological Reflections on the Works of Elie Wiesel*. Middletown: Wesleyan UP, 1979.

Berkovits, Eliezer. *With God in Hell: Judaism in the Ghettos and Deathcamps*. New York: Sanhedrin, 1979.

Bernard-Donals, Michael, and Richard Glejzer. *Between Witness and Testimony: The Holocaust and the Limits of Representation*. Albany: State U of New York P, 2001.

Bettelheim, Bruno. *"Surviving," and Other Essays*. New York: Knopf, 1979.

Blanchot, Maurice. *The Writing of the Disaster*. Trans. Ann Smock. Lincoln: U of Nebraska P, 1995.

Bloom, Harold, ed. *Modern Critical Interpretations: Elie Wiesel's* Night. Philadelphia: Chelsea, 2001.

Borowski, Tadeusz. "This Way for the Gas, Ladies and Gentlemen." *"This Way for the Gas, Ladies and Gentlemen"; and Other Stories*. Trans. Barbara Vedder. New York: Viking, 1967. 29–49.

Braham, Randolph. *The Hungarian Jewish Catastrophe: A Selected and Annotated Bibliography*. 2nd ed. New York: Inst. for Holocaust Studies, City U of New York, 1984.

———. "Hungary: Jews during the Holocaust." *The Encyclopedia of the Holocaust*. Ed. Israel Gutman. Vol. 2. New York: Macmillan, 1990. 698–703.

———. *The Politics of Genocide: The Holocaust in Hungary*. Rev. ed. New York: Rosenthal Inst. for Holocaust Studies, 1994.

Bretholz, Leo, and Michael Olesker. *Leap into Darkness: Seven Years on the Run in Wartime Europe*. Baltimore: Woodholme, 1998.

Brockman, John, ed. *The Next Fifty Years: Science in the First Half of the Twenty-First Century.* New York: Vintage, 2002.

Brown, Robert McAfee. *Elie Wiesel: Messenger to All Humanity.* Rev. ed. Notre Dame: U of Notre Dame P, 1989.

Browning, Christopher R. "Before the 'Final Solution': Nazi Ghettoization Policy in Poland (1940–1941)." *Ghettos 1939–1945: New Research and Perspectives on Definition, Daily Life, and Survival.* Washington: Center for Advanced Holocaust Studies / United States Holocaust Memorial Museum, 2005. 1–14.

Cargas, Harry J. *Harry James Cargas in Conversation with Elie Wiesel.* New York: Paulist, 1976.

———, ed. *Responses to Elie Wiesel: Critical Essays by Major Jewish and Christian Scholars.* New York: Persea, 1978.

Caruth, Cathy. "Unclaimed Experience: Trauma and the Possibility of History." *Yale French Studies* 79 (1991): 182–91.

Cesarani, David, ed. *The Final Solution: Origins and Implementation.* New York: Routledge, 1994.

Charney, Israel. "Teaching the Violence of the Holocaust." *Jewish Education* 38 (1969): 15–24.

Dante. *The Inferno.* Trans. Robert Pinsky. New York: Farrar, 1994.

Davis, Colin. *Elie Wiesel's Secretive Texts.* Gainesville: UP of Florida, 1994.

Dawidowicz, Lucy. *The War against the Jews, 1933–45.* New York: Holt, Rinehart, 1975.

Dawkins, Richard. *A Devil's Chaplain.* New York: Mariner, 2003.

Delbo, Charlotte. *Aucun de nous ne reviendra.* Paris: Minuit, 1965.

———. *Auschwitz and After.* Trans. Rosetta C. Lamont. New Haven: Yale UP, 1995.

———. *Auschwitz et après.* Paris: Minuit, 1970.

———. *Une connaissance inutile.* Paris: Minuit, 1970.

———. *Le convoi du 24 janvier.* Paris: Minuit, 1965. Trans. as *Convoy to Auschwitz: Women of the French Resistance.* Trans. Carol Cosman. Boston: Northeastern UP, 1997.

———. *Mesure de nos jours.* Paris: Minuit, 1971.

Des Pres, Terrence. *The Survivor: An Anatomy of Life in the Death Camps.* New York: Oxford UP, 1976.

Dostoyevsky, Fyodor. *The Brothers Karamazov.* Trans. Constance Garnett. New York: Heritage, 1949.

Dwork, Debórah, and Robert Jan van Pelt. *Auschwitz: 1270 to the Present.* New York: Norton, 1996.

Edelheit, Abraham, and Hershel Edelheit. *Bibliography on Holocaust Literature.* Boulder: Westview, 1986.

Eliach, Yaffa. *Hasidic Tales of the Holocaust.* New York: Oxford UP, 1982.

Encyclopedia Judaica. 16 vols. Jerusalem: Keter, 1971–72.

Estes, Ted. *Elie Wiesel.* New York: Ungar, 1980.

Ezrahi, Sidra DeKoven. *By Words Alone: The Holocaust in Literature.* Chicago: U of Chicago P, 1980.

Feig, Konnilyn. *Hitler's Death Camps: The Sanity of Madness.* New York: Holmes, 1979.

Felman, Shoshana. "Education in Crisis; or, The Vicissitudes of Teaching." *Trauma.* Ed. Cathy Caruth. Baltimore: Johns Hopkins UP, 1995. 13–60.

Felman, Shoshana, and Dori Laub. *Testimony: Crises of Witnessing in Literature, Psychoanalysis, and History.* New York: Routledge, 1992.

Fine, Ellen. *Legacy of* Night: *The Literary Universe of Elie Wiesel.* Fwd. Terrence Des Pres. Albany: State U of New York P, 1982.

Fink, Ida. *Traces: Stories.* Trans. Philip Boehm and Francine Prose. New York: Metropolitan, 1997.

Fleischner, Eva. "Mauriac's Preface to *Night*—Thirty Years Later." Rittner 116–19.

Franciosi, Robert, ed. *Elie Wiesel: Conversations.* Jackson: UP of Mississippi, 2002.

Frankl, Viktor. *Man's Search for Meaning.* Boston: Beacon, 1959.

Freud, Sigmund. *An Outline of Psychoanalysis.* New York: Norton, 1949.

Fried, Hedi. *The Road to Auschwitz: Fragments of a Life.* Ed. and trans. Michael Meyer. Lincoln: U of Nebraska P, 1990.

Friedlander, Henry. *On the Holocaust: A Critique of the Treatment of the Holocaust in History Textbooks Accompanied by an Annotated Bibliography.* New York: ADL, 1973.

Friedman, Philip. "The Jewish Ghettos of the Nazi Era." *Roads to Extinction: Essays on the Holocaust.* Ed. Ada June Friedman. Introd. Salo Wittmayer Baron. New York: Jewish Pub. Soc., Conference on Jewish Social Studies, 1980. 59–87.

Fromm, Erich. *Escape from Freedom.* New York: Holt, Rinehart, 1941.

Frost, Christopher J., and Rebecca Bell-Metereau. *Simone Weil: On Politics, Religion, and Society.* London: Sage, 1998.

Frost, Kathryn M., and Christopher J. Frost. "On Loss and Melancholy: An Autobiographical Essay." *Journal of Loss and Trauma* 7 (2002): 185–201.

Gerlach, Christian. "The Wannsee Conference, the Fate of German Jews and Hitler's Decision in Principle to Exterminate All European Jews." *Journal of Modern History* 70 (1998): 759–812.

Gilbert, Martin. *The Holocaust: A History of the Jews of Europe during the Second World War.* New York: Holt, Rinehart, 1985.

Glatstein, Jacob, Israel Knox, and Samuel Margoshes, eds. *Anthology of Holocaust Literature.* Philadelphia: Jewish Pub. Soc., 1969.

Goldhagen, Daniel Jonah. *Hitler's Willing Executioners.* New York: Knopf, 1996.

Grade, Chaim. "My Quarrel with Hersh Rasseyner." *A Treasury of Yiddish Stories.* Ed. Irving Howe and Eliezer Greenberg. New York: Viking, 1989. 624–51.

———. *The Seven Little Lanes.* Trans. Curt Leviant. New York: Bergen Belsen Memorial Press, 1967.

Greenberg, Gershon. "The Suffering of the Righteous according to Shlomo Zalma Unsdorfer of Bratislava, 1939–1944." *Remembering for the Future.* Ed. John K. Roth and Elisabeth Maxwell. Vol. 1. Basingstoke: Palgrave, 2001. 422–38.

Greene, Joshua M., and Shiva Kumar, eds. *Witness: Voices from the Holocaust.* New York: Free, 2000.

Gross, Jan. *Neighbors: The Destruction of the Jewish Community in Jedwabne, Poland.* Princeton: Princeton UP, 2001.

Guide to Yale University Holocaust Video Testimonies. New Haven: Yale UP, 1994.

Gutman, Yisrael, and Michael Berenbaum, eds. *Anatomy of the Auschwitz Death Camp.* Bloomington: Indiana UP, 1994.

Hackett, David A., ed. *The Buchenwald Report.* Boulder: Westview, 1995.

Halivni, David Weiss. *The Book and the Sword: A Life of Learning in the Shadow of Destruction.* New York: Westview, 1996.

Halperin, Irving. "From *Night* to *The Gates of the Forest.*" Cargas, *Responses* 45–82.

———. *Messengers from the Dead: Literature of the Holocaust.* Philadelphia: Westminster, 1970.

Hartman, Geoffrey. *Scars of the Spirit: The Struggle against Inauthenticity.* New York: Palgrave, 2002.

Heilman, Anna. *Never Far Away: The Auschwitz Chronicles of Anna Heilman.* Calgary: U of Calgary P, 2001.

Hellman, Peter. *The Auschwitz Album.* New York: Random, 1981.

Hilberg, Raul. *The Destruction of the European Jews.* Chicago: Quadrangle, 1961.

———. "German Railroads, Jewish Souls." *The "Final Solution."* Marrus 3: 520–56.

———. *Sonderzüge nach Auschwitz.* Frankfurt am Main: Ullstein, 1987.

Hillesum, Etty. *An Interrupted Life: The Diaries, 1941–1943; and, Letters from Westerbork.* Trans. Arnold J. Pomerans. New York: Henry Holt, 1996.

The Holy Scriptures. Philadelphia: Jewish Pub. Soc., 1917.

Horowitz, Sara R. "Voices from the Killing Ground." *Holocaust Remembrance: The Shapes of Memory.* Ed. Geoffrey Hartman. Oxford: Blackwell, 1994. 42–58.

———. *Voicing the Void: Muteness and Memory in Holocaust Fiction.* Albany: State U of New York P, 1997.

Horváth, Rita. "Jews in Hungary after the Holocaust: The National Relief Committee for Deportees, 1945–1950." *Journal of Israeli History* 19 (1998): 69–91.

Howe, Irving. "Writing and the Holocaust." Lang, *Writing* 175–99.

Isacovici, Salomon, and Juan Manuel Rodríguez. *Man of Ashes.* Trans. Dick Gerdes. Lincoln: U of Nebraska P, 1999.

Isakovitch, Samuel [Salomon Isacovici]. "Interview with David Boder, July 30, 1946." *Voices of the Holocaust.* <http://voices.iit.edu>.

Jäckel, Eberhard. "On the Purpose of the Wannsee Conference." Pacy and Wertheimer 39–49.

Johnson, Mary, and Margot Stern Strom. *Facing History and Ourselves: Elements of Time.* Brookline: Facing History and Ourselves, 1989.

Kant, Immanuel. *Critique of Judgment.* Trans. Werner Pluhar. Indianapolis: Hackett, 1987.

Ka-Tzetnik 135633 [Yehiel De-Nur]. *House of Dolls.* Trans. Moshe M. Kohn. New York: Simon, 1955.

———. *Sunrise over Hell.* Trans. Nina De-Nur. London: Allen, 1977.

"Ka-Zetnik." *Leksikon.*

Kertész, Imre. *Fateless*. Trans. Christopher C. Wilson and Katharina M. Wilson. Evanston: Northwestern UP, 1996.

———. *Fatelessness*. Trans. Tim Wilkinson. New York: Vintage, 2004.

King, Martin Luther, Jr. "Letter from Birmingham Jail." *Nobel Prize Internet Archive*. 1963. 9 Aug. 2006 <http://almaz.com/nobel/peace/MLK-jail.html>.

Kitov, Eliyahu. *The Book of Our Heritage*. Trans. Nathan Bulman. Vol. 1. New York: Feldheim, 1973.

Klüger, Ruth. *Still Alive: A Holocaust Girlhood Remembered*. New York: Feminist, 2001.

Kogon, Eugen. *The Theory and Practice of Hell: The German Concentration Camps and the System behind Them*. Trans. Heinz Norden. Rev. ed. New York: Farrar, 2006.

Kolbert, Jack. *The Worlds of Elie Wiesel: An Overview of His Career and His Major Themes*. Selinsgrove: Susquehanna UP, 2001.

Kraft, Robert N. *Memory Perceived: Recalling the Holocaust*. Westport: Praeger, 2002.

Kritzman, Lawrence D., ed. *Auschwitz and After: Race, Culture, and "the Jewish Question" in France*. New York: Routledge, 1995.

Kugelmass, Jack, and Jonathan Boyarin, eds. *From a Ruined Garden: The Memorial Books of Polish Jewry*. New York: Schocken, 1983.

Kuperhand, Miriam, and Saul Kuperhand. *Shadows of Treblinka*. Urbana: U of Illinois P, 1998.

LaCapra, Dominick. *Representing the Holocaust: History, Theory, Trauma*. Ithaca: Cornell UP, 1994.

———. *Writing History, Writing Trauma*. Baltimore: Johns Hopkins UP, 2001.

Lang, Berel. *Holocaust Representation: Art within the Limits of History and Ethics*. Baltimore: Johns Hopkins UP, 2000.

———. *Post-Holocaust: Interpretation, Misinterpretation, and the Claims of History*. Bloomington: Indiana UP, 2005.

———, ed. *Writing and the Holocaust*. New York: Holmes, 1988.

Langer, Lawrence. *The Holocaust and the Literary Imagination*. New Haven: Yale UP, 1975.

———. *Holocaust Testimonies*. New Haven: Yale UP, 1998.

Langfus, Anna. *Les bagages de sable*. Paris: Gallimard, 1962. Trans. as *The Lost Shore*. Trans. Peter Wiles. New York: Pantheon, 1964.

———. *Saute, Barbara*. Paris: Gallimard, 1965.

———. *Le sel et le soufre*. Paris: Gallimard, 1960. Trans. as *The Whole Land Brimstone*. Trans. Peter Wiles. New York: Pantheon, 1962.

Lao-tzu. *Tao Te Ching*. New York: Vintage, 1972.

Leksikon fun der nayer yidisher literatur ["Biographical Dictionary of Modern Yiddish Literature"]. New York: Congress for Jewish Culture, 1956–81.

Levi, Primo. *Collected Poems*. Trans. Ruth Feldman and Brian Swann. London: Faber, 1988.

———. *The Drowned and the Saved*. Trans. Raymond Rosenthal. New York: Vintage Intl., 1989.

——. *Survival in Auschwitz: The Nazi Assault on Humanity*. 1961. Trans. Stuart Woolf. New York: Simon, 1996.

Lewin, Abraham. *A Cup of Tears: A Diary of the Warsaw Ghetto*. Ed. Antony Polonsky. Trans. Christopher Hutton. Oxford: Blackwell, 1988.

Liebsch, Burkhard. "Giving Testimony." *Contemporary Portrayals of Auschwitz: Philosophical Challenges*. Ed. Alan Rosenberg. Amherst: Humanity, 2000. 69–77.

Longerich, Peter. *The Unwritten Order: Hitler's Role in the Final Solution*. Charleston: Tempus, 2001.

Luckmann, Thomas. *The Invisible Religion: The Problem of Religion in Modern Society*. New York: Macmillan, 1964.

Lyotard, Jean-François. *The Differend: Phrases in Dispute*. Trans. Georges Van den Abbeele. Minneapolis: U of Minnesota P, 1988.

Marrus, Michael R., ed. *The Nazi Holocaust: Historical Articles on the Destruction of European Jews*. 9 vols. Westport: Meckler, 1989.

Mary R. Interview with Lucy Stanovick. Mar.–Apr. 1997. Transcript.

Mass, Wendy, ed. *Readings on* Night. San Diego: Greenhaven, 2000.

Mauriac, François. Foreword. Wiesel, *Night* (2006) xvii–xxi.

Mierzejewski, Alfred C. *The Most Valuable Asset of the Reich: A History of the German National Railway*. Chapel Hill: U of North Carolina P, 2000.

——. "A Public Enterprise in the Service of Mass Murder: The Deutsche Reichsbahn and the Holocaust." *Holocaust and Genocide Studies* 15 (2001): 33–46.

Moss-Coane, Marty. "Interview with Elie Wiesel." Franciosi 160–73.

Neufeld, Michael, and Michael Berenbaum, eds. *The Bombing of Auschwitz: Should the Allies Have Attempted It?* Lawrence: U of Kansas P, 2003.

Niewyk, Donald L., ed. *The Holocaust: Problems and Perspectives of Interpretation*. Boston: Houghton, 1997.

Niewyk, Donald, and Francis Nicosia. *The Columbia Guide to the Holocaust*. New York: Columbia UP, 2000.

Niger, Shmuel. "Tendentsn in der nayster yidisher literatur." *Jewish Book Annual*. Vol. 13. New York: Jewish Book Council, 1955. 3–8.

Nomberg-Przytyk, Sara. *Auschwitz: True Tales from a Grotesque Land*. Trans. Roslyn Hirsch. Chapel Hill: U of North Carolina P, 1985.

Ozick, Cynthia. "The Rights of History and the Rights of Imagination." *Commentary* 107.3 (1999): 22–27.

Pacy, James S., and Alan P. Wertheimer, eds. *Perspectives on the Holocaust: Essays in Honor of Raul Hilberg*. Boulder: Westview, 1995.

Pascal, Roy. *Design and Truth in Autobiography*. Cambridge: Harvard UP, 1960.

Patterson, David. *Sun Turned to Darkness: Memory and Recovery in the Holocaust Memoir*. Syracuse: Syracuse UP, 1998.

Perl, Gisella. *I Was a Doctor in Auschwitz*. New York: Intl. Universities, 1948.

Polen, Nehemia. *The Holy Fire: The Teachings of Rabbi Kalonymus Kalman Shapira, the Rebbe of the Warsaw Ghetto*. Northvale: Aronson, 1994.

Rashi. *Pentateuch with Targum Onkelos, Haphtaroth, and Rashi's Commentary*. Trans.

M. Rosenbaum and A. M. Silbermann. Vol. 2. Jerusalem: Silbermann, 1930. 5 vols.

Reitlinger, Gerald. *The Final Solution: The Attempt to Exterminate the Jews of Europe.* London: Vallentine-Mitchell, 1953.

Rittner, Carol, ed. *Elie Wiesel: Between Memory and Hope.* New York: New York UP, 1990.

Rittner, Carol, and John K. Roth, eds. *Different Voices: Women and the Holocaust.* New York: Paragon, 1993.

Robbins, Tom. *Jitterbug Perfume.* New York: Bantam, 1984.

Robinson, Jacob. *The Holocaust and After: Sources and Literature in English.* Jerusalem: Israel Universities P, 1973.

Robinson, Jacob, and Philip Friedman. *Guide to Jewish History under Nazi Impact.* New York: YIVO, 1960.

Roseman, Mark. "Surviving Memory: Truth and Inaccuracy in Holocaust Testimony." *Journal of Holocaust Education* 8 (1999): 1–20.

———. *The Wannsee Conference and the Final Solution: A Reconsideration.* New York: Metropolitan, 2002.

Rosen, Alan. "Elie Wiesel." *Holocaust Literature: An Encyclopedia of Writers and Their Work.* Ed. S. Lillian Kremer. New York: Routledge, 2003: 1315–25.

Rosenfeld, Alvin, and Irving Greenberg, eds. *Confronting the Holocaust: The Impact of Elie Wiesel.* Bloomington: Indiana UP, 1978.

Roskies, David, ed. *The Literature of Destruction: Jewish Responses to Catastrophe.* Philadelphia: Jewish Pub. Soc., 1988.

———. "Scribes of the Ghetto." *Against the Apocalypse: Responses to Catastrophe in Modern Jewish Culture.* Cambridge: Harvard UP, 1984. 196–224.

Roth, John K. *A Consuming Fire: Encounters with Elie Wiesel and the Holocaust.* Philadelphia: Westminster, 1979.

Rothberg, Michael. *Traumatic Realism: The Demands of Holocaust Representation.* Minneapolis: U of Minnesota P, 2000.

Rousset, David. *L'univers concentrationnaire.* Paris: Minuit, 1965.

Rozit, Rachel, and Alvin Goldfarb, eds. *Theatrical Performance during the Holocaust.* Baltimore: Johns Hopkins UP, 1999.

Rubenstein, Richard L. "Elie Wiesel and Primo Levi." Pacy and Wertheimer 145–65.

Sable, Martin. *Holocaust Studies: A Directory and Bibliography of Bibliographies.* Greenwood: Penkevill, 1987.

Schindler, Pesach. *Hasidic Responses to the Holocaust in Light of Hasidic Thought.* Hoboken: Ktav, 1990.

Scholem, Gershom. *Major Trends in Jewish Mysticism.* New York: Schocken, 1946.

Schuster, Ekkehard, and Reinhold Boschert-Kimmig. *Hope against Hope: Johann Baptist Metz and Elie Wiesel Speak Out on the Holocaust.* Trans. J. Matthew Ashley. New York: Paulist, 1999.

Schwarz, Daniel R. *Imagining the Holocaust.* New York: St. Martin's, 1999.

Schwarz, Jan. "Dos Poylishe Yidntum, 1945–1956." *Memory of the Holocaust.* Ed.

Gabriel Finder, Natalia Aleksiun, Antony Polonsky, and Schwarz. Oxford: Littman, 2007. 173–96. Vol. 20 of *Polin: Studies in Polish Jewry*.

Seidman, Naomi. "Elie Wiesel and the Scandal of Jewish Rage." *Jewish Social Studies* 3 (1996): 1–19.

Semprun, Jorge. *The Long Voyage*. Trans. Richard Seaver. New York: Grove, 1964.

———. *What a Beautiful Sunday!* Trans. Alan Sheridan. San Diego: Harcourt, 1982.

Sibelman, Simon. *Silence in the Novels of Elie Wiesel*. New York: St. Martin's, 1995.

Simonin, Anne. *Les Editions de Minuit, 1942–1955: Le devoir d'insoumission*. Paris: IMEC, 1994.

———. Personal communication to Alan Rosen. March 2006.

Sorell, Dora Apsan. *Tell the Children: Letters to Miriam*. San Rafael: Sighet, 1996.

Stern, Ellen Norman. *Elie Wiesel: Witness for Life*. New York: Ktav, 1982.

Stone, Dan. "Holocaust Testimony and the Challenge to the Philosophy of History." *Social Theory After the Holocaust*. Ed. Robert Fine and Charles Turner. Liverpool: Liverpool UP, 2000. 219–34.

Strigler, Mordechai. *Maydanek*. Dos poylishe yidntum 20. Buenos Aires: Tsentral-Farband fun Poylishe Yidn in Argentine, 1947.

Suleiman, Susan Rubin. "Do Facts Matter in Holocaust Memoirs? Wilkomirski/Wiesel." *Obliged by Memory: Literature, Religion, Ethics*. Ed. Steven T. Katz and Alan Rosen. Syracuse: Syracuse UP, 2006. 21–42.

———. "War Memories: On Autobiographical Reading." Kritzman 47–62.

Sutzkever, Avraham. *Selected Poetry and Prose*. Trans. Barbara Harshav and Benjamin Harshav. Introd. Benjamin Harshav. Berkeley: U of California P, 1991.

Szonyi, David, ed. *The Holocaust: An Annotated Bibliography and Resource Guide*. Hoboken: Ktav, 1985.

Talmud Bavli. Vilna: Romm, 1886.

Trunk, Isaiah. *Judenrat: The Jewish Councils in Eastern Europe under Nazi Occupation*. New York: Macmillan, 1972.

Vishniac, Roman, ed. *A Vanished World*. Fwd. Elie Wiesel. New York: Farrar, 1983.

von Kues, Nikolaus. *Mutmaßungen (De coniecturis)*. Hamburg: Meiner, 2002.

Weintraub, Karl. *The Value of the Individual: Self and Circumstance in Autobiography*. Chicago: U of Chicago P, 1978.

White, Hayden. "Historical Emplotment and the Problem of Truth." *Probing the Limits of Representation: Nazism and the "Final Solution."* Ed. Saul Friedlander. Cambridge: Harvard UP, 1992. 37–53.

Wiesel, Elie. *The Accident*. Trans. Anne Borchardt. New York: Hill, 1962.

———. *All Rivers Run to the Sea: Memoirs*. Trans. Jon Rothschild. New York: Knopf, 1995.

———. *And the Sea Is Never Full: Memoirs, 1969–*. Trans. Marion Wiesel. New York: Knopf, 1999.

———. *Ani Maamin: A Song Lost and Found Again*. Trans. Marion Wiesel. New York: Random, 1973.

———. *L'aube*. Paris: Seuil, 1960.

———. *Dawn*. Trans. Frances Frenaye. New York: Hill, 1961.

———. "Exile and the Human Condition." Abrahamson 1: 179–83.

———. *The Forgotten*. Trans. Stephen Becker. New York: Summit, 1992.

———. *From the Kingdom of Memory*. Trans. Marion Wiesel. New York: Summit, 1990.

———. *The Gates of the* Forest. Trans. Frances Frenaye. New York: Holt, Rinehart, 1966.

———. "Have You Learned the Most Important Lesson of All?" *Parade* 24 May 1992: 3–6.

———. "The Holocaust as Literary Inspiration." *Dimensions of the Holocaust*. Ed. Elliot Lefkowitz. Evanston: Northwestern UP, 1990. 5–19.

———. "An Interview unlike Any Other." Wiesel, *A Jew Today* 14–19.

———. *A Jew Today*. Trans. Marion Wiesel. New York: Random, 1978.

———. *Le jour*. Paris: Seuil, 1961.

———. *Legends of Our Time*. New York: Schocken, 1982.

———. "Marginal Thoughts on Yiddish." *Telling the Tale: A Tribute to Elie Wiesel*. Ed. Harry Cargas. Saint Louis: Time Being, 1993. 33–35.

———. *Night*. Trans. Stella Rodway. Fwd. François Mauriac. 1960. Pref. Robert MacAfee Brown. New York: Bantam, 1986.

———. *Night*. Trans. Marion Wiesel. Fwd. François Mauriac. Pref. Elie Wiesel. New York: Hill, 2006.

———. *The* Night *Trilogy*. New York: Hill, 1987.

———. *La nuit*. Paris: Minuit, 1958.

———. *The Oath*. Trans. Marion Wiesel. New York: Random, 1973.

———. "A Plea for the Dead." Wiesel, *Legends* 174–97.

———. "Recalling Swallowed-Up Worlds." *Christian Century* 27 May 1981: 609–12.

———. *Souls on Fire: Portraits and Legends of Hasidic Masters*. New York: Summit, 1972.

———. *The Town beyond the Wall*. Trans. Stephen Becker. New York: Holt, Rinehart, 1964.

———. *Un di velt hot geshvign*. Dos poylishe yidntum 117. Buenos Aires: Tsentral-Farband fun Poylishe Yidn in Argentine, 1956.

———. "Why I Write." Trans. Rosette C. Lamont. Rosenfeld and Greenberg 200–06.

———. *Zalman; or, The Madness of God*. Trans. Nathan Edelman. New York: Random, 1975.

Wiesel, Elie, and Richard D. Heffner. *Conversations with Elie Wiesel*. Ed. Thomas J. Vinciguerra. New York: Schocken, 2001.

"Wiesel, Eliezer." *Leksikon*.

Yahil, Leni. *The Holocaust: The Fate of European Jewry, 1932–1945*. Trans. Ina Friedman and Haya Galai. New York: Oxford UP, 1990.

Yerushalmi, Yosef. *Zakhor: Jewish History and Jewish Memory*. Seattle: U of Washington P, 1984.

Zapruder, Alexandra, ed. *Salvaged Pages: Young Writers' Diaries of the Holocaust*. New Haven: Yale UP, 2002.

Audiovisual Materials

Challenge of Memory. Brookline: Facing History and Ourselves, 1989.

Elie Wiesel Goes Home. Narr. William Hurt. Choices, 1994.

Facing Hate. With Elie Wiesel and Bill Moyers. Mystic Films / Public Affairs TV, 1991.

First Person Singular. By Elie Wiesel. Narr. William Hurt. PBS, 2002.

Fortunoff Video Archives for Holocaust Testimonies. Sterling Memorial Lib., Yale U, New Haven.

The Grey Zone. Dir. Tim Blake Nelson. Lions Gate, 2001.

Guidall, George, narr. *Night*. By Elie Wiesel. Trans. Marion Wiesel. Recorded Books, 2006.

Memory of the Camps. London: Ministry of Information, 1945. Frontline, 1985.

Nuit et brouillard. Dir. Alain Resnais. France, 1955.

Rosenblatt, Jeffrey, narr. *Night*. By Elie Wiesel. Audio Bookshelf, 2000.

Sighet, Sighet. Narr. Elie Wiesel. Alden Films, 1967.

INDEX

Modern Language Association of America
Approaches to Teaching World Literature
Joseph Gibaldi, series editor

Shorter Elizabethan Poetry. Ed. Patrick Cheney and Anne Lake Prescott. 2000.

Ellison's Invisible Man. Ed. Susan Resneck Parr and Pancho Savery. 1989.

English Renaissance Drama. Ed. Karen Bamford and Alexander Leggatt. 2002.

Works of Louise Erdrich. Ed. Gregg Sarris, Connie A. Jacobs, and
     James R. Giles. 2004.

Dramas of Euripides. Ed. Robin Mitchell-Boyask. 2002.

Faulkner's The Sound and the Fury. Ed. Stephen Hahn and Arthur F. Kinney. 1996.

Flaubert's Madame Bovary. Ed. Laurence M. Porter and Eugene F. Gray. 1995.

García Márquez's One Hundred Years of Solitude. Ed. María Elena de Valdés and
     Mario J. Valdés. 1990.

Gilman's "The Yellow Wall-Paper" and Herland. Ed. Denise D. Knight and
     Cynthia J. Davis. 2003.

Goethe's Faust. Ed. Douglas J. McMillan. 1987.

Gothic Fiction: The British and American Traditions. Ed. Diane Long Hoeveler
     and Tamar Heller. 2003.

Hebrew Bible as Literature in Translation. Ed. Barry N. Olshen and
     Yael S. Feldman. 1989.

Homer's Iliad and Odyssey. Ed. Kostas Myrsiades. 1987.

Ibsen's A Doll House. Ed. Yvonne Shafer. 1985.

Henry James's Daisy Miller and The Turn of the Screw. Ed. Kimberly C. Reed and
     Peter G. Beidler. 2005.

Works of Samuel Johnson. Ed. David R. Anderson and Gwin J. Kolb. 1993.

Joyce's Ulysses. Ed. Kathleen McCormick and Erwin R. Steinberg. 1993.

Kafka's Short Fiction. Ed. Richard T. Gray. 1995.

Keats's Poetry. Ed. Walter H. Evert and Jack W. Rhodes. 1991.

Kingston's The Woman Warrior. Ed. Shirley Geok-lin Lim. 1991.

Lafayette's The Princess of Clèves. Ed. Faith E. Beasley and
     Katharine Ann Jensen. 1998.

Works of D. H. Lawrence. Ed. M. Elizabeth Sargent and Garry Watson. 2001.

Lessing's The Golden Notebook. Ed. Carey Kaplan and Ellen Cronan Rose. 1989.

Mann's Death in Venice and Other Short Fiction. Ed. Jeffrey B. Berlin. 1992.

Medieval English Drama. Ed. Richard K. Emmerson. 1990.

Melville's Moby-Dick. Ed. Martin Bickman. 1985.

Metaphysical Poets. Ed. Sidney Gottlieb. 1990.

Miller's Death of a Salesman. Ed. Matthew C. Roudané. 1995.

Milton's Paradise Lost. Ed. Galbraith M. Crump. 1986.

Molière's Tartuffe and Other Plays. Ed. James F. Gaines and
     Michael S. Koppisch. 1995.

Momaday's The Way to Rainy Mountain. Ed. Kenneth M. Roemer. 1988.

Montaigne's Essays. Ed. Patrick Henry. 1994.

Novels of Toni Morrison. Ed. Nellie Y. McKay and Kathryn Earle. 1997.

Murasaki Shikibu's The Tale of Genji. Ed. Edward Kamens. 1993.

Pope's Poetry. Ed. Wallace Jackson and R. Paul Yoder. 1993.

Proust's Fiction and Criticism. Ed. Elyane Dezon-Jones and
    Inge Crosman Wimmers. 2003.
Novels of Samuel Richardson. Ed. Lisa Zunshine and Jocelyn Harris. 2006.
Rousseau's Confessions and Reveries of the Solitary Walker. Ed. John C. O'Neal
    and Ourida Mostefai. 2003.
Shakespeare's Hamlet. Ed. Bernice W. Kliman. 2001.
Shakespeare's King Lear. Ed. Robert H. Ray. 1986.
Shakespeare's Othello. Ed. Peter Erickson and Maurice Hunt. 2005.
Shakespeare's Romeo and Juliet. Ed. Maurice Hunt. 2000.
Shakespeare's The Tempest and Other Late Romances. Ed. Maurice Hunt. 1992.
Shelley's Frankenstein. Ed. Stephen C. Behrendt. 1990.
Shelley's Poetry. Ed. Spencer Hall. 1990.
Sir Gawain and the Green Knight. Ed. Miriam Youngerman Miller and
    Jane Chance. 1986.
Song of Roland. Ed. William W. Kibler and Leslie Zarker Morgan. 2006.
Spenser's Faerie Queene. Ed. David Lee Miller and Alexander Dunlop. 1994.
Stendhal's The Red and the Black. Ed. Dean de la Motte and Stirling Haig. 1999.
Sterne's Tristram Shandy. Ed. Melvyn New. 1989.
Stowe's Uncle Tom's Cabin. Ed. Elizabeth Ammons and Susan Belasco. 2000.
Swift's Gulliver's Travels. Ed. Edward J. Rielly. 1988.
Thoreau's Walden and Other Works. Ed. Richard J. Schneider. 1996.
Tolstoy's Anna Karenina. Ed. Liza Knapp and Amy Mandelker. 2003.
Vergil's Aeneid. Ed. William S. Anderson and Lorina N. Quartarone. 2002.
Voltaire's Candide. Ed. Renée Waldinger. 1987.
Whitman's Leaves of Grass. Ed. Donald D. Kummings. 1990.
Wiesel's Night. Ed. Alan Rosen. 2007.
Woolf's To the Lighthouse. Ed. Beth Rigel Daugherty and Mary Beth Pringle. 2001.
Wordsworth's Poetry. Ed. Spencer Hall, with Jonathan Ramsey. 1986.
Wright's Native Son. Ed. James A. Miller. 1997.